The Economics of the Family

The Economics of the Family

How the Household Affects Markets
and Economic Growth

Volume 2

Esther Redmount, Editor

 PRAEGER

AN IMPRINT OF ABC-CLIO, LLC
Santa Barbara, California • Denver, Colorado • Oxford, England

Library of Congress Cataloging-in-Publication Data

The economics of the family : how the household affects markets and economic growth / Esther Redmount, editor.

volumes ; cm

Includes bibliographical references and index.

ISBN 978–1–4408–0055–9 (hard copy : alk. paper) — ISBN 978–1–4408–0056–6 (ebook) 1. Families—Economic aspects. 2. Households—Economic aspects. I. Redmount, Esther, editor.

HQ519.E386   2015

306.850973—dc23   2014024403

ISBN: 978–1–4408–0055–9
EISBN: 978–1–4408–0056–6

19 18 17 16 15   1 2 3 4 5

This book is also available on the World Wide Web as an eBook.
Visit www.abc-clio.com for details.

Praeger
An Imprint of ABC-CLIO, LLC

ABC-CLIO, LLC
130 Cremona Drive, P.O. Box 1911
Santa Barbara, California 93116-1911

This book is printed on acid-free paper ∞

Manufactured in the United States of America

Contents

Introduction to Volume Two

This two-volume set is motivated by the desire to understand the interaction between households and markets. Volume One was devoted to defining what constitutes a family in today's world. Volume Two concentrates on market responses to the new and rapidly evolving family structures; it then turns around and takes another look at how these self-same families are adapting to the new pressures coming from the market. Because the changes on both ends have been so dramatic, social scientists have begun in earnest to collect data on what is happening to families and what is happening in markets and to tease out how the two are connected. Many of the essays in this volume make use of those new and innovative surveys to arrive at a deeper understanding of family economics. Indeed, for some readers, this may be their first exposure to such data sets.

Understanding how the household works enables us to analyze the interaction between households and resource allocations, including labor supply and work effort, consumption, education, and savings. Decisions not to educate girls, for example, have grave implications for society, but may be grounded in a family calculus that gives low priority to this use of resources.

Decisions made at home are especially influential for issues of labor force participation and gender equity, care of the elderly, population growth, and capital formation. How the new family responds to recessions and other shocks to the economy will shape the business cycle and influence how successful government policies can be in promoting economic growth.

The first chapter in Volume Two is an introduction by Esther Redmount to the debate about the internal nature of the household. Is the domestic entity best described as having a single head who takes the resources available to the household and doles them out to family members? Or is the family a collective of individuals coming together for some joint purpose, bargaining among themselves, and using the resources available to each to satisfy the goals and desires of the group? The answers to these questions will be extremely important for understanding how markets work and how effective policies can be.

Chapter 2, by Solomon W. Polachek and Jun Xiang, examines a longstanding and important feature of household income—namely, the gender pay gap between men and women. That women earn less in labor markets is uncontestable, but families are doing more to prepare girls for the market and governments are doing more to ensure fair play in employment. Polachek and Xiang look at a number of different data sets to see if there is evidence of a declining gender pay gap. Their regression-based analysis is able to identify some of the factors driving that decline.

In Chapter 3, Rachel Connelly and Jean Kimmel use the American Time Use Survey to explore how men and women in traditional families (and those not in traditional families) are dividing up their time between home work, market work, and personal time. A new feature of the data set allows them to explore the feelings of well-being associated with newly emerging patterns of time use and to comment on whether men's days and women's days now look more equal than they did previously.

Given the myriad demands on the modern woman's day—market work, home work, and personal time—something has to give. Chapter 4 by Karine Moe documents the rising demand for workplace flexibility (which has multiple dimensions) and the responses of employers to workers' needs to be accommodated. Moe considers the possibility that the gender revolution, which in part sparked the dramatic transformations in the family, will stall out if the market does not respond extensively and appropriately to the changing nature of family.

In Chapter 5, Joyce P. Jacobsen writes about the technologies of household production. Household production refers to those goods and services that a family provides for itself: home-cooking, lawn care, and the births and rearing of children, among so many other activities. Labor-saving devices, market innovations (such as fast food and birth-control pills), and access to water and electricity have the power to transform lives within the household and to enable the household to participate fully in the market economy. Jacobsen explores the causes and consequences of these changes for the family.

Political and social changes have expanded the definition of what constitutes a family. In Chapter 6, Lisa K. Jepsen looks at how sexual orientation and the ability and desire to "marry" affect family formation. She finds a whole new class of families have come into existence. Same-sex partnerships, same-sex marriages, and cohabiting opposite-sex couples have profound implications for personal well-being. The demands and supplies associated with these new families may transform labor markets, housing markets, and urban landscapes in ways we are just beginning to understand.

Families have traditionally provided life's early-stage and late-stage caregiving. Now that the family is undergoing profound changes, it is unclear whether it will be able to absorb the demands for care by a growing elderly population worldwide. Susan L. Averett, Asia Sikora, and Laura M. Argys consider the decision to provide care in the home and examine who bears the burden of that choice. They close by asking how governments committed to pension systems such as Social Security can sustain these programs if the family structure on which they rely is in flux.

The final essay, written by Mark C. Kelly and Ronald S. Warren, Jr., appears even as the United States is grappling with a deep and enduring recession. Unemployment remains stubbornly high and labor force participation rates have declined precipitously. Recognizing that the decision to work and to look for work is one taken by individuals at the household level, these authors consider whether the differences between microeconomic estimates of labor supply elasticities and the macroeconomic estimates might be due to the changing nature of the household.

Chapter 1

Who's in Charge Here? Decision Making in the Family

Esther Redmount

Once Upon a Time—which is the way all good stories begin—it was assumed (or maybe just devoutly hoped) that people fell in love, moved in together, with or without parental blessing or benefit of state or clergy, and then lived happily ever after. The "happily ever after" part of this equation suggests shared values, common goals and desires, and long-term commitments to each other and to the "marriage" regardless of shocks to income (for richer or poorer) or physical well-being (in sickness and in health). In the fairy-tale versions, there was no marital strife or at least nothing irreconcilable. There was no infidelity. One partner did not throw the other over when their best years were behind them. One partner did not abuse or neglect the other. And then, beyond all those good individual-level outcomes, there was a social equilibrium in which the very young were raised, educated, and socialized, and the elderly spent their later years in comfort and dignity. The state prospered and the economy grew.

When many of the features of the happy ending failed to materialize and massive changes began to occur in the nature of marriage and household formation, economists turned their attention to the mechanics behind the fairy tale. How did individuals meet and enter into long-term relations and for what purpose? What kind of work went into the relationship and its outcomes? How was it decided who was responsible for which task and with what compensation?

When adversity struck or good fortune materialized, how did the relationship adjust? Could the family be counted on to care for society's most vulnerable members? Was the wealth of the family equitably distributed within the household—and if equity or equality were not the goals, did each individual in the family realize at least part of his or her desires? What causes divorce and household dissolution? Finally, when, from time to time, the family needs help, which form should the intervention take?

Exploring the answers to these questions is the purpose of this chapter. The field of the economics of the family has grown too rich and too massive to do more than highlight some interesting results. Also, whoever reads beyond this point should remember that this is a survey of economists thinking and talking about some of the most intimate issues in a human life. Economists are nothing if not analytical. There may seem to be a certain aloofness and disinterestedness in their discourse. But make no mistake: economists assume this distance to lend clarity and precision to what they are trying to say. They are not disinterested. The concerns underlying their research are very real and economists want to be sure at the end of the day they truly understand what is going on.

To understand how the family works, we must first consider how it is formed, so this chapter begins with a discussion of courtship and the gains to be had from marriage (or other formal partnership). Once the household has formed, the next question to ask is how it functions. Initially, economists assumed that the family was a "little commonwealth." That meant that there was a clearly defined head who made all the economic decisions for the family. Economic models that presume a single decision maker are known as *unitary*. This chapter first reviews those models, as they serve as a benchmark for the discussions that follow. Critiques of the unitary model were not long in coming, so economists considered the possibility of multiple decision makers, thereby creating a new class of models of the household that we call *non-unitary*.

There are two major categories of non-unitary models. The language gets a bit messy, but for the sake of the discussion here, following Chiappori (1988, 1992), I will call the first category *collective*. In this class of models, each decision maker weighs the wants and desires of the other(s) even as they make choices for themselves. Households, in turn, are assumed to negotiate among themselves, choosing and revising their choices, so that there is no reallocation of resources that would make any member better off without damaging the well-being of another. This is the famous Pareto criterion for efficiency; hence the collective household is a Pareto-efficient household. We assume this point right from the start and then see where that assumption takes us.

The second category of models comes to us from the field of game theory. In these models, there is no presumption that the households we observe are Pareto efficient. Instead, we think of them as engaged in a competition for resources constrained only by members' feelings for the well-being of the other(s) in the household. In the worst case, the outcome really is like that of a hard-fought game. Households that behave in this manner are called *noncooperative*. In the best-case scenario, when the game is played repeatedly and the players come to understand that there is a path along which they might all benefit if they choose differently, households become *cooperative*. Cooperative and collective outcomes may thus be indistinguishable from each other in reality, but analytically we get to those outcomes in quite different ways that may matter for our understanding of how families function. The chapter closes with a brief examination of why we care about how families function.

HOW FAMILIES FORM: COURTSHIP AND THE GAINS FROM PARTNERSHIPS OR MARRIAGE

Courtship is a search process. Gary Becker (1973) outlined that process for economists in his highly influential paper, "Theory of Marriage: Part 1." Out of all the potential matches, some are highly eligible, others barely so, and the remainder not at all desirable. Two aspects of this matching process stand out. First, we can characterize the motivation of the principals. Of course, who the principals actually are is a question of interest, too. Parents may contract unions for their children with goals in mind that serve the purposes of the extended family and its older generations. Alternatively, children may contract unions for themselves, with or without the blessing of their elders (Edlund and Lagerlof 2006). Here, I consider only the case where two consenting adults arrange a marriage on their own behalf.

If men or partners of the first part bring to a union some profile of characteristics x, and the second partners, perhaps women, bring a profile of characteristics y, those characteristics intermingle to generate some household outputs captured by the mathematical expression $h(x, y)$. Both more x and *more y* make for greater marital output, whether that output comprises socioeconomic status, higher-quality children, greater longevity, or whatever else matters to (i.e., is in the utility functions of) the individuals involved. How the attributes in x and the attributes in y match up depends on whether individuals are looking for persons complementary to themselves, in which case *positive* assortative mating takes place (like marries like), or substitutes for themselves in household processes, in which case *negative* assortative mating occurs (opposites attract). In an efficient marriage market, where maximizing the marital output is the purpose, the process of matching should lead to positive assortative mating. Conversely, if partnerships are formed to share risk, highly risk-averse men may seek out very risk-tolerant women in a process of negative assortative mating that provides the ultimate insurance policy (Chiappori and Reny, 2005). More recent work in this area explores whether pairings are better when couples seek to match on more than a single attribute (among the most recent work are the papers by Galichon and Salanié [2012] and Cacioppo et al. [2013]).

Consider what happens if an individual does not find a match. That person's household output then depends on his or her own efforts alone. We express this as $h(x, 0) = h(x)$ or $h(0, y) = h(y)$. The mathematics suggests that most of us are capable of surviving on our own. We have positive output, but it is also true that for most of us, the joint product will be greater than the individual product. This is the conclusion that there are positive gains from marriage.

Gains from marriage entail more than just the outcomes of the marital output function $h(x, y)$. Additional terms in our marital output function may capture matches on other attributes—for example, religion, caste, social norms, musical taste, or beauty. These attributes may enhance the enjoyment of the match, yet be inessential for the production of the main outputs for which the marriage is arranged. Fisman et al. (2006) examine the role of preferences in dating. They find women care about intelligence and race, whereas men care about physical attractiveness, but are put off by higher intelligence and greater ambitiousness than their own. In a follow on study, Fisman et al. (2008) delve further into racial preferences by controlling for neighborhood and state effects associated with this preference. Bisin et al. (2004) look at religious intermarriage and find strong preferences for mates who will allow one to have children who share one's religious identity.

Banerjee et al. (2013) are among the latest set of authors to look at the impact of caste on marriage markets, explicitly through the placing of and response to newspaper ads for partners. They call the attributes that enhance the enjoyment of the match without increasing its marital output "horizontal factors." Caste would be a horizontal factor in many instances. The attributes that shift the marital output directly are referred to as "vertical factors" by Banerjee et al. Educational attainments of the spouses would be one example of a vertical factor. Choosing a mate based on a vertical factor may be "marrying up." Banerjee et al., as well as the authors mentioned previously, find a strong preference for remaining within one's in-group. Indeed, individuals will trade off other characteristics, such as advanced education or beauty, to find a partner in their own caste, race, or religious affiliation.

The second aspect of the matching process has to do with the sheer availability of eligible mates (those with the desired characteristics) and the likelihood of meeting them. This is the classic matching problem (Roth and Sotomayor 1990). Speed dating, online dating services, and marriage brokers are some of the many intermediaries that exist to help individuals make the match of their dreams, though many people still rely on luck.

Participants in a match can be indexed by the level of the respective amounts of their attributes x and y that go into marital production. A match will be made when the searcher can find the highest value mate for himself or herself while committing to provision of at least the minimum of what is required for the other. If the first pairing does not satisfy expectations or desire, switching partners could enable the seeker to find a better match. A "better match" is defined as a partnership that increases the individual's own contribution to marital output because of the positive interaction between what the potential mate brings to the union and what the seeker brings to the union. If there is no appreciable gain from switching, we say that the current match is stable.

Imagine a continuum of men and of women, who can be rank-ordered on the basis of their respective attributes x and y. The men and women at the bottom of everyone's list may find themselves having to promise away any gains from the marriage simply to secure the match. Keep in mind that at the margin, remaining single may not be a bad alternative to marriage. In a world where there is a sexual imbalance, one partner type is in short supply. The type in short supply will be able to extract greater concessions from potential spouses. If women outnumber men, the men at the bottom of the ranking may bring almost nothing to the marriage while the women, just to be married, may accept the same level of utility they would get as a singletons, yielding the remainder of the marital output to their husbands. In some societies, that lower bound, especially for women, is very low indeed.

If, in contrast, women can trade up the profile of eligible matches (the sex ratio moves in their favor), they can expect to enhance their position in two ways. The marital output itself may be larger, as the complementarity of their y with the potential mate's x is stronger. Being in shorter supply also ensures that women obtain a larger share of the marital output. Chiappori, Fortin, and Lacroix (2002, 66) found that an increase in the ratio of men to women increased women's share of the household's resources by $2,163 (in 1988) and that a change in divorce laws in women's favor caused husbands to transfer $4,310 toward their wives.

In a world of imbalance, even high-status women might have to assign away almost all of the benefits that marriage confers on them. Alternatively, there may be a payment from the bride's family to the groom's family to protect the bride against subsequent extraction of surplus once the marriage contract is made (Zhang and Chan 1999). Rao (1993) found an upward trajectory in dowry payments in rural India over a 40-year period as a spurt in population growth dramatically increased the availability of nubile young women, turning the sex ratio against them in marriage markets. If men outnumber available women, a bride price or dower might be necessary to clinch the deal between the groom and the bride and still protect the groom (Anderson 2007).

Much of within-household decision making and sharing may, in fact, be determined before the couple even comes together. Women put at a disadvantage by their relative numbers or relative incomes (what Browning, Chiappori, and Weiss [2011, 342–350] call distributional factors) may find themselves accepting meager shares of the household product. Men put at a disadvantage by their rankings in a profile of desirable traits may surrender their power to decide when it comes to how the household is run. Monetary transfers before marriage may obviate the disadvantages of one party or the other, but remain little studied in economics (Anderson 2007). Even the legal profession is undecided about how premarital agreements—let alone compensatory transfers—affect the success or failure of the subsequent union (Bix 1998). Explicit payments still exist in many places, but there is a widespread perception that such payments decline as economic development increases and authorities are often anxious to hasten their disappearance (Anderson 2007).

HOW FAMILIES FUNCTION

Once the match is made, how the members of that household conduct themselves at home and abroad is of even greater interest to economists and social scientists. The financial as well as emotional well-being of the family is tied up with the management of its economic resources. Households are the repository of a nation's assets, its agents, and its hopes for the future. The economic activities of households constitute approximately 70 percent of a country's gross domestic product and intra-household allocations of resources are the bedrock of distributive justice in a society.

In many societies, even in the so-called progressive West, women surrendered their personhood on entering into the marital state. To quote the famous English legal theorist, William Blackstone:

> By marriage, the husband and wife are one person in law: that is, the very being or legal existence of the woman is suspended during the marriage, or at least incorporated and consolidated into that of the husband, under whose wing, protection and cover, she performs everything.[1]

This is perhaps the strongest definition of what constitutes a unitary household. Nevertheless, it will be useful to give this some economic content, so that we can better understand later departures from this model. Much of what follows focuses on the two-person household or family for simplicity of exposition. Nevertheless, research on the multiple-person household does exist, and where possible I will allude to it. I will try to be gender neutral. I will use the term "marriage" interchangeably with "formal partnership," while fully recognizing that they may not be exactly equivalent yet.

THE ECONOMICS OF UNITARY MODELS

When we examined the matching process earlier, we were primarily concerned with the marital production function, $h(x, y)$—that is, what could be gained by working together. Very little was said about the actual output from that process. Now we turn to the outputs of production and the preferences of individuals within the household for those outputs.

Preferences or tastes are described for economists by utility functions. Utility (or well-being or satisfaction) is derived from the quantities and qualities of the particular commodities and services we desire. Economists distinguish between two general sets of commodities. "Private" goods are consumed by us alone. What I wear, what I eat, my haircut, and my appendectomy are all private; they are rival goods and exclusive in consumption. Having once consumed them, there is nothing left over for anyone else. I alone derive the benefit from private goods.

"Public" goods are those in which we can share—what Samuelson (1954) called collective consumption goods. These goods are nonrival and nonexclusive in consumption. The warmth of a fire, certain aspects of shelter, the joys and sorrows of children—all can be thought of as public goods at the household level, because one individual's experience of them does not automatically impair another's ability to partake of the same goods. Strictly speaking, such goods may be only quasi-public; a house holds just so many people, for example. Nevertheless, up to the capacity of a dwelling, we can share in the shelter which it provides. Public goods are often big-ticket items and require joint participation to provide, so their provision is the logical reason for which marriage is ordained. Goods such as national defense and public safety are public goods as well, but they are beyond the scope of the household; their provision belongs to the public sphere.

Goods may have both private and public aspects. Fong and Zhang (2001) focus on individuals' leisure or free time. They hypothesize a private leisure and then what they call spousal leisure. In a partnership, having free time together has many aspects of a public good, but leisure may also be quite private—for example, the contemplative time I spend alone. In the discussion that follows, goods are treated as strictly public or strictly private, though the mathematics of the situation can be adjusted to reflect the more complicated reality of jointness.

Modern technology has made it easier to achieve some goods by ourselves, but children are probably still the ultimate public good that grows out of a partnership. Marital output, $h(x, y)$, should therefore produce in abundance private and public goods for the principals. Of course, the question is, how do we allocate the time and monetary resources of the individuals to generate the maximum (utility) of private and public goods for the family? And if there is a lack of agreement between the principals about exactly what and how much of the private goods and how much of the public goods are to be produced, how are those disputes resolved and whose will prevails?

Economists label as *unitary* a model of the household in which a single decision maker and his (or her) preferences prevail over all other members. The head is assumed to maximize his own utility function and his alone—which may incorporate arguments for the well-being of the others—subject to the income at his command. The major predictions of this model are that the household acts like an individual in all matters economic, even though multiple individuals constitute that household, and that the resources available to the head are the pooled incomes of all members. Who actually earned those incomes is irrelevant for the choices the "household" makes. Behind the veil of maximization must be some decision-making process by which other members have input into the choices made, but these models are silent on that matter. The outcomes need not be harsh; Gary Becker (1991) posits an "altruistic Patriarch" working hard to satisfy "Rotten Kids." Even so, these models do not fare well when put to the empirical test.

It is worthwhile at this point to say a little about the empirical tests, because those tests form a large literature in their own right. Moreover, other "more realistic models" are subjected to the same sorts of tests to see if they better fit the data we have on family behavior. Recall that the unitary model makes two major predictions. The first, which is often called the "income pooling hypothesis," essentially states that incomes are co-mingled so that household consumption patterns are independent of who earns what. Income can be transferred back and forth between family members so that each gets his or her negotiated share. The ratio of husband's earnings to wife's earnings should not predict how much of a private good or a public good is actually purchased.

Over the last decade this hypothesis has been tested dozens of times. Browning, Chiappori, and Weiss (2011, 225) tabulate an extensive list of articles in this area; the authors of these articles tested for how relative earnings affect labor supply, family savings, food, tobacco and alcohol consumption, child health, and actual family farm production. For example, Lundberg, Pollak, and Wales (1997) found that government payments for child welfare in the United Kingdom, when redirected from fathers to mothers, resulted in a concomitant increase in spending on children. That constitutes a failure of the income pooling hypothesis. In her study of South African households, Duflo (2003) showed that pension payments to grandmothers (rather than grandfathers) enhanced the health of granddaughters relative to their status quo ante. This is also evidence against income pooling, since the hypothesis of income pooling predicts that it should not matter for outcomes who actually receives the income.

The second major prediction of the unitary model is that the unitary household should behave like an individual behaves when one looks at its demands in the marketplace. The short-hand term for this prediction is "testing for Slutsky conditions," after the technical conditions that should characterize individual demand. If households did, indeed, behave like individuals, they should exhibit demand functions that obey the law of demand, have expenditure shares for each commodity that sum to total household expenditure, and display well-ordered substitution (and complementarity) behaviors among commodities (Slutsky symmetry). Then economists could use their well-developed toolkit to evaluate how exogenous forces alter behaviors and affect human welfare. If households do not behave like individuals, however, we will need a new toolkit—or at least new tools—to judge what is going on. In general, analysts find that individual behaviors follow the predictions of Slutsky, but households' behaviors do not. Deviations from Slutsky symmetry bring us to other models that may better capture what is going on behind closed doors.

NON-UNITARY MODELS OF HOUSEHOLD DECISION MAKING

Non-unitary models belong to one of two general categories, but in all cases they acknowledge that the household includes more than one decision maker. For simplicity, this chapter concentrates on households with two adult decision makers, but other papers consider multiple decision makers. Bourguignon (1999) considers a three-person household, consisting of two altruistic parents and a child.

The child is not an independent decision maker, but the child's preferences are strongly represented by the parents. Dauphin et al. (2008) explore whether sons and daughters ages 16–22 and "children" older than age 22 who are also still at home are independent decision makers. The presence of the relative income of the child in various household demands convinces these authors that 16- to 22-year-olds are influential in their respective households, and that daughters are always so regardless of their age. The most general discussion of the multiple decision-maker household from a collective perspective comes from Chiappori and Ekeland (2009). Threats to depart give decision-making adolescents their power in noncooperative models of household decision making (Bergstrom, 1996).

In a very interesting twist on multiple decision makers, Ermisch and Pronzato (2008) consider how child support payments from the father are affected when he forms a new family with a new partner even as his children live with his ex-wife and her new partner (if she has one). Potentially there are four decision makers here. Not surprisingly, second wives resent diversion of household resources to the first wife's children. In fact, an organization called "The British Second Wives Club" lobbies for limits on child support payments to first wives; it has a U.S. counterpart as well (349). We discuss Ermisch and Pronzato's article in more detail later in this chapter.

Non-unitary, Collective Models

What distinguishes collective models from the noncooperative models is the presumption that any outcome we observe is efficient in the sense that there are no obvious changes to be made that will enhance the well-being of one party without damaging the well-being of the other party. This is the well-known Pareto criterion. It applies in these models, because the underlying assumption of matching between partners suggests that households that do not satisfy the needs of both partners have been or shortly will be dissolved. In other words, people will prefer to live singly or will find new partners if household decisions do not meet their desires. At any point in time that we look, of course, some households may not be Pareto efficient, but we expect those to be in a minority and to disappear over time.

If the family is a collective entity, economists assume that it maximizes some combination of the utilities of both of its members:

$\mu U_1 + (1 - \mu)U_2$, where μ lies between 0 and 1. The word "maximizes" here leaves opaque to the outside observer exactly which process leads to the efficient outcome, but it emphasizes that the outcome will be the best that can be achieved (or else the union will dissolve).

In discussing the matching process earlier, we considered the possibility that the value of μ a person gets in a marriage would depend on his or her relative strengths in the matching process. We were particularly concerned that when women are in excess supply (i.e., the sex ratio favors men), women would settle for lower values of their share. Women's shares could even be zero, as long as the husband's utility function contains an argument for some minimal consumption for their wives. Of course, then wives' consumption would depend solely on the weight their husbands assign to the wife's preferences and not on the wife's preferences directly—the ultimate in patriarchal outcomes.

When distribution factors favors women, they can extract higher values of μ. Values of μ may also vary with prices, wages, and incomes, in which case exogenous changes that send pensions or child welfare payments to women rather than to men would alter household expenditures (the rejection of the income pooling hypothesis). If, for example, children figure more prominently in women's utility functions, then researchers will see the household's expenditure on children increase because women have the power (μ) to make that happen. If $\mu = \frac{1}{2}$, then each individual's utility function would carry equal weight in decision making.

It would be useful at this point to say something about the preferences, U_1 and U_2. If preferences are *egotistical*, then person 1's utility function contains only his or her own private consumption q_1 and the public good Q, which is indivisible and nonexclusive in consumption. Recall that the public goods obtained through marriage may be one of the main reasons to marry. Children, a home, and care in adversity and old age may all be public goods. If person 2 were egotistical, his or her utility function would contain only q_2 and Q. Two egotists could still opt to form a household, because together they might be able to provide more of the public good for themselves and enjoy no less of the private good than they do alone. Being egotistical is not an insuperable barrier to marriage.

Alternatively, we could imagine a union of altruists. In such a union, each person cares about the other's utility as well as his or her own. The partners may care equally for themselves and the other; they may care more for the other; or they may care more for themselves. Nevertheless, person 1's utility function contains the utilities and not just the consumption level of the other. One possible mathematical definition of altruism would be $U_j = U_j [U_1(q_1, Q) + U_2(q_2, Q)]$, where individual j ($j = 1$ or 2) cares not only about his own utility, but also about the utility of his or her partner. This situation—what Chen and Woolley (2001) call *caring* preferences—is simply one way in which we might describe altruistic behavior. There are many functions to describe caring preferences.

We observe neither a partner's utility function nor the value of μ that governs that individual's share of household resources and, therefore, defines his or her relative power. All we observe when we look at the data households generate is what the household actually buys or the labor it chooses to supply to the market. Even so, a lot of information about the household can be extracted from such expenditure survey data. If some goods are *exclusive* to one partner or the other—men's versus women's clothing may be the best example here—we can make inferences about how powerful one partner or the other is by observing how much of the budget goes to an exclusive good (Donni and Chiappori 2011). Other goods may not be exclusive but rather be *assignable* based on some *a priori* notions we bring to an analysis. In the olden days, it was assumed that only men consumed the tobacco products purchased by a household. Commodities such as diapers and day care probably belong to children's consumption. We can use these observations on household expenditures to make inferences about what is going on behind the scenes as long as we also have information on nonexclusive, nonassignable goods against which to compare.

Labor supply (and its mirror image, demand for leisure) forms one category where we may have the kind of detailed behavior for each individual that is necessary to recover the sharing rule. Time use studies are particularly helpful in this regard. Of course, the labor market has rigidities to it: one may not have flexible hours, for example, and some large segment of the population may not be in the labor force at any given moment. These facts of life complicate the recovery of sharing rules and the underlying utilities, but do not necessarily prohibit discovery (Blundell, Chiappori, and Meghir 2005; Donni and Moreau 2007).

Focusing on labor supplies raises the possibility of household production. Families may be engaged in producing output for their own consumption or to take to market. These supplementary activities also convey information about decision making within the household. In an influential piece from the development literature where we have information on household production, Udry (1996) observes that approximately 6 percent of output is lost because household labor is not allocated across cultivated plots in a gender-blind manner. In Udry's study, plots controlled by women had much lower productivity because female labor can be applied only to plots controlled by women. Consequently, women's land was worked much more intensively by women. Output could be increased if some of the female laborers could be transferred to plots controlled by men, but that would violate gender norms. The role that societal norms play in decision making will be considered again when we look at the idea of "separate spheres" later in the chapter.

Behind the idea of the collective model is something like the following narrative (Apps and Rees 1997). The spouses discuss in a first stage the level of the households' public goods they want. This is not hard to imagine: husbands and wives talk about how many children they want, how big a house they want to live in, and when to retire. After they are agreed on the level of the public good, they decide how to allocate the remainder of household resources between them so that each partner can maximize utility over their own private consumption. That is a how-to story, the kind economists tell. It gives a rough and ready sketch of how the optimization is accomplished and how intra-household resource allocation might, indeed, be Pareto efficient.

Can we test the underlying efficiency assumption that is such an important aspect of these models? It turns out that we can to some degree. The technical discussion of these tests goes beyond the bounds of this chapter, but the intuition is accessible. All the factors that determine μ—the household balance of power—should affect household demands in roughly the same (proportional) way, assuming this model captures the reality. Thus, if we estimate demand functions, we should see that the distribution factors that determine μ (sex ratios, relative incomes) show up in those demand functions. With a high degree of care, we can even extend these models to intertemporal demands and supplies and demands under conditions of uncertainty. If something like the sex ratio and the relative earning powers of the spouses are not influential in those estimations, then that is evidence against the collective model.

Non-unitary, Noncooperative, or Game Theoretic Models

Ultimately the justification behind the collective models we examined was that they had to be Pareto efficient. Marital sorting should assure that this condition is met. Many analysts, however, do not buy this argument. They prefer (as more realistic) a narrative different from the one offered by Apps and Rees.

In noncooperative or game theoretic models, we assume that the family is maximizing the utilities of its members, subject to the amount of income they have brought to the union. A noncooperative household is not a unitary household, but neither is there an agreement on the level of the public good before each individual decides on his or her own private consumption. Each individual chooses for himself or herself own private consumption and the amount that person intends to contribute to the public good (housing, child care).

Private consumptions are chosen in tandem with the choice of contribution to the public good. Each individual perceives that the public good costs him or her directly, where that cost is the own private consumption foregone. Because a public good generates benefits for both parties, but each party individually takes no account of those spillover effects, the value of such goods is routinely underestimated and underprovided. That condition is also what makes this a Cournot-Nash equilibrium rather than the best-response, cooperative equilibrium. Moreover, it is why households do not meet the Pareto efficiency criterion (the assumption underlying collective models) even though family members are maximizing their own welfare.

Students of game theory will recognize this Cournot-Nash game, as it closely resembles the one we see between firms in imperfectly competitive markets. In Cournot-Nash equilibria, especially one-shot games, the players cannot see beyond their own selfish, short-term interests. In a long term game however, with very patient players, it is possible (folk wisdom even says it is likely) that the Pareto-efficient outcome will finally emerge and be sustained (Lundberg and Pollak 1993, 1994). Of course, in the face of shocks to the family, the infidelity of one member being an example, players may revert to a noncooperative behavior with a loss of welfare to all. Del Boca and Flinn (2011) find that almost one-fourth of families experiencing an infidelity in the partnership can be characterized as noncooperative after the event.

Threat points may be built in to help keep game-theoretic families away from the Nash-Cournot (noncooperative) outcomes. Partners maximize over the product of their own and their partner's utility, but each of those utilities has a lower bound built into it. If either individual ever finds that the choice of the partner causes his or her own utility to drop below a certain threshold, that individual will leave the relationship, sending the value of the partnership to zero. Manser and Brown (1980) and McElroy and Horney (1981) call that lower bound a threat point. For both of their analyses, the threat point is measured as the utility that can be obtained when single. Threat points need not be as drastic as divorce, however. They may, for example, be defined as the utility that could be achieved by something like resistance or sabotage (the outcome of a noncooperative game) that stops short of actual departure.[2]

If we posit the existence of threat points, we have a model in which each partner maximizes his or her own utility constrained by the existence of the threat. This formulation still allows Pareto-efficient behaviors to emerge, but it does not impose such behaviors *a priori* on the model.

In general, the outcomes to noncooperatives games are *not* Pareto efficient. The household could do better if its members sat down together and agreed to provide a larger amount of the public good and then divvied up what was left of their joint income between them. Why do they not follow this path? The answer from the game theory literature is that there is a commitment problem. A commitment problem—in a marriage? Well, yes, because these families are imagined to consist of egotistical individuals maximizing their own utilities constrained only by the "threats" from the other. If one forgoes what maximizes one's own utility, in the hope that the partner will match this altruism, it creates an opportunity for the partner to take advantage. If the partner forgoes taking advantage, that person is counting on the fact that the first player will not then pounce. An ongoing stream of altruistic moves requires a suspension of the selfish motives of each partner. That requires a long-term commitment—an "until death does them part" commitment. It is possible to have such a commitment, but it is not a foregone conclusion in any marriage.[3] And should one partner or the other slip, game theory tells us that there must be a punishment and repentance mechanism by which the family can come back from the brink.

Noncooperative Models and the Idea of Separate Spheres

In Udry's (1996) analysis of agricultural households, we encountered noncooperative, Pareto-inefficient households because social norms prevent efficient use of resources. Household production and consumption may be segregated along gender lines because social norms dictate that division. Keeping home and hearth and rearing small children were thought in many places and many times somehow to be the special province of women. Men, who were deemed more fit for combat and the public sphere, were expected to "go out to work," earning the family's income to support that very separate life "at home." The segregation of women and children is ancient and widespread, although the valorization of the idea of separate spheres is a Victorian English innovation (Davidoff and Hall 1987).Whether separate spheres are imposed on the household exogenously through social and religious forces (Lundberg and Pollak 1993) or whether they arise endogenously from the preferences and incomes in the household, the notion of separate spheres implies that public goods provision will be limited by the sphere in which those goods are used (Browning, Chiappori, and Lechene 2009).

A caveat is in order. One might think that policies designed to affect one sphere rather than the other could be targeted to one spouse rather than the other. Browning, Chiappori, and Lechene (2009) find, however, that over some range of incomes, income pooling prevails—as in the unitary models—in the provision of household resources. This factor will make targeting ineffective, as all funds go into a single family pot. In contrast, when incomes are vastly unequal, as they might have been in Victorian times, income pooling does not occur, so targeting policies might have reached the recipients for whom they are intended.

Hybrid Models: An Example

We may also have hybrid models that partake of aspects of both cooperative and noncooperative behaviors. For a particularly interesting example, let us return to the essay mentioned earlier by John Ermisch and Chiara Pronzato (2008). In their model, there are potentially four decision makers. In the ex-wife's new family, decisions on child expenditure grow out of a cooperative model between her new partner and the mother. Similarly, in the ex-husband's new household, decisions on his contributions to child support grow out of a cooperative model between his second wife and the father. The decision making between households is decidedly noncooperative (the ex-wife has no leverage over her ex-husband), so that we end up with a game theoretic outcome. If the bargaining that takes place between the two households leaves the sharing rule within each of the new households unchanged, then child support payments appear to come out of the "pooled" income of the two households. If the sharing rule within households is changed by the bargaining between households, the amount of child support forthcoming depends on the relative power of the father in his new household.

How can researchers distinguish among the different models of household behavior? So far, the best tests involve looking for income pooling and Slutsky symmetry. If who earns the income affects the pattern of expenditure, then we must reject the hypothesis that income is pooled. Income pooling is a major attribute of the unitary models, so we would reject the unitary model of the household if we reject income pooling. Of course, as noted earlier, we might fail to reject income pooling in certain noncooperative models as well, so it becomes important to look at the family's demand behavior. When households are not run by a single decision maker, then what is bought and by whom it is bought will depend on the relative power of that individual within the household. Because relative power depends on distribution factors—sex ratios, relative income, and gender, to name a few—those distribution factors will prove to be important explanatory variables in estimating demand. Every student of economics is taught that demand essentially depends on the levels of prices and incomes. Sex ratios should not matter in the purchase of shirts and blouses. If they do, then we have evidence for a non-unitary structure to the household.[4]

CONCLUSION: HAPPILY EVER AFTER?

Of all the models of family decision making examined in this chapter, which is correct: the unitary model, the collective model, or the game theoretic models? Most researchers acknowledge that the unitary model may once have provided an adequate explanation of family behavior, but is no longer applicable. Indeed, it is routinely rejected in empirical tests. Historically and in traditional societies, women had limited power to control their own fates. On entering marriage, whatever status they had had as unmarried daughters was surrendered to their husbands. That changed in Western societies at the turn of the 20th century. Married women's property rights, freer access to divorce, and rising educational levels and labor force participation can be credited with transforming women into decision makers—if not the equals of their husbands—within their own families (Waller 2010, 324–330).

That brings us to models of the family that take seriously the idea of multiple economic agents within the family. One set, known as *collective* models, begins with the presumption that households are Pareto efficient. Decision makers bargain over levels of the public, shared goods they want, and any resources left over are then shared between or among them according to some sharing "rule" so that they may satisfy their own private needs. Justification for this set of models rests on the efficacy of marital sorting—individuals pair up with mates who share many of their own attributes—and the ease of dissolving any relationship that is not working. The observer then concludes that, on average, the households are indeed efficient. Empirical tests that repudiate the unitary model have lent credence to the collective story, but cannot establish those models unequivocally. This is due in part to a second class of multiple-decision-maker models offered as an alternative to the collective story.

This second set of models of multiple-decision-maker families comes to us from the game theory literature. These models do not carry the *a priori* assumption of Pareto efficiency, but instead assume some competition occurs inside the family for the available resources. When families play "nice," the outcomes we observe are difficult to distinguish from those predicted by the collective models. When families do not play "nice," we observe what game theorists call noncooperative outcomes, which are decidedly not Pareto efficient. Research continues to see if we can better distinguish between these two sets of models.

Why do we care what goes on behind closed doors? The short answer is that if households do not achieve Pareto-efficient outcomes, it is possible to do things differently so that at least one family member is made better off without making anyone else worse off. All of economics is organized around this principle, described colloquially as the notion that "money should not be left on the table." In other words, inefficiencies should not prevail. If a child could be better fed or better educated, or if an adult could get the health care she needs or the hous-ing he wants or just a night on the town, or if we could divvy up what we have more effectively, then that is a change we want to make.

Some of the changes we want to make are so important—health, education, and nutrition—that a government policy to improve family welfare might be warranted. Targeting of support payments is at least as old as the Fabians, who firmly believed that government should be involved in promoting family welfare (Pember-Reeves 1913). At the turn of the last century, the Fabians dispensed small weekly sums directly to new mothers to show that infants might have fresh food and untainted milk if a targeted transfer program were put in place. Whether targeting as a policy instrument works is something that better knowledge of intra-family decision making can tell us.

In economies where females have meager prospects in labor mar-kets or are simply not the preferred sex of child desired by their parents, women's and girls' intra-household power is severely lim-ited, as is their consumption and overall well-being. Social, political, and environmental factors that enhance the power of women in these households may be influential in improving the prospects of their daughters (Duflo 2003; Li and Wu 2011). Closer to home, Farmer and Tiefenthaler (1996) argue that policies that strengthen women's bar-gaining power in the family may be instrumental in reducing domes-tic violence. A better understanding of who the decision makers are and how the balance of power is determined would enable us to make strides toward greater efficiency and greater equality.

What transpires within households may also enable us to make bet-ter sense of macroeconomic phenomena, although this area of research remains in its infancy. One area in which some research has been done focuses on trends in economy-wide inequality. Fernandez et al. (2005) explore how positive assortative mating and the families that form from that process may lead to greater inequality in the economy, as high performers pair off with other high performers and lower per-formers are left to match with other lower performers. Lise and Seitz (2011) suggest that there has been a decline in intra-household inequality in the United Kingdom since 1970, which they attribute to rising labor force participation by wives that subsequently leads to a more equal sharing of resources within the family.

Once we open the door, it becomes obvious that many decisions that affect the economy are made within the household. The economic theory that explores intra-household decision making holds true to the methodological individualism inherent in economics, but also builds on the very real perception that the family is not a monolithic union. How families are formed and who is most influential within them will matter for production and consumption, employment and unemployment, and inequality and fairness.

NOTES

1. Quoted in Maureen Waller, *The English Marriage* (London, UK: John Murray, 2009), 2. The original is from Sir William Blackstone, "By Marriage," in *Commentaries on the Law of England: The Rights of Persons* (Philadelphia, PA: 1900 [reprint]), 442.

2. Generally, threat points would depend on the earnings of each partner, the costs of divorce, and the factor affecting the probabilities of remarriage. It should also be noted that these lower bounds are not observable to the researcher, although it may be possible for one spouse to send a credible signal of unhappiness to the other about an intention to leave (Farmer and Tiefenthaler, 1996).

3. Of course, intertemporal cooperative models and models under uncertainty require something similar. A changing balance of power over time can inflict inefficiencies as individuals take advantage of increases in their power to push through outcomes more beneficial to themselves (Donni and Chiappori 2007; Mazzoco 2005). The reference here should be Donni and Chiapport 2011, and that is already in the reference list. See above.

4. Slutsky symmetry describes how an individual's demands respond to all price changes: own price, substitute prices, and complement prices. The degree to which households depart from Slutsky symmetry depends on the number of decision makers in the household. Browning and Chiappori (1998) show that in a k-member cooperative household, there is an additional set of $k - 1$ responses that can be thought of as augmenting the individual's responses. In noncooperative households, there should a different and distinguishable augmenting response from that one encountered in the cooperative household (Lechene and Preston 2000).

REFERENCES

Anderson, Siwan. "The Economics of Dowry and Bride Price." *Journal of Economic Perspectives* 21, no. 4 (2007): 151–174.

Apps, Patricia, and Ray Rees. "Collective Labour Supply and Household Production." *Journal of Political Economy* 105, no. 1 (1997): 178–190.

Banerjee, Abhijit, Esther Duflo, Maitreesh Ghatak, and Jeanne Lafortune. "Marry for What? Caste and Mate Selection in Modern India." *American Economic Journal: Microeconomics* 5, no. 2 (2013): 33–72.

Becker, Gary S. "A Theory of Marriage: Part I." *Journal of Political Economy* 81, no. 4 (1973): 813–846.

Becker, Gary S. *A Treatise on the Family.* Cambridge, MA: Harvard University Press, 1991.

Bergstrom, Theodore. "Economics in a Family Way." *Journal of Economic Literature* 34, no. 4 (1996): 1903–1934.

Bisin, Alberto, Giorgio Topa, and Thierry Verdier. "Religious Intermarriage and Socialization in the United States." *Journal of Political Economy* 112, no. 3 (2004): 615–664.

Bix, Brian. "Bargaining in the Shadow of Love: The Enforcement of Premarital Agreements and How We Think about Marriage." *William and Mary Law Review* 40, no. 1 (1998): 145–207.

Blundell, Richard, Pierre-André Chiappori, and Costas Meghir. "Collective Labor Supply with Children." *Journal of Political Economy* 113, no. 6 (2005): 1277–1306.

Bourguignon, Francois. "The Cost of Children: May the Collective Approach to Household Behavior Help?" *Journal of Population Economics* 12, no. 4 (1999): 503–522.

Browning, Martin, and Pierre-André Chiappori. "Efficient Household Allocation: A Characterization and Tests." *Econometrica* 66 (1998): 1241–1278.

Browning, Martin, Pierre-André Chiappori, and Valerie Lechene. "Distribution Effects in Household Models: Separate Sphere and Income Pooling." *Economic Journal* 120 (2009): 786–799.

Browning, Martin, Pierre-André Chiappori, and Yoram Weiss. "Family Economics." 2011. http://www.cemmap.ac.uk/resources/chiappori/paper_1.pdf.

Cacioppo, John T., Stephanie Cacioppo, Gian C. Gonzaga, Elizabeth L. Ogburn, and Tyler J. VanderWeele. "Marital Satisfaction and Break-ups Differ across On-line and Off-line Meeting Venues." *Proceedings of the National Academy of Sciences* 110, no. 25 (2013): 10135–10140.

Chen, Zhiqi, and Frances Woolley. "A Cournot-Nash Model of Family Decision Making." *Economic Journal* 111 (2001): 722–748.

Chiappori, Pierre-André. "Rational Household Labor Supply." *Econometrica* 56 (1988): 63–89.

Chiappori, Pierre-André. "Collective Labor Supply and Welfare." *Journal of Political Economy* 100 (1992): 437–467.

Chiappori, Pierre-André, and Ivar Ekeland. "The Microeconomics of Efficient Group Behavior: Identification." *Econometrica* 77, no. 3 (2009): 763–790.

Chiappori, Pierre-André, Bernard Fortin, and Guy Lacroix. "Marriage Market, Divorce Legislation and Household Labour Supply." *Journal of Political Economy* 110, no. 1 (2002): 37–72.

Chiappori, Pierre-André, and Philip J. Reny. *Matching to Share Risk.* Working paper. New York, NY: Columbia University, September 2005.

Dauphin, Anyck, Abdel-Rahmen El Lahga, Bernard Fortin, and Guy Lacroix. *Are Children Decision-Makers within the Household.* IZA Discussion Paper 3728. Bonn, Germany: Institute for the Study of Labor, 2008.

Davidoff, Leonore, and Catherine Hall. *Family Fortunes: Men and Women of the English Middle Class, 1780–1850.* Chicago, IL: University of Chicago Press, 1987.

Del Boca, Daniela, and Christopher Flinn. "Endogenous Household Interaction." *Journal of Econometrics* 166 (2011): 49–65.

Donni, Olivier, and Pierre-André Chiappori. "Nonunitary Models of Household Behavior: A Survey of the Literature." In *Household Economic Behaviors*, edited by José Alberto Molina, 1–40. New York, NY: Springer, 2011.

Donni, Olivier, and Nicolas Moreau. "Collective Labor Supply: A Single Equation Model and Some Evidence from French Data." *Journal of Human Resources* 42, no. 1 (2007): 214–246.

Duflo, Esther. "Grandmothers and Granddaughters: Old Age Pension and Intra-household Allocation in South Africa." *World Bank Economic Review* 17, no. 1 (2003): 1–25.

Edlund, Lena, and Nils-Petter Lagerlof. "Individual versus Parental Consent in Marriage: Implications for Intra-household Resource Allocation and Growth." *American Economic Review* 96, no. 2 (May 2006): 304–307.

Ermisch, John, and Chiara Pronzato. "Intrahousehold Allocation of Resources: Inferences from Non-residential Fathers' Child Support." *Economic Journal* 118 (2008): 347–362.

Farmer, Amy, and Jill Tiefenthaler. "Domestic Violence: The Value of Services as Signals." *American Economic Review* 6, no. 2 (1996): 274–279.

Fernandez, Raquel, Nezih Gruner, and John Knowles. "Love and Money: A Theoretical and Empirical Analysis of Household Sorting and Inequality." *Quarterly Journal of Economics* 120, no. 1 (2005): 273–344.

Fisman, Raymond, Sheena S. Iyengar, Emir Kamenica, and Itamar Simonson. "Gender Differences in Mate Selection: Evidence from a Speed Dating Experiment." *Quarterly Journal of Economics* 121, no. 2 (2006): 673–697.

Fisman, Raymond, Sheena S. Iyengar, Emir Kamenica, and Itamar Simonson. "Racial Preferences in Dating." *Review of Economic Studies* 75, no. 1 (2008): 117–132.

Fong, Yuk-fai, and Junsen Zhang. "The Identification of Unobservable and Spousal Leisure." *Journal of Political Economy* 109, no. 1 (2001): 191–202.

Galichon, Alfred, and Bernard Salanié. *Cupid's Invisible Hand: Social Surplus and Identification in Matching Models.* Economics Department Working Paper. Paris, France: Sciences Po, September 2012.

Lechene, Valerie, and Ian Preston. *Departures from Slutsky Symmetry in Noncooperative Household Demand Models.* University of Oxford Discussion Papers No. 52. Oxford, UK: University of Oxford, December 2000.

Li, Lixing, and Xiaoyu Wu. "Gender of Children, Bargaining Power and Intra-household Resource Allocation in China." *Journal of Human Resources* 46, no. 2 (2011): 295–316.

Lise, Jeremy, and Shannon Seitz. "Consumption Inequality and Intra-household Allocations." *Review of Economic Studies* 78, no. 1 (2011): 328–355.

Lundberg, Shelly J., and Robert A. Pollak. "Separate Spheres Bargaining and the Marriage Market." *Journal of Political Economy* 101 (1993): 988–1010.

Lundberg, Shelly J., and Robert A. Pollak. "Noncooperative Bargaining Models of Marriage." *American Economic Review* 84, no. 2 (1994): 132–137.

Lundberg, Shelly J., Robert A. Pollak, and Terence J. Wales. "Do Husbands and Wives Pool Their Resources? Evidence from the U.K. Child Benefit." *Journal of Human Resources* 32, no. 3 (1997): 463–480.

Manser, Marilyn, and Murray Brown. "Marriage and Household Decision-Making." *International Economic Review* 21, no. 1 (1980): 31–44.

Mazzoco, Maurizio. "Savings, Risk Sharing and Preferences for Risk." *American Economic Review* 94 (2005): 1169–1180.

McElroy, Marjorie, and Mary Jean Horney. "Nash Bargained Household Decisions: Towards a Generalization of the Theory of Demand." *International Economic Review* 22, no. 2 (1981): 333–349.

Pember-Reeves, Maud. *Round about a Pound a Week.* London, UK: Bell and Sons, 1913. Reprinted London, UK: Virago Press, 1979.

Rao, Vijayendra. "The Rising Price of Husbands: A Hedonic Analysis of Dowry Increases in Rural India." *Journal of Political Economy* 101, no. 4 (1993): 666–677.

Roth, Alvin, and Marilda A. Oliveira Sotomayor. *Two Sided Matching: A Study in Game Theoretic Modeling and Analysis.* Econometric Society Monograph No. 18. Cambridge, UK: Cambridge University Press, 1990.

Samuelson, Paul. "The Pure Theory of Public Expenditure." *Review of Economic Studies* 36 (1954): 387–389.

Udry, Christopher. "Gender, Agricultural Production and the Theory of the Household." *Journal of Political Economy* 104 (1996): 1010–1046.

Waller, Maureen. *The English Marriage: Tales of Love, Money and Adultery.* London, UK: John Murray, 2010.

Zhang, Junsen, and William Chan. "Dowry and Wife's Welfare: A Theoretical and Empirical Analysis." *Journal of Political Economy* 107, no. 4 (1999): 786–808.

Chapter 2

The Gender Pay Gap across Countries: A Human Capital Approach

Solomon W. Polachek and Jun Xiang

This chapter concentrates on labor market institutions that are related to female lifetime work that affects the gender wage gap across countries. Using International Social Survey Programme (ISSP), Luxembourg Income Study (LIS), and Organization for Economic and Cooperative Development (OECD) wage data for 35 countries covering 1970–2002, we show that the gender pay gap is positively associated with the fertility rate, positively associated with the husband-wife age gap at first marriage, and positively related to the top marginal tax rate—all factors that negatively affect women's lifetime labor force participation. In addition, we show that collective bargaining, as found in previous studies, is negatively associated with the gender pay gap.

The fact that women earn less than men is a consistent and widely observed phenomenon. Explaining this pay gap has attracted much attention, not just because the gender part of the pay gap is intrinsically interesting, but also because discriminatory wage practices could lead to an inefficient resource allocation. Here, we compute the gender wage gap as the difference between the male and female log of mean or median wages (O'Neill and O'Neill, 2006). In what follows, wages are measured at the median of the wage distribution, using raw wage data for the sample of full-time workers. As such, the gender wage gap has been studied throughout the last several decades using many data sets, various estimation methods, and numerous employee subgroups (Weichselbaumer and Winter-Ebmer 2003). Despite the large number of studies, scholars continue to debate the causes and consequences of the gender wage gap.

To date, relatively little attention has been paid to comparative studies across countries. Blau and Kahn have conducted most of the studies on this subject and found striking international variations in the gender pay gap (Blau and Kahn 1996a, 1996b, 2002). Countries such as Australia, Belgium, Czech Republic, Hungary, Italy, Poland, and Sweden exhibited a gender pay gap of approximately 20 percent over the period 1970–2000 based on OECD data. Other countries such as Austria, Canada, South Korea, and Japan maintained gender pay gaps as large as 40 to 50 percent. During this time period, there were dramatic demographic and institutional changes that may help explain how and why women's relative labor market success varied across these countries. If so, one can use these international differences to better understand the gender wage gap.

Previous comparative studies mostly focused on wage-setting institutions (Blau and Kahn 2003; Weichselbaumer and Winter-Ebmer 2002). In particular, Weichselbaumer and Winter-Ebmer (2003) performed a meta-analysis comparing 363 studies that collectively examined gender wage differences for 67 particular countries. As a meta-analysis, their study analyzed secondary data. Blau and Kahn (2003) utilized micro-data from the ISSP for 22 countries over the 1985–1994 period. They found that countries with a more compressed male wage structure (a narrower male earnings distribution) were associated with a lower gender pay gap. Also, they report that greater collective bargaining coverage was negatively related to the gender pay gap.

One important demographic factor that may be relevant is the *family* wage gap. Male-female wage differences are relatively small (usually less than 10 percent) for single (especially never married) men and women, but considerably larger (roughly 40 percent) for married men and women (Blau and Kahn 1992), and even greater for those men and women with children (Harkness and Waldfogel 2003), especially when those children are spaced widely apart (Polachek 1975a). To explain this pattern Polachek (1975a) and Becker (1985) resort to division of labor in the home. Division of labor in the home implies married men expect to work more years in the market (and with greater effort) over their lifetime than do married women.

As a result, married men purchase more human capital than married women (especially those married women with children), so married men have higher wages. Single (especially never-married childless) men and women earn roughly similar wages and exhibit roughly comparable lifetime work histories.

Proving that household division of labor is an important factor instigating the gender wage gap is particularly complicated. Division of labor increases incentives for husbands to invest in *marketable* human capital, yet increases incentives for wives to invest in less remunerative home activities. The problem is that actual human capital investments are not directly observable. Most data sets contain years of schooling and some contain actual work experience, but few data sets are detailed enough to contain specifics such as subjects studied, quality of schooling, or types of on-the-job training. Thus, although these more-subtle factors are important determinants of human capital investment, they are rarely available when explaining the gender wage gap (Weinberger and Kuhn 2005).

Given the difficulty in incorporating precise measures of human capital, it makes sense to validate the implications of the division of labor in the home in some other way. One possibility is to explore whether the theory's predictions regarding lifetime work and wages are upheld in comparative data across countries. Within a number of specific countries (e.g., Germany, United Kingdom, United States, and Austria), there is a direct link between lifetime work and earnings, as illustrated by the previously mentioned relationship between the gender wage gap and marital status (Blau and Kahn 1992). Another approach is to test whether the theory's inferences hold *between* countries. This can be done by examining whether cross-country *differences* in institutional variables that affect lifetime labor force participation and the incentive to invest in human capital are related to cross-country differences in the gender wage gap.

In this chapter, we introduce three innovations. First, we expand the information used by incorporating a greater number of years of ISSP data (1985–2002) than in past studies. Second, we introduce new data obtained from the Luxembourg Income Study as well as the OECD. Third, we concentrate on hypotheses emanating from the division of labor within the home. In particular, we explore whether differences in women's incentive for labor force participation can account for variations in the gender pay gap across countries and over time. More specifically, because women (especially married women) were historically, and still are, more likely than men to specialize in household activities, they may invest less effort in market-related activities than do men because of a greater preoccupation with household responsibilities (Becker, 1991). If such is the case, then women's incentive for lifetime work (in terms of both work time and work effort) may be an important determinant of female wages relative to men. For this reason, we expect women who reside in countries that offer fewer incentives for women's market work to have lower wages relative to men, and vice versa for women residing in countries with greater work incentives Becker, 1964. Variables such as the fertility rate, the age gap between husband and wife at their first marriage, the top marginal income tax rate, and female relative educational attainment—all of which affect women's incentive for labor force participation relative to men's—may be important in determining this relationship.

BRIEF BACKGROUND LITERATURE

Donald Treiman and Patricia Roos (1983) were the first to investigate gender pay differences within a cross-national framework. They ran standard $\log_e$-linear wage regressions for full-time workers aged 20–64 in each of nine industrialized countries. They then decomposed wage differences in each country, parceling out the gap between education, potential experience, and occupation, and found significant "unexplained" differences in each country. Rachel Rosenfeld and Arne Kalleberg (1990) adopted a similar approach, but concentrated on only four countries (United States, Canada, Norway, and Sweden). Using slightly more refined demographic variables (e.g., number of children instead of simply marital status) and concentrating on two sets of countries with different labor market structures (Scandinavian countries with more centralized wage determination and North American countries with decentralized wage systems), they also reported significant unexplained wage differences in each country. However, both of these studies confined their analysis to decomposing wage differences *within* each country rather than comparing differences *across* countries.

Blau and Kahn were the first to compare gender pay gap differences systematically across countries. In a series of papers (1992, 1995, 1996b, 2003), they focused on cross-country variations in market returns from skills, both measured and unmeasured. They found the gender pay gap to be higher in countries with a larger overall wage inequality because generally female workers are more likely to be located at the bottom of the wage distributions. To show this, Blau and Kahn (1996b) adopted the Juhn, Murphy, and Pierce (1993) methodology to decompose the intercountry differences in the gender wage gap into a number of components reflecting gender differences in worker attributes and what they call "wage structure" (1992, 538). They reaffirmed this result in a later study, stating, "more compressed wage structures . . . are associated with a lower gender pay gap" (2003, 138–139). Because a country's wage-setting institution determines wage structure, these authors also concentrated on particular labor market institutions. In particular, they report that collective bargaining coverage is significantly negatively related to the gender pay gap (2003, 106).

Blau and Kahn's decomposition presents at least two problems, however. First, this decomposition can lead to erroneous conclusions when the statistical assumptions about earnings dispersion underlying their approach are violated (Suen 1997). One can attribute gender wage differences to changes in a country's wage structure when, in reality, such changes occur only because male earnings are becoming more dispersed. This is not unreasonable, given that many countries are now exhibiting widening (more unequal) male wage distributions (Macdhin and Manning, 1994).

Second, this decomposition (as well as the Blinder-Oaxaca decomposition, which will be discussed later, Oaxaca, 1973; Blinder, 1973; Jones, 1983; Oaxaca and Ransom, 1994) can lead to erroneous conclusions because it assumes the same earnings structure for *both* men and women, when different remuneration structures may actually be warranted (Yun 2007). This is especially true if measured female and male characteristics have a different meaning for men and women. For example, being married may imply *steeper* age-earning profiles for men because division of labor in the home causes them to specialize in market human capital investment, whereas being married may yield *flatter* age-earnings profiles for women because division of labor could imply specialization in household human capital rather than marketable human capital (Polachek 1975a).

Because of these potential biases, which preclude one from distinguishing between discrimination and wage structure, it makes sense to identify particular country institutions and test directly their effects on the gender wage gap. Blau and Kahn did so by exploring the role of a particular wage setting scheme: collective bargaining. They report collective bargaining to be negatively associated with the gender pay gap, which stands to reason because collective bargaining tends to set high wage floors, thereby equalizing earnings. Blau and Kahn also tested for other institutional factors (unemployment insurance duration and replacement rates, an index of protective regulation for permanent and temporary workers, an index of gender occupational segregation, and a measure of relative female labor supply), but these factors turned out to be statistically insignificant in their analysis (2003, 136, Table 8).

Weichselbaumer and Winter-Ebmer (2003) adopted a different approach. Their meta-analysis pooled the results of 363 papers from which they obtained 1,532 data points on 67 countries. From these data, they regressed the wage gap on a host of variables (including characteristics pertaining to each study's author, such as whether the study's author was female). These authors report that ratification of international conventions supporting equal treatment of male and female workers has a negative and significant effect on the gender pay gap. At the same time, countries with greater economic competition measured by the Economic Freedom Index display lower gender pay gaps based on Becker (1957)'s argument that in the long run, competitive markets eliminate gender discrimination when firms try to minimize their costs.

Neither of these sets of studies concentrated on the implications of gender differences in expected lifetime labor force participation coming about because of division of labor in the home. This model was originally developed by Ben-Porath (1967) and later modified so it could be applied to account for how interrupted lifetime work links expected lifetime labor force participation to one's incentive to acquire marketable training (Polachek 1975a). Such training, which is acquired both in school and on the job, determines earnings potential. Thus, according to this approach, expected lifetime work history is the important motivating ingredient in one's ability to eventually achieve high earnings. As will be illustrated, this model is consistent with each of the stylized facts governing the gender wage gap.

Concentrating on factors related to expected lifetime labor force participation is even more important because it sheds new light on another labor economics paradox. When data are examined over time, one important finding is that the gender pay gap is narrowing in spite of the growing overall wage inequality. (This narrowing is unexpected because, as discussed earlier, Blau and Kahn [2003] show that wider wage inequality leads to a *greater* gender pay gap.) We suggest that the diminishing gender pay gap is a result in recent decades of women's increased incentive to participate over their lifetime in the labor market. Higher expected participation leads to larger female rates of return to education, steeper female earnings profiles, greater female wage dispersion, higher female wages relative to males, and smaller overall gender wage differences. As it turns out, our empirical evidence shows a wider male wage dispersion *is* associated with a larger gender wage gap, but its effect is mitigated when the female wage dispersion also increases.

THE STYLIZED FACTS

The U.S. female-male wage ratio is now approximately 78 percent, but an intriguing pattern emerges when examining this gender wage gap for different marital status groups. For *single* men and women, the wage gap is generally less than 10 percent, implying single women on average earn more than 90 percent of what men earn. *Married* women, however, earn *far* less than married men. Here the wage ratio is typically in the 60 to 70 percent range, implying a 30 to 40 percent wage gap. Further deconstruction illustrates that children play a major role in the gender wage gap. Married women with children earn less than married women without children (Harkness and Waldfogel 2003). Married women who space their births widely apart receive even lower wages (Polachek 1975a). Opposite patterns regarding marital status and family hold for men. Married men with children earn more, and spacing children at wide intervals is associated with even higher husband earnings (Polachek 1975b). Thus the wage gap varies by marital status, children, and spacing of children. As it turns out, these demographic variables are more important predictors of the gender wage gap than any other explanatory factors.

There is now more than ample evidence of these family effects, as numerous studies have corroborated this "motherhood" penalty. For example, Korenman and Neumark (1992) find that typical econometric estimates understate the negative effect of children on wages. Waldfogel (1998) shows that having children lowers a women's pay by about 10 percent, after controlling for age, education, experience, race, ethnicity, and marital status. Budig and England (2001) find an approximately 7 percent wage penalty per child. Using the National Longitudinal Survey Panel, Baum (2002, 2) confirms the finding that "interrupting work to give birth has a negative effect on wages" but notes that "this negative effect is at least partially eliminated when [controlling for] whether the mother returns to work at her pre-childbirth job." Berger et al. (2003, 309) find evidence that "the forces towards specialization become stronger as the number of children increase, so that the spouse specializing in childcare [has] some combination of lower wages, hours worked and fringe benefits." Similarly, looking at British data, Joshi, Paci, and Waldfogel (1999, 543) show "women who broke their employment at childbirth were subsequently paid less pay than childless women [whereas] mothers who maintained their employment continuously were as well paid as childless women." Using the European Household Panel Survey, the German Socio-Economic Panel, and the British Household Panel, Davies and Pierre (2005) show a family wage gap for 11 European nations. Paull (2006) makes similar inferences.

Male and female age-earnings profiles also diverge from each other over the life cycle. Male profiles are higher and generally steeper, and men experience more rapid earnings growth than women. Whereas male earnings profiles tend to be concave (rising steeply early in one's work career and then tapering off), women's earnings functions are often non-monotonic. Female earnings rise moderately early in the career, then flatten out or decline during the childrearing period, and finally rise often at a rate equal or exceeding men's (Mincer and Ofek 1982; Polachek 1975b). Thus, the gender earnings gap is relatively small when men and women begin to work after graduating from school. It widens in mid-life during childbearing periods, but then decreases somewhat when women return to the labor market at older ages. While originally observed using cross-section analysis, these results have been verified using a cohort-based analysis following age groups across the 1960–2000 U.S. Decennial Censuses. Weinberger and Kuhn (2005) report that the 43 percent wage gap for 23- to 32-year-olds in 1959 rose to 57 percent in 1969 when these workers were 33 to 42 years old, but eventually returned to 46 percent when they were 53 to 62 years old in 1989. This same gender wage gap pattern is replicated within other cohorts.

Married women's labor force participation rose dramatically over the 20th century, from 4.6 percent in 1890 to 61.0 percent in 2003.

This rapid rise in female labor force participation probably constitutes the single most noteworthy labor market trend in the United States over the last century (Goldin and Polachek, 1987;Smith and Ward,1989). Women are now approximately 15 times more likely to be in the labor force than their counterparts 100 years ago. At the same time, men's labor force participation declined moderately from 84.3 percent in 1890 to 73.5 percent in 2003.[1] Concomitant with these two labor force participation trends, the female-to-male wage ratio rose (albeit more erratically) from 34 percent in 1890 to about 76 percent in 2003, and again to 78 percent today.[2]

HOUSEHOLD DIVISION OF LABOR, WOMEN'S LIFETIME LABOR FORCE PARTICIPATION, AND THE GENDER WAGE GAP

A distinct feature of women's labor force participation is intermittent periods of work and nonwork over the lifetime. Never-married white women who were 30 to 44 years old in 1967 worked 14.5 years out of a possible 16 years. In contrast, married-spouse-present women worked only 6.4 years out of about 16.8 years (Mincer and Polachek 1974). Although somewhat less starkly, these same patterns have emerged in more recent data. Using the 1980 Panel Study of Income Dynamics Data (PSID), Carole Miller (1993) found that married women averaged 10.04 years out of the labor force. Equivalently, using a panel of 2,659 individuals from the 1976–1987 PSID data, Polachek and Kim (1994) found that women averaged 9.62 years out of the labor force relative to men's 2.22 years. Also, using the National Longitudinal Survey Spivey (2005, 124) found that in 1994 only 57 percent of women worked more than 70 percent of the time after the start of their careers, whereas the comparable figure for men was 79 percent. Data for foreign countries are comparable. For example, using Canadian data, Simpson (2000) found that in 1993 married women with children averaged 7.6 years (or 36.4 percent of their work years) out of the labor force, whereas single women spent 1.5 years (or 12.9 percent) of their work years out of the labor force. For men, the corresponding figure was 0.9 year (or 8.1 percent). Data within narrow professions yielded similar results. Catalyst (2003) found that only 29 percent of women MBA graduates had worked full-time continuously since graduation, compared to 69 percent of men; similarly, only 35 percent of women law graduates had worked continuously since graduation compared to 61 percent of men. Clearly, lifetime labor force participation differs by gender and marital status.

Division of labor in the home is one explanation why men work throughout their life, while even nowadays women (especially married women) often drop out to bear and raise children. Whereas this division of labor may come about because of "efficient" allocation in the home, it can also result from a wife's inferior bargaining power within a marriage (Ott 1995), high marginal tax rates on wives' earnings (Kumar 2005), the unavailability of daycare centers (Kreyenfeld and Hank 2000), or simply cultural norms (Coltrane 2000). But whatever the reason, less time in the workforce over one's lifetime decreases one's incentive to invest in marketable human capital (Weiss and Gronau, 1981). In turn, smaller human capital investment decreases one's wage. This relationship can be exacerbated because even while at work, division of labor may cause women to work less intensely, thereby receiving less on-the-job training (Becker 1985).

One way to explain these patterns is to model households as efficient economic units that maximize the discounted value of production throughout the course of their marriage subject to human capital accumulation and asset constraints (Polachek 1975a). Obviously, marriage length is not known with certainty. The model is more applicable the longer one expects the marriage to last. Another approach is to maximize household utility or—even better—the gain in utility from being married, which can be analyzed in a Nash equilibrium-type model derived by McElroy and Horney (1981) and Manser and Brown (1980). Either way, such a model entails a complex decision-making process within the household. In each time period, the household must determine both the husband's and wife's allocation of time to the household and to labor market work, as well as the husband's and wife's allocation of time to human capital investment (Greenwood and Guner, 2004).

The solution to such a model depends on both the system's initial conditions and the precise functional forms of the human capital and commodity production functions. The model assumes symmetry between both husband and wife as inputs to the model. It also implies identical husband and wife labor force participation, investment, and wages throughout the marriage, assuming husbands and wives are equally efficient in producing household goods and human capital, have the same human capital going into their marriages, and have the same rental (wage) rates per unit of human capital. However, assuming equality at the outset of marriage is highly unrealistic.

There are a number of reasons why husbands and wives differ and equality in marriage is not realized. First, men and women could differ in household productivity. Second, discrimination could cause men to have higher wages per unit of human capital. But even without discrimination or differing husband-wife productivity, equality at the outset of marriage is unlikely because men and women bring different amounts of human capital to the marriage—namely, education. In the United States, 32.7 percent of husbands graduate from college compared to 29 percent of wives. Also, husbands are, on average, 2.1 years older than their spouses.[3] Being older and more educated at the outset of marriage indicates that husbands have enjoyed opportunities to acquire greater amounts of human capital than their younger, less-educated wives(Polachek, 1995; Polachek, 2006; Polachek, 2012). At least with respect to age at first marriage, these same patterns emerge worldwide. In the 38 countries represented in the ISSP, LIS, and OECD data that we examine in this study, in every case husbands are older than their wives. In 209 United Nations (UN) member-countries, husbands are also older than their wives in every country, except San Marino. There, wives' age exceeds husbands' age by 0.2 year. In all other countries, the difference in mean age at marriage varies from 0.3 year in Belize to 9.2 years in Gambia. Whether these initial conditions are caused by societal preconditioning or result from efficient mating processes, these demographic differences at the outset of marriage are sufficient to cause the symmetry of the model to break down (Bergstrom and Bagnoli, 1993).

Given that age and education are positively related to human capital and earnings, the differences in husband-wife age and education imply greater human capital for husbands (Mincer, 1974; Lemieux, 2006). In turn, differences in the market value of human capital lead to specialization whereby the spouse with the greater market earnings potential (in this case, the husband) concentrates more on market activities. This spouse works in the market a greater proportion of time over the course of the marriage, and as a result reaps greater gains from human capital investment. As expected, this spouse invests more in human capital. Thus, despite the reasons for these initial differences, even if husbands are equal in all respects except initial endowment at the onset of marriage, efficient behavior (based on maximization of the present value of family income over time) dictates specialization so that the husband (or the spouse with the greater lifetime work) invests more in the market than in the home compared to his wife (or the spouse with lower lifetime work). Accordingly, greater human capital investments lead to higher wages.

DATA

One critical issue in a comparative study is the choice of data. A representative sample can avoid biased conclusions induced by a nonrandom sample. However, data limitations are a common problem for researchers doing international comparisons of labor markets. This is particularly true for gender difference analyses because often many variables are computed for the aggregate population, rather than broken down by gender. Because comprehensive information is mostly collected in developed countries, inferences are usually drawn from these nations (Blau and Kahn 1996b). Few data are available for developing countries, so they are omitted from the sample. In our study, we utilize the International Social Survey Programme data, the Luxembourg Income Survey, and OECD data.

The ISSP, which began in 1985, is an ongoing survey conducted annually for a sample of 39 countries. The topics emphasized on the survey vary each year, as do the participating countries.[4] In each survey, standardized questions are asked about social attitudes as well as respondents' age, sex, schooling years, earnings, and weekly working hours. Some country-years are omitted because of lack of crucial information (either earnings or weekly working hours). After excluding a few outlier country-years, we have a total of 250 observations.

It turns out that most of these sample countries are also OECD countries and have a relatively high development level. Also, the number of years for which data are available varies a great deal across sample countries: it ranges from 1 year to 16 years. In a significant proportion of the sample, earnings are reported as midpoints of categories. Such categorical reporting smoothes earnings measures, which could either narrow or exaggerate the gender pay gap depending on how wages fit into the categories. For example, the measured gender pay gap would be smaller if women are likely to have earnings in low percentiles of a category whereas men have earnings in high percentiles of the same category. Conversely, the gender pay gap would be exaggerated if men and women were in two adjacent earnings categories—say, if women were in high percentiles of the low category while men were in low percentiles of the high category. This categorical data limitation could be more serious than omitting taxes, because compared to taxes, earnings smoothing based on categorical data is more likely to have asymmetric effect on men and women.

We offer the following numerical example to illustrate. Suppose two reported earnings categories are $0 to $20,000 and $20,001 to $40,000. Because the ISSP data report the category midpoints, a worker's earnings is shown as $10,000 in the first category and as $30,000 in the second one. When a male worker earns $18,000 and a female worker earns $9,000, both are reported to earn a wage of $10,000 in the data. In this case, the calculated gender pay gap is underestimated. In contrast, if a male worker earns $25,000 and a female worker earns $15,000, the data are reported as $30,000 and $10,000, respectively. In this case, the calculated pay gap is inflated.

Another issue is that earnings are not calculated per hour. Because women are more likely to work part-time, ignoring working hours is likely to overestimate the gender pay gap. The ISSP data contain information on weekly working hours, but do not collect data on weeks worked. We focus on the sample of full-time workers (defined as working at least 30 hours per week, set by the OECD in 1997, OECD 1997.) to maintain consistency with the two other data sets we use in this study. Correlation coefficients comparing each gender pay gap measure are as high as 0.9 and regression coefficients are close to 1 when one measure is regressed on the other one.

The Luxembourg Income Study is a collection of household-level data compiled from ongoing statistical surveys in 29 countries widely spread across Europe, America, Asia, and Oceania. The LIS began in 1983 and is now jointly sponsored by the Luxembourg government and the Centre for Population, Poverty, and Policy Studies (CEPS), Centre Universitaire (CU) de Luxembourg. The data are standardized to facilitate comparative research. Data include country-specific labor force surveys over various labor market structures and include demographic, income, and expenditure information on three different levels: household, person, and child. In our study, we extract information on gender, earnings, and weekly working hours from the LIS person files.[5] To maintain consistency with ISSP data, we confine ourselves to those country-years that contain information on weekly working hours. Fewer countries and years are covered by the LIS than by the ISSP; for our purposes, LIS data yield a total number of 71 observations. Again, OECD countries account for most of the sample. As before, we restrict our sample to full-time workers who work at least 30 hours per week.

The OECD collects pretax (gross) wage data on full-time workers from surveys conducted by governments for each country.[6] The sample includes 21 countries and a varying number of years. The earliest data start in 1950 for France, but most countries begin to have data in the 1970s and the 1980s. For each country and gender, the mean and median, as well as wage data, for the 10th to the 90th percentiles, plus the 25th and the 75th percentiles, and 11 percentile groups are reported. There are 292 observations at the 50th percentile measure and 322 observations at the mean value measure.

The current literature generally concentrates on both mean and median measures of the gender pay gap. As such, we compute the gender pay gap as a difference between the male and female log of wages for each of the three data sets (and do so both for means and medians). The antilogarithm is the female-to-male pay ratio. Because the time periods of the three data sets overlap, we are able to compute correlation matrices measuring the data's consistency between data sets. The correlation matrices show that the LIS and OECD gender pay gap measures are the most similar, whereas the LIS and ISSP data are the least similar (correlation coefficients of 0.80 and 0.75 versus 0.36 and 0.31, respectively).[7]

To further test the consistency of the data, we examine each country's time series trends from the early 1970s to 2002 for each of the three data sets (for France, we have data from 1950). Examples of these are plotted in Figures 2.1 through 2.5.

Just as Blau et al. (2006) observe a declining gender gap in the United States, so we find the gender wage gap to be getting smaller for most countries. This is especially true for Canada, Hungary, Korea, Northern Ireland, Slovenia, and Switzerland, where the wage gap is declining relatively more quickly than in the other countries (Table 2.1).

Generally the decline follows a smooth pattern for the OECD and LIS data, but the ISSP data appear a bit more erratic, oscillating from year to year. This year-to-year change seems implausible and we suspect two possible reasons for its existence. First, the sample composition changes in the ISSP, which arise because each year's survey concentrates on a different particular survey topic, may explain the variation. Second, the categorical reporting of earnings data in ISSP may be a factor. This weakness is consistent with the correlation

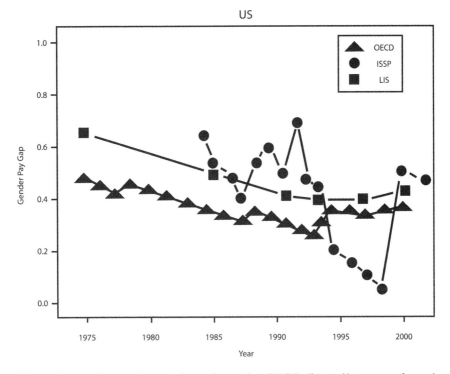

Figure 2.1   (Data adapted from from the OECD (http://stats.oecd.org/Index.aspx?DatasetCode=DEC_I), LIS (http://www.lisdatacenter.org/data -access/), and ISSP from ICPSR (www.icpsr.umich.edu).)

matrixes that show the ISSP data to have the least linear relationship with the other two data sets.

The preceding results lead to the conclusion that the best candidate for the calculation of gender pay gap is the OECD data set. Compared to the ISSP data set, it is much more consistent over time. Compared to the LIS data set, it has many more observations. Nevertheless, we use all three data sets for our analyses, but include a variable denoting which of the three data sets we are actually using so that we can take into account the reliability of each data set.

HOW WOMEN'S INCENTIVES FOR LABOR FORCE PARTICIPATION AFFECT THE GENDER PAY GAP: MEASURES OF WOMEN'S LABOR FORCE PARTICIPATION INCENTIVES

In the previous section we argued that expectations regarding lifetime labor force participation could affect human capital

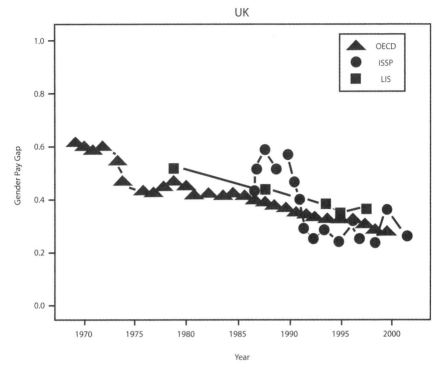

Figure 2.2   (Data adapted from from the OECD (http://stats.oecd.org/ Index.aspx?DatasetCode=DEC_I), LIS (http://www.lisdatacenter.org/data-access/), and ISSP from ICPSR (www.icpsr.umich.edu).)

accumulation and consequently the gender wage gap. The division of labor in the family was considered to be the underlying reason for low work incentives, especially for married women with children. Generally these incentives are unobservable, but one way to capture them is through observable factors that have a direct influence on women's expected lifetime work. In the following discussion, we examine country attributes that we expect to affect women's lifetime work incentives and hence the gender pay gap.

Perhaps the variable that has the greatest influence on women's (and men's) lifetime work behavior is fertility (Becker, 1960; Willis, 1973). The greater the number of children in a family, the more pronounced the division of labor. Two observable consequences appear from high fertility. First, women are expected to drop out of the labor force more frequently, which suggests they will accrue less market experience and less human capital investment (Mincer and Polachek 1974).

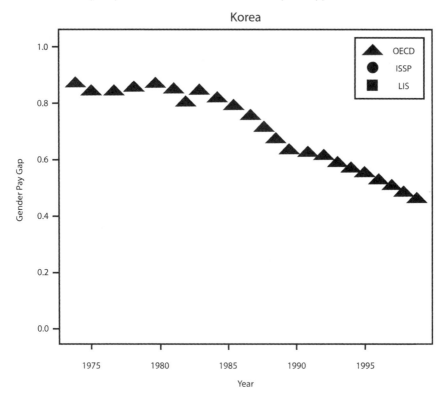

Figure 2.3   (Data adapted from from the OECD (http://stats.oecd.org/ Index.aspx?DatasetCode=DEC_I), LIS (http://www.lisdatacenter.org/data- access/), and ISSP from ICPSR (www.icpsr.umich.edu).)

Second, women are likely to exert less effort in market work (Becker 1985). Both factors may eventually lead to a larger gender pay gap.

Empirical evidence for an inverse relationship between the fertility rate and female labor force participation (and earnings) abounds. Eckstein and Wolpin (1989) use the National Longitudinal Survey's mature women's cohort to estimate a dynamic model of married women's labor force participation and fertility; they conclude that an increase in the population of children younger than age six substan- tially reduces women's labor force participation. Using the 1980 Popu- lation Census of Japan, Yamada and Yamada (1984) find higher fertility rates to have a negative labor supply impact for married women. Based on a cohort of more than 2,000 women in the Cebu Longitudinal Health and Nutrition Survey, Adair, Guilkey, Bisgrove, and Gultiano (2002) conclude that having an additional child younger

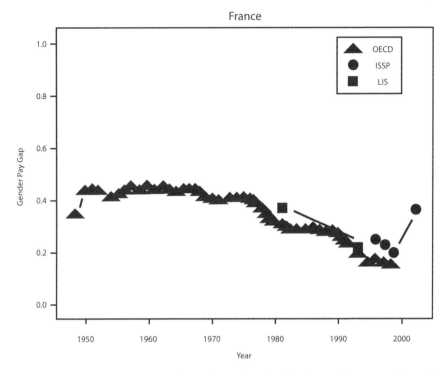

Figure 2.4   (Data adapted from from the OECD (http://stats.oecd.org/
Index.aspx?DatasetCode=DEC_I), LIS (http://www.lisdatacenter.org/data-
access/), and ISSP from ICPSR (www.icpsr.umich.edu).)

than age two would reduce women's working hours and that wom-
en's earnings are substantially decreased if they have two or more
additional children. Assaad and Zouari (2003) find that women
(in urban Morocco) decrease their participation in all types of wage
work (e.g., public and private wage work) in the presence of school-
age children. Many other case studies similarly support this inverse
relationship (e.g., Psacharopoulos and Tzannatos 1992).

A second variable that captures women's incentive to participate in
the labor market is the age gap between husband and wife. Generally
older males are likely to have accumulated more wealth and have
higher wages than their wives.[8] The larger this age gap, the more pronounced the division of labor within the family, because relatively
higher human capital for husbands leads them to specialize in market
activities. As a result, women in countries with larger husband-wife
age gaps are likely to have a lower incentive to invest in the labor market. Despite husbands being universally older than their wives, there

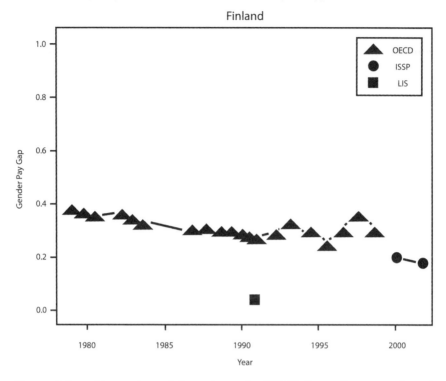

Figure 2.5   (Data adapted from from the OECD (http://stats.oecd.org/Index.aspx?DatasetCode=DEC_I), LIS (http://www.lisdatacenter.org/data-access/), and ISSP from ICPSR (www.icpsr.umich.edu).)

is no empirical evidence relating this age differential to the gender pay gap. Based on the preceding argument, the gender pay gap would be expected to be smaller in countries where the difference in a husband's and wife's ages is smallest, holding all other factors constant.

Country-specific fiscal policies such as income tax rates can influence one's incentive to work. This is especially true for women because women's labor supply is more elastic and, therefore, more sensitive to such tax rates. Married women might find it advantageous to specialize in household activities when a large proportion of the secondary earner's income must go toward paying taxes. By the same token, a low income tax regimen is likely to exert a positive effect on women's incentive to consistently participate in the labor market. In this circumstance, the gender pay gap can diminish. The effect of tax rates on women's labor force participation has been studied in a number of papers. Baffoe-Bonnie (1995) investigates the effect of the

Table 2.1 Annualized Percent Change in the Gender Wage Gap

Country[1]	Annualized Percent Change[2]
Australia*	−0.40%
Austria*	−0.69%
Belgium	−0.28%
Bulgaria	1.23%
Canada*	−1.12%
Chile	1.27%
Cyprus	0.38%
Czech Republic	−0.75%
Denmark	−0.59%
East Germany*	−0.80%
Finland*	−0.63%
France*	−0.51%
Germany*	−0.67%
Hungary*	−1.30%
Ireland	−1.13%
Israel*	−0.98%
Italy	−0.09%
Japan*	−0.34%
Korea*	−1.76%
Latvia	−0.70%
Luxembourg	0.27%
Netherlands*	−0.31%
New Zealand	−0.31%
Northern Ireland*	−2.10%
Norway	0.38%
Philippines	−0.24%
Poland*	−1.41%
Portugal	−0.14%
Russia	0.89%
Slovak Republic	0.19%
Slovenia*	−2.43%
Spain*	2.64%
Sweden	−0.03%
Switzerland*	−1.48%
United Kingdom*	−0.99%
United States*	−1.02%

*Denotes statistical significance at the 5% level. Computed from the b coefficient of the following regression: $Ln(\text{Pay Gap}) = a + b \text{ year} + c \text{ LIS} + d \text{ ISSP}$.

Author adapted these from data: OECD (http://stats.oecd.org/Index.aspx?DatasetCode=DEC_I), LIS (http://www.lisdatacenter.org/data–access/), and ISSP from ICPSR (www.icpsr.umich.edu).

negative income tax on the labor supply of different family members and finds that females are likely to reduce their labor supply at all levels of tax rates, whereas males increase their labor supply at certain program parameter levels. Another study based on a sample of married women in the Antwerp district in Belgium found that women's labor supply decreased more than 20 percent if they received an individual transfer of 15,000 Belgian francs per month while simultaneously facing an increase in the income tax rate (Kesenne 1990). Additionally, based on data from the United Kingdom, Denmark, Ireland, and Germany, Smith, Dex, Vlasblom, and Callan (2003) find that women's labor force participation rates are highly influenced by the design of tax schemes (e.g., joint taxation versus separate taxation).

Another variable that measures women's work incentive is female educational attainment. Female educational attainment affects the gender pay gap in two ways. First, the pay gap is expected to decrease as a direct result of a larger female human capital stock. Second, more schooling instigates higher labor force participation. These higher labor force participation rates are evident in primary data (e.g., Table D in *OECD Employment Outlook*, 2002, OECD 2002) as well as in secondary analysis. When Chaykowski and Powell (1999) examined the progress of Canadian women in the labor market during the period 1978–1998, they found women's educational attainment to be one of the major factors contributing to the increase in women's labor force participation. Eckstein and Wolpin (1989) also report that an "increase in the level of schooling has the largest (positive) impact on participation" (389). In turn, higher labor force participation increases on-the-job training and wages such that the higher women's education relative to men's education, the higher women's wages and the smaller the wage gap.

Finally, in our study, we include four institutional characteristics used in the literature on cross-country comparisons: centralized collective bargaining, economic competition, the public/private employment ratio, and overall earnings dispersion (Pontusson, Rueda and Way, 2002; Rueda and Pontusson, 2000; Gornick and Jacobs, 1998). In addition, we extend Rhum's (1998, 2000) parental leave data from 9 to 17 countries. However, because of the limited number of observations using the data (and the inability to distinguish between countries with zero parental leave weeks and missing values), we report results incorporating this parental leave variable in a footnote later in the chapter. Iversen (1999), Wallerstein (1999), and Blau and Kahn (2003) argue that bargaining centralization reduces wage differentials among different firms and sectors because bargaining includes more firms and sectors into a common wage settlement. This development is relevant to the gender pay gap because in the real world we observe female workers in less remunerative sectors. Centralized bargaining tends to equalize these sectoral differences and, as such, we expect the gender pay gap to be negatively associated with this labor market institution. Economic competition has been suggested to negatively affect the gender pay gap by causing firms to eliminate discrimination against women in an attempt to minimize their costs in a highly competitive market (Becker 1957; Weichselbaumer and Winter-Ebmer 2002). Public employment is another indicator of wage compression: public-sector employers are more inclined than private-sector employers to equalize wages for their employees (Kolberg 1991). Finally, we include direct measures of the 90th percentile minus 10th percentile wage gap for males and for females. Blau and Kohn (2003) use the 50–10 wage gap as an independent variable in a regression to show that a more compressed male wage structure decreases the gender pay gap.

The sources for the previously mentioned variables are given in Appendix 1. Summary statistics for each of these variables appear in Table 2.2.

The first two variables are measures of the difference between the male and female log of (median and mean) wages, our dependent variable. The average wage gap exceeds 30 percent. Thus women are consistently in a disadvantaged wage position, but their situation varies significantly across countries and years. The median measure of the gender pay gap is smaller than the mean measure, suggesting that the male wage distribution tends to be more right skewed when compared to the female wage distribution, implying a larger proportion of high-earning males compared to high-earning females.

Summary statistics for the independent variables follow. The fertility rate, defined as births per woman, is used to capture the effect of children on lifetime labor supply and wages. As can be seen from the range of this variable, women in some country-years have total fertility rates three times as high as women in other country-years, although most country-years are associated with relatively low fertility rates. On average, men are 2.6 years older than their wives, but here, too, there is a great deal of variation, although this variable is more symmetrically distributed than the fertility rate. The top

Table 2.2 Variable Summaries Based on Each Data Set

Variable	OECD Number of Observations	OECD Mean	LIS Number of Observations	LIS Mean	ISSP Number of Observations	ISSP Mean	Total Number of Observations	Total Mean	Total Standard Deviation	Total Minimum	Total Maximum
Gender Pay Gap_50th	292	0.306	71	0.31	250	0.328	613	0.315	0.162	0.19	1.79
Gender Pay Gap_Mean	322	0.374	71	0.338	250	0.341	643	0.357	0.15	0.032	1.36
Fertility Rate	341	1.77	71	1.67	200	1.68	612	1.73	0.381	1.09	3.71
Age Gap at the First Marriage	330	2.62	70	2.52	204	2.71	604	2.64	0.543	1.2	6.8
Top Marginal Income Tax Rate	312	58	70	53	222	47	604	53	12.4	13	89
Female Educational Attainment	304	0.859	62	0.963	204	1.02	570	0.926	0.237	0.21	1.77
Bargaining Centralization	201	0.264	24	0.217	59	0.27	284	0.261	0.16	0.071	0.647
Economic Competition	331	6.8	70	7.1	227	6.9	628	6.9	0.96	3.6	8.6
Public Employment Ratio	275	10.98	44	10.58	114	11.46	433	11.07	4.41	5.57	24.97
90–10 Male Wage Gap	243	3.00	36	3.08	87	3.22	366	3.06	0.684	2.02	4.75
90–10 Female Wage Gap	253	2.70	38	2.89	90	2.97	381	2.78	0.626	1.64	4.29
Parental Leave	38	28.26	6	23.5	13	30.77	57	28.33	16.879	10	68

[1] Variable Definitions: **Gender Pay Gap_50th:** The difference between log of males' median wage and log of females' median wage based on the full-time sample. **Gender Pay Gap_Mean:** The difference between log of males' mean wage and log of females' mean wage based on the full-time sample. **Fertility Rate:** Births per women. **Age Gap at the First Marriage:** Mean age gap between husband and wife at the first marriage. **Top Marginal Income Tax Rate:** Top marginal income tax rate as a percentage. **Female Educational Attainment:** The ratio of females to males at the "third level" post-secondary education level. **Bargaining Centralization:** An index of the degree to which collective bargaining is centralized. **Economic Competition:** The Economic Freedom Index. **Public Employment Ratio:** Civilian government employment as a percentage of the working age population (15–64 years).

[2] Author adapted these from data: **Gender Pay Gap_50th, Gender Pay Gap_Mean, 90/10 Male Wage Gap,** and **90/10 Female Wage Gap** from OECD (http://stats.oecd.org/Index.aspx?DatasetCode=DEC_I), LIS (http://www.lisdatacenter.org/data-access/), and ISSP from ICPSR (www.icpsr.umich.edu); **Fertility Rate** from World Development Indicators; **Age Gap at the First Marriage** and **Female Educational Attainment** from *United Nations Women's Indicators and Statistics Database;* **Top Marginal Income Tax Rate** and **Economic Competition** from *Economic Freedom of the World 2004 Annual Report;* **Bargaining Centralization** from Torben Iversen, "Wage Bargaining, Central Bank Independence and the Real Effects of Money," *International Organization* 52 (Summer 1998); **Public Employment Ratio** from *Comparative Welfare States Dataset;* and **Parental Leave** from (1) Christopher J. Ruhm, "Parental Leave and Child Health," *Journal of Health Economics* 19 (2000): 931–960; (2) Christopher J. Ruhm, "The Economic Consequences of Parental Leave Mandates: Lessons from Europe," *Quarterly Journal of Economics* 113, no. 1 (1998): 285–317, Table 2; and (3) Sakiko Tanaka, "Parental Leave and Child Health across OECD Countries," *Economic Journal* 115, no. 501 (2005): Table 2. Precise definitions and data sources are given in Appendix 1.

marginal income tax rate averages 53 percent, but varies from 13 percent to 89 percent. Marginal tax rates increase the gender wage gap to the extent they discourage women, as secondary earners, from engaging in labor market activity. Female educational attainment is defined as a ratio of females to males at the "third level," which essentially translates into the ratio of women to men in post-secondary education. This variable measures women's relative human capital stock. The primary and secondary educational attainment ratios for men and women are similar; only the gender ratios of third-level education exhibit sufficient variation to use in analysis.

THE STATISTICAL MODEL

We use a multivariate regression analysis to reveal how international differences in institutional variables are related to the gender wage gap. The estimation model we use is

$$y_{ijt} = x_{ijt}\,\beta + D_j\gamma_j + v_i + \varepsilon_{ijt}$$

where y_{ijt} represents the gender earnings difference for country i using data set j in year t (for which we use two measures), x_{ijt} represents the set of independent time-varying institutional variables for country i using data set j in year t, D_j reflects which of the three data sets was used to obtain the information, v_i is a country error term depicting innate random differences between countries, and ε_{ijt} is a country/ data set/time-varying random term reflecting measurement or other errors intrinsic within the data.

There is precedent to claim that over relatively short periods of time, within-country variance is smaller than between-country variance; thus it makes sense to study how the wage gap varies across countries rather than within them (Baltagi and Griffin 1984). Consequently, it is important to perform the analysis by concentrating on the between-country differences rather than small changes within countries over time. For this reason, we primarily focus on the between-country differences, which we estimate assuming a random effects (RE) GLS model, rather than a fixed-effect (FE) approach (Greene 2012).

RESULTS OF THE COMPARATIVE STUDY

We examine two measures of the gender pay gap: the mean $\log_e$ pay difference and the median $\log_e$ pay difference (to avoid the effect of outliers). Under each measure, several specifications are designed to test robustness.

We adopt four models for each of the two gender pay gap measures. The first model examines how a country's fertility rate, the husband-wife age difference at first marriage, and the top marginal income tax rate are related to the gender wage gap. Female educational attainment is not included in the first model because its effect on the gender pay gap is twofold. First, a higher educational level increases women's wages directly; second, higher education works to raise women's incentives for more lifetime labor force participation, which in turn increases women's wages indirectly through more human capital investment. By excluding the direct effect of the educational attainment variable, the first model shows how female labor force participation (perhaps including education if education influences labor force participation) affects the gender pay gap. The direct role of education is captured in the second model, in which all four independent variables are included. Model 3 incorporates centralized bargaining, economy-wide competition, and the economy's proportion of public employment. Model 4 incorporates the 90–10 male and 90–10 female pay dispersion measures.

We begin by considering the regression results on the entire sample (Table 2.3). They generally support the argument that the larger the gender pay gap, the smaller women's incentives to work over their lifetimes. In Model 1, all three independent variables have positive and statistically significant coefficients. This suggests that variables connected to low lifetime labor force participation are associated with a bigger gender pay gap.

By using an international cross-section made up of heterogeneous countries, these results regarding the fertility rate generalize past findings based on data from specific countries (such as the United States) regarding fertility's negative impact on female-versus-male earnings. The results related to the husband-wife age gap at first marriage (new to the literature) suggest that one fundamental determinant of the gender pay gap can be traced to specialization between family members.

Table 2.3 Effects of Women's Incentive for Labor Force Participation on the Gender Pay Gap, Based on the OECD, LIS, and ISSP Data

Dependent variable:	In_mean_male_female				In_50_male_female			
	Model 1	Model 2	Model 3	Model 4	Model 1	Model 2	Model 3	Model 4
Fertility Rate	0.0977***	0.0787***	0.0607	0.0342	0.109***	0.0874***	-0.0144	0.0823*
	(0.0227)	(0.0228)	(0.0465)	(0.0322)	(0.0340)	(0.0337)	(0.0632)	(0.0327)
Age Gap at first Marriage	0.0806***	0.0602***	-0.00975	0.0284	0.138***	0.116***	-0.0699*	0.0505**
	(0.0201)	(0.0215)	(0.0271)	(0.0226)	(0.0242)	(0.0258)	(0.0366)	(0.0236)
Top Marginal Income Tax Rate	0.00239***	0.000346	0.00177*	0.00162**	000184***	-0.000794	0.00156	0.00185**
	(0.000465)	(0.000656)	(0.000983)	(0.000696)	(0.000564)'	(0.000809)	(0.00133)	(0.000709)
Female Educational Attainment		-0.275***	-0.246***	-0.205***		-0.348***	-0.151	-0.187***
		(0.0628)	(0.0673)	(0.0601)		(0.0758)	(0.0989)	(0.0628)
Centralized Bargaining			-0.107*				-0.0535	
			(0.0571)				(0.0789)	
Economic Freedom			0.0308				0.0258	
			(0.0215)				(0.0290)	
Public Employment Ratio			-0.00146				0.0143	
			(0.00307)				(0.00483)	
LIS Data	0.0323**	0.0334**	0.0248	0.0512***	0.0293**	0.0287*	0.0505***	0.0478***
	(0.0133)	(0.0138)	(0.0173)	(0.0135)	(0.0149)	(0.0154)	(0.0197)	(0.0132)
ISSP Data	0.0534***	0.0581***	0.0751***	0.0703***	0.0596***	0.0637***	0.0625***	0.0671***
	(0.0100)	(0.0103)	(0.0129)	(0.00971)	(0.0114)	(0.0117)	(0.0143)	(0 00946)

ln90_10male				0.919***				1.079***
				(0.179)				(0.182)
ln90_10female				0.318***				1.027***
				(0.193)				(0.197)
int_ln90_10mf				−0.674***				−0.928***
				(0.148)				(0.151)
Constant	−0.195***	0.265**	0.207	−0.584**	−0.361***	0.211	−.00445	−1.073***
	(0.0679)	(0.127)	(0.241)	(0.252)	(0.0904)	(0.160)	(0.324)	(0.257)
Observations	542	514	238	348	528	500	232	366
R-squared	-	-	-	-	-	-	-	-
Number of countryjd	35	34	15	21	35	34	15	21

Dependent variable depict the percent gender difference in mean (columns 1–4) and median (columns 5–8) earnings.
Other variables defined in the text.
Robust standard errors in parentheses.
***>0.01, **>0.05, *>0.1

Author adapted these from data: Dependent variables, LIS Data, ISSP Data, Ln90_10male, Ln90_10female, and int_ln90_10mf from OECD (http://stats.oecd.org/Index.aspx?DatasetCode=DEC_I), LIS (http://www.lisdatacenter.org/data- access/), and ISSP from ICPSR (www.icpsr.umich.edu); Fertility Rate from World Development Indicators; Age Gap at the First Marriage and Female Educational Attainment from United Nations Women's Indicators and Statistics Database; Top Marginal Income Tax Rate and Economic Freedom from Economic Freedom of the World 2004 Annual Report; Centralized Bargaining from Torben Iversen, "Wage Bargaining, Central Bank Independence and the Real Effects of Money," International Organization 52 (Summer 1998); and Public Employment Ratio from Comparative Welfare States Dataset.

A higher top marginal income tax rate raises the gender pay gap asymmetrically, reducing women's labor force participation relative to men's participation (Jaumotte 2003).[9] Adding a measure of women's educational attainment in Model 2 leaves the results largely unchanged, but female educational attainment coefficients appear to support the argument that relatively more schooling for women reduces the gender pay gap across countries. As a group, these four variables lend empirical support to the argument that women's incentives for labor force participation decrease the gender pay gap.

Model 3 adds three institutional variables. As can be seen, centralized bargaining is associated with a reduced gender wage gap, but economic competition is associated with an increased gap. The public employment ratio is statistically insignificant.

Interacting the economic competition and public employment variable (not presented) yields a significantly negative interaction term. Thus, public employment appears to mitigate larger pay differentials brought about by competition. In light of the work by Gary Becker (1957), these results are consistent with economically adverse consequences for men because economic competition is associated with a wider (not smaller) gender wage gap. Market intervention through country-wide collective bargaining and public employment decreases (not increases) the gap. More specifically, the results show that public-sector employment helps eradicate women's pay differences—as long as competition in the economy increases rather than decreases the gender pay gap.

Incorporating the 90–10 overall male and female earnings spreads (Model 4) does not qualitatively alter the results. As demonstrated by Blau and Kahn (2003), we find greater male or female wage dispersion is associated with a wider gender pay gap. This holds true for both the male and female wage dispersions, but given the interaction term, the positive effect on the gender wage gap is mitigated when either the male or female wage dispersion increases.

Worth mentioning in Table 2.3 is the coefficient for the ISSP data. The range of the positive coefficients (2.6 percent to 8.1 percent) indicates that the ISSP consistently overestimates the gender pay gap compared to the OECD. Similarly, the LIS overstates the wage gap by between zero and 5.5 percent. As a final note, in Table 2.3, the top marginal income tax rate is seen to have a strong effect on the gender pay gap. Because this variable specifically refers to the tax rate at top wage percentiles, a further test is needed to examine its effect on the gender pay gap measured at other wage percentiles.

Table 2.4   The Effect of Top Marginal Income Tax Rate on the Gender Pay Gap, Measured at Different Percentiles

	10th	20th	25th	30th	40th	50th	60th	70th	75th	80th	90th
Top Marginal Income Tax Rate	−0.0002	0.0002	0.0015***	0.0004	0.0007	0.0012***	0.0019***	0.0022***	0.0035***	0.0021***	0.001
	(0.0007)	(0.0005)	(0.0006)	(0.0005)	(0.0005)	(0.0004)	(0.0005)	(0.0005)	(0.0006)	(0.0005)	(0.0006)
Country Dummies	Yes	Yes	Yes	Yes	Yes	Yes	Yes	Yes	Yes	Yes	Yes
Number of Observations	247	231	160	231	231	252	231	231	160	231	236
Probability > F	0	0	0	0	0	0	0	0	0	0	0

***P < 0.01, ** P < 0.05, * P < 0.10. Standard errors are in parentheses.

[1] Robust standard errors are experimented, and the statistical significance of the variables holds, despite the small decrease in the t-values

[2] In addition to the top marginal income tax rate, the independent variables include fertility rate, age gap at the first marriage, and female educational attainment.

[3] Author adapted these from data: **Dependent variables** from OECD (http://stats.oecd.org/Index.aspx?DatasetCode=DEC_I); **Fertility Rate** from World Development Indicators; **Age Gap at the First Marriage** and **Female Educational Attainment** from *United Nations Women's Indicators and Statistics Database*; **Top Marginal Income Tax Rate** from *Economic Freedom of the World 2004 Annual Report*.

We predict that the top marginal income tax rates will have the strongest effects in reducing wives' incentives to work, thereby decreasing their human capital investment and widening the gender wage gap. The regression results obtained at 11 other wage percentiles generally support this prediction (Table 2.4). The coefficient of this tax variable is much more likely to be statistically significant in cases above the 50th wage percentile. Furthermore, the coefficient magnitude increases with a higher wage percentile.

CONCLUSIONS

This study described in this chapter has tested the argument that women's incentive for lifetime labor force participation is an important determinant of the gender pay gap. Using a 40-country data set covering the years 1970–2002, we find that the fertility rate, the age gap between husband and wife at first marriage, and the top marginal income tax rate are all positively associated with the gender pay gap, while female educational attainment is negatively related to the gap. Because current comparative studies on the gender pay gap tend to focus on institutional factors affecting wage structures between countries, our study adds new findings by examining demographic variables using a wider set of data than in the past.

Our results underscore the roles of demographic variables—particularly those affecting lifetime work, which in turn influences human capital investment—in understanding the gender wage gap in a comparative country format. The evidence shows that the gender pay gap, at least in part, results from factors affecting women's lifetime labor force participation. In turn, this finding sheds light on the currently paradoxical finding that the gender wage gap is narrowing despite a wider dispersion in the overall wage structure. We argue that higher expected female lifetime labor force participation leads to higher female rates of return, higher female earnings, a wider female wage dispersion, and a smaller gender pay gap.

APPENDIX 1

Definitions and Sources of Independent Variables

Fertility rate: The total fertility rate, defined as births per woman. Source: *World Development Indicators*, World Bank CD-ROM, 2004.

Data are available for most years. Linear interpolation is used to create a time series.

Age gap at the first marriage: Mean age gap between husband and wife at the first marriage. Source: *United Nations Women's Indicators and Statistics Database*, version 4, United Nations 1999. Data on mean age at the first marriage by sex are available for 1970, 1980, 1990, and the latest year (around 1995). Linear interpolation is used to create a time series.

Top marginal income tax rate: Top marginal income tax rate as a percentage. Source: Economic *Freedom of the World 2004 Annual Report*, edited by James Gwartney and Robert Lawson. Data are available at five-year intervals. Linear interpolation is used to create a time series.

Female educational attainment: The ratio of female educational attainment over male educational attainment at the third level (educational attainment was originally defined as third-level students per 100,000 population by sex). Source: *United Nations Women's Indicators and Statistics Database*, version 4, United Nations 1999. Data on third-level students per 100,000 population by sex are available for 1970, 1980, 1990, and the latest year (around 1995). Linear interpolation is used to create a time series.

Bargaining centralization: The Index of Centralization. Source: Torben Iversen, "Wage Bargaining, Central Bank Independence and the Real Effects of Money," *International Organization* 52 (Summer 1998).

Economic competition: The Economic Freedom Index. Source: *Economic Freedom of the World 2004 Annual Report*, edited by James Gwartney and Robert Lawson. Data are available at five-year intervals. Linear interpolation is used to create a time series.

Public employment ratio: Civilian government employment as a percentage of the working-age population (15–64 years). Source: *Comparative Welfare States Dataset, 2004* (downloaded from Luxembourg Income Study). Find the Original Sources in the Comparative Welfare States Dataset.

NOTES

1. The 1890 data are from *Historical Statistics of the United States from Colonial Times until 1970*, Series D49-62, p. 133. The data from 2003 are from the 2004–2005 *Statistical Abstract of the United States*, Table 57 (p. 371) for males and Table 578 (p. 376) for females.

2. The 1830 figure is based on Claudia Goldin (1990, 60–61); the 2003 figure is based on June O'Neill and Dave O'Neill (2006).

3. These data are computed from Table 2 in Nock (2001) and based on the 1999 March *Current Population Survey* (CPS) Demographic Supplement.

4. The ISSP survey topics were as follows: role of government in 1985, 1990, and 1996; social networks in 1986; social inequality in 1987, 1992, and 1999; family and changing gender roles in 1988, 1994, and 2002; work orientations in 1989, 1997, and 2005; religion in 1991 and 1998; environment in 1993 and 2000; national identity in 1995 and 2003; citizenship in 2004; and social relations and support systems in 2001. Data are downloadable from Inter-University Consortium for Political and Social Research (ICPSR), except for the years 1999 and 2001 and the years after 2002.

5. Data for weeks worked are available for a proportion of the sample in LIS. This information is omitted here to keep the data consistent with the other two data sets examined in this study. Computing gender pay gaps based on hourly earnings produces very similar regression results.

6. The exception for the definition of full-time workers is Austria, which uses information of both full-time and part-time employees. Also, the exception for the definition of gross earnings is France, which uses net earnings.

7. This observation is strengthened by the P value; it is not significant at 1 percent level between the LIS and ISSP data.

8. Under the assumption that economic roles of males are more varied than the roles of females, Bergstrom and Bagnoli (1993) find in their model that in equilibrium, "males with poor prospects marry at an early age, whereas those who expect success will marry later in life. All females marry relatively early in life. The more desirable females marry successful older males and the less desirable females marry the young males who do not expect to prosper" (186).

9. Incorporating parental leave data, as mentioned earlier, yielded a regression with only 49 observations for Model 1, 44 observations for Model 2, and 19 observations for Models 3 and 4. Thus we do not report there regressions in Tables 2.4 and 2.5. However, we find a smaller gender wage gap in counties with greater parental leave opportunities. This result is statistically significant in Model 1, and consistent with our overall hypothesis that country policies favoring

increased female lifetime labor force participation result in a smaller gender wage gap.

REFERENCES

Adair, Linda, David Guilkey, Eilene Bisgrove, and Socorro Gultiano. "Effect of Childbearing on Filipino Women's Work Hours and Earnings." *Journal of Population Economics* 15, no. 4 (2002): 625–645.

Assaad, R., and S. Zouari. "Estimating the Impact of Marriage and Fertility on the Female Labor Force Participation When Decisions Are Interrelated: Evidence from Urban Morocco." *Topics in Middle Eastern and North African Economies* 5 (September 2003). http://www.luc.edu/publications/academic/.

Baffoe-Bonnie, John. "Negative Income Tax and Family Labor Supply in Canada." *Eastern Economic Journal* 21, no. 2 (1995): 197–213.

Baltagi, Badi, and James Griffin. "Short and Long Run Effects in Pooled Models." *International Economic Review* 25, no. 3 (1984): 631–645.

Baum, Charles. "The Effect of Work Interruptions on Women's Wages." *Labour* 16, no. 1 (2002): 1–36.

Becker, Gary S. *The Economics of Discrimination*. Chicago, IL: University of Chicago Press, 1957.

Becker, Gary S. "An Economic Analysis of Fertility." In *Demographic and Economic Change in Developed Countries*, 209–240. Universities National Bureau Conference Series. Princeton, NJ: Princeton University Press, 1960.

Becker, Gary S. *Human Capital*. New York, NY: Columbia University Press, 1964.

Becker, Gary S. "Human Capital, Effort, and the Sexual Division of Labor." *Journal of Labor Economics* 3, no. 1 (Pt 2) (1985): S33–S58.

Becker, Gary S. *A Treatise on the Family*, enlarged ed. Cambridge, MA: Harvard University Press, 1991.

Ben-Porath, Yoram. "The Production of Human Capital over the Life Cycle." *Journal of Political Economy* 75 (1967): 352–365.

Berger, Mark, Dan Black, Amitabh Chandra, and Frank Scott. "Children, Non-discriminatory Provision of Fringe Benefits, and Household Labor Market Decisions." *Research in Labor Economics* 22 (2003): 309–349.

Bergstrom, Theodore C., and Mark Bagnoli. "Courtship as a Waiting Game." *Journal of Political Economy* 101, no. 1 (1993): 185–202.

Blau, Francine, Mary Brinton, and David Grusky, eds. *The Declining Significance of Gender.* New York, NY: Russell Sage Foundation, 2006.

Blau, Francine D., and Lawrence M. Kahn. "The Gender Earnings Gap: Learning from International Comparisons." *American Economic Review* 82 (1992): 533–538.

Blau, Francine D., and Lawrence M. Kahn. "The Gender Earnings Gap: Some International Evidence." In *Differences and Changes in Wage Structures,* edited by Richard Freeman and Lawrence Katz, 105–143. Chicago, IL: University of Chicago Press, 1995.

Blau, Francine D., and Lawrence M. Kahn. "International Differences in Male Wage Inequality: Institutions versus Market Forces." *Journal of Political Economy* 104 (1996a): 791–837.

Blau, Francine D., and Lawrence M. Kahn. "Wage Structure and Gender Earnings Differentials: An International Comparison." *Economica* 63 (1996b): S29–S62.

Blau, Francine D., and Lawrence M. Kahn. *At Home and Abroad U.S. Labor-Market Performance in International Perspective.* New York, NY: Russell Sage Foundation, 2002.

Blau, Francine D., and Lawrence M. Kahn. "Understanding International Differences in the Gender Pay Gap." *Journal of Labor Economics* 21, no. 1 (2003): 106–144.

Blinder, Alan S. "Wage Discrimination: Reduces Form and Structural Estimates." *Journal of Human Resources* 8, no. 4 (1973): 436–455.

Budig, Michelle, and Paula England. "The Wage Penalty for Motherhood." *American Sociological Review* 66, no. 2 (2001): 204–225.

Catalyst. "Workplace Flexibility Is Still a Women's Advancement Issue." 2003. http://64.233.167.104/u/Catalyst?q=cache:BGumQK H8saEJ:www.catalystwomen.org/bookstore/files/view/Workplace %2520Flexibility%2520Is%2520Still%2520a%2520Women%27s %2520Advancement%2520Issue.pdf+mba+and+men+and+women &hl=en&ie=UTF-8.

Chaykowski, Richard P., and Lisa M. Powell. "Women and the Labour Market: Recent Trends and Policy Issues." *Canadian Public Policy* 25, no. 0 (1999): S1–S25.

Coltrane, Scott. "Research on Household Labor: Modeling and Measuring the Social Embeddedness of Routine Family Work." *Journal of Marriage and Family* 62, no. 4 (2000): 1208–1233.

Davies, Rhys, and Gaëlle Pierre. "The Family Gap in Europe: A Cross-Country Study." *Labour Economics* 12, no. 4 (2005): 469–486.

Eckstein, Zvi, and Kenneth I. Wolpin. "Dynamic Labour Force Participation of Married Women and Endogenous Work Experience." *Review of Economic Studies* 56, no. 3 (1989): 375–390.

Goldin, Claudia. *Understanding the Gender Gap: An Economic History of American Women.* Oxford, UK: Oxford University Press, 1990.

Goldin, Claudia, and Solomon Polachek. "Residual Differences by Sex: Perspectives on the Gender Gap in Earnings." *American Economic Review, Papers and Proceedings* 77, no. 2 (May 1987): 143–151.

Gornick, Janet, and Jerry Jacobs. "Gender, the Welfare State and Public Employment." *American Sociological Review* 63, no. 5 (October 1998): 688–710.

Greene, William H. *Econometric Analysis, 7th ed.* Saddle River, NJ: Pearson publishing as Prentice Hall, 2012.

Greenwood, Jeremy, and Nezih Guner. *Marriage and Divorce since World War II: Analyzing the Role of Technological Progress on the Formation of Household.* Research Report No. 8. Rochester, NY: University of Rochester, 2004.

Gwartney, James, and Robert Lawson, eds. *Economic Freedom of the World 2004 Annual Report.* Vancouver, Canada: Fraser Institute, 2004.

Harkness, Susan, and Jane Waldfogel. "The Family Gap in Pay: Evidence from Seven Industrialized Countries." *Research in Labor Economics* 22 (2003): 369–414.

Iversen, Torben. *Contested Economic Institutions.* New York, NY: Cambridge University Press, 1999.

Jaumotte, Florence. "Labour Force Participation of Women: Empirical Evidence on the Role of Policy and Other Determinants in OECD Countries." *OECD Economic Studies* 37, no. 2 (2003): 51–108.

Jones, F. L. "On Decomposing the Gender Wage Gap; A Critical Comment on Blinder's Decomposition." *Journal of Human Resources* 18, no. 1 (1983): 126–130.

Joshi, Heather, Pierella Paci, and Jane Waldfogel. "The Wages of Motherhood: Better or Worse." *Cambridge Journal of Economics* 23, no. 5 (1999): 543–564.

Juhn, Chinhui, Kevin M. Murphy, and Brooks Pierce. "Wage Inequality and the Rise in Returns to Skill." *Journal of Political Economy* 101, no. 3 (1993): 410–442.

Kesenne, S. L. J. "Basic Income and Female Labour Supply: An Empirical Analysis." *Cahiers Economiques de Bruxelles* 0, no. 125 (1990): 81–92.

Kolberg, Jon Eivind. "The Gender Dimension of the Welfare State," *International Journal of Sociology* 21, no. 2 (1991): 119–148.

Korenman, Sanders, and David Neumark. "Marriage, Motherhood, and Wages." *Journal of Human Resources* 27, no. 2 (1992): 233–255.

Kreyenfeld, Michaela, and Karsten Hank. "Does the Availability of Child Care Influence the Employment of Mothers? Findings from Western Germany." *Population Research and Policy Review* 19, no. 4 (2000): 317–337.

Kumar, Anil. *Lifecycle Consistent Estimation of Effect of Taxes on Female Labor Supply in the U.S: Evidence from Panel Data*. Federal Reserve Bank of Dallas Working Paper. Dallas, Texas: Federal Reserve Bank of Dallas, 2005.

Lemieux, Thomas. "The 'Mincer Equation' Thirty Years after *Schooling, Experience, and Earnings*." In *Jacob Mincer: A Pioneer of Modern Labor Economics*, edited by Shoshana Grossbard. New York, NY: Springer Science, 2006.

Macdhin, Stephen, and Alan Manning. "The Effects of Minimum Wages on Wage Dispersion and Employment: Evidence from the U.K. Wage Councils." *Industrial and Labor Relations Review* 47, no. 1 (1994): 319–329.

Manser, Marilyn, and Murray Brown. "Marriage and Household Decisions Making: A Bargaining Analysis." *International Economics Review* 21, no. 1 (1980): 31–44.

McElroy, Marjorie, and Mary Horney. "Nash Bargained Household Decisions." *International Economic Review* 22, no. 2 (1981): 333–349.

Miller, Carole. "Actual Experience, Potential Experience or Age, and Labor Force Participation by Married Women." *Atlantic Economic Journal* 21, no. 4 (1993): 60–66.

Mincer, Jacob. *Schooling, Experience, and Earnings*. New York, NY: Columbia University Press, 1974.

Mincer, Jacob, and Haim Ofek. "Interrupted Work Careers: Depreciation and Restoration of Human Capital." *Journal of Human Resources* 17, no. 1 (1982): 3–24.

Mincer, Jacob, and Solomon Polachek. "Family Investment in Human Capital: Earnings of Women." *Journal of Political Economy* 82, no. 2 (1974): S76–S108.

Nock, Steven. "The Marriages of Equally Dependent Spouses." *Journal of Family Issues* 22, no. 6 (2001): 755–775.

Oaxaca, Ronald. "Male-Female Wage Differentials in Urban Labor Markets." *International Economic Review* 14, no. 3 (1973): 693–709.

Oaxaca, Ronald, and Michael Ransom. "On Discrimination and the Decomposition of Wage Differentials." *Journal of Econometrics* 61, no. 1 (1994): 5–21.

O'Neill, June, and Dave O'Neill. "What Do Wage Differentials Tell Us about Labor Market Discrimination." *Research in Labor Economics* 24 (2006): 293–357.

Organization for Economic Cooperation and Development, *OECD Employment Outlook*, OECD, Paris 1997.

Organization for Economic Cooperation and Development, *OECD Employment Outlook*, OECD, Paris, 2002.

Ott, Notburga. "Fertility and the Division of Work within the Family." In *Out of the Margin*, edited by Edith Kuiper and Jolande Sap, 80–99. London, UK/New York, NY: Routledge Press, 1995.

Paull, Gillian. "The Impact of Children on Women's Paid Work." *Fiscal Studies* 27, no. 4 (2006): 473–512.

Polachek, Solomon. "Potential Biases in Measuring Male-Female Discrimination." *Journal of Human Resources* 10, no. 2 (1975a): 205–229.

Polachek, Solomon. "Differences in Expected Post-School Investment as a Determinant of Market Wage Differentials." *International Economic Review* 16 (1975b): 451–470.

Polachek, Solomon. "Human Capital and the Gender Wage Gap." In *Out of the Margin*, edited by Edith Kuiper and Jolande Sap, 61–79. London, UK/New York, NY: Routledge Press, 1995.

Polachek, Solomon. "How the Human Capital Model Explains Why the Gender Wage Gap Narrowed." In *The Declining Significance of Gender*, edited by F. Blau, M. Brinton, and D. Grusky, 102–124. New York, NY: Russell Sage Foundation, 2006.

Polachek, Solomon. "A Human Capital Account of the Gender Wage Gap." In *The New Gilded Age*, edited by D. Grusky and T. Kricheli-Katz, 161–188. Stanford, CA: Stanford University Press, 2012.

Polachek, Solomon, and Moon-Kak Kim. "Panel Estimates of the Gender Earnings Gap: Individual Specific Intercept and Individual Specific Slope Models." *Journal of Econometrics* 61, no. 1 (1994): 23–42.

Pontusson, Jonas, David Rueda, and Christopher R. Way. "Comparative Political Economy of Wage Distribution: The Role of Partisanship and Labour Market Institutions." *British Journal of Political Science* 32 (2002): 281–308.

Psacharopoulos, George, and Zafiris Tzannatos, eds. *Case Studies on Women's Employment and Pay in Latin America*. Washington, DC: World Bank, 1992.

Rosenfeld, Rachel, and Arne Kalleberg. "A Cross-National Comparison of the Gender Gap in Income." *American Journal of Sociology* 96, no. 1 (1990): 69–106.

Rueda, David, and Jonas Pontusson. "Wage Inequality and Varieties of Capitalism." *World Politics* 52 (2000): 350–383.

Ruhm, Christopher. "The Economic Consequences of Parental Leave Mandates: Lessons from Europe." *Quarterly Journal of Economics* 113, no. 1 (1998): 285–317.

Ruhm, Christopher. "Parental Leave and Child Health." *Journal of Health Economics* 19, no. 6 (2000): 931–960.

Simpson, Wayne. "Intermittent Work Activities and Earnings." *Applied Economics* 32, no. 14 (2000): 1777–1786.

Smith, James, and Michael Ward. "Women in the Labor Market and in the Family." *Journal of Economic Perspectives* 3, no. 1 (1989): 9–23.

Smith, Nina, Shirley Dex, Jan Dirk Vlasblom, and Tim Callan. "The Effects of Taxation on Married Women's Labour Supply across Four Countries." *Oxford Economic Papers* 55, no. 3 (2003): 417–439.

Spivey, Christy. "Time off at What Price? The Effects of Career Interruptions on Earnings." *Industrial and Labor Relations Review* 59, no. 1 (2005): 119–140.

Suen, Wing. "Decomposing Wage Residuals: Unmeasured Skill or Statistical Artifact?" *Journal of Labor Economics* 15, no. 3 (1997): 555–566.

Tanaka, Sakiko. "Parental Leave and Child Health across OECD Countries." *Economic Journal* 115, no. 501 (2005): F7–F28.

Treiman, Donald, and Patricia Roos. "Sex and Earnings in Industrial Society: A Nine-Nation Comparison." *American Journal of Sociology* 89, no. 3 (1983): 612–650.

Waldfogel, Jane. "Understanding the 'Family Gap' in Pay for Women with Children." *Journal of Economic Perspectives* 12, no. 1 (1998): 137–156.

Wallerstein, Michael. "Wage-Setting Institutions and Pay Inequality in Advanced Industrial Societies." *American Journal of Political Science* 43, no. 3 (1999): 649–680.

Weichselbaumer, Doris, and Rudolf Winter-Ebmer. *The Effects of Competition and Equal Treatment Laws on the Gender Wage Differential.* Working Paper No. 0307. Linz, Austria: Johannes Kepler University, Department of Economics, 2002.

Weichselbaumer, Doris, and Rudolf Winter-Ebmer. *A Meta-analysis of the International Gender Wage Gap.* Working Paper No. 0311. Linz, Austria: Johannes Kepler University, Department of Economics, 2003.

Weinberger, Catherine, and Peter Kuhn. *The Narrowing of the U.S. Gender Earnings Gap, 1969–1999: A Cohort-Based Analysis.* Working Paper. Santa Barbara, CA: University of California Santa Barbara, 2005.

Weiss, Yoram, and Reuben Gronau. "Expected Interruptions in Labor Force Participation and Sex Related Differences in Earnings Growth." *Review of Economic Studies* 48, no. 4 (1981): 607–619.

Willis, Robert J. "A New Approach to the Economic Theory of Fertility Behavior." *Journal of Political Economy* 81, no. 2 (Pt 2) (1973): S14–S64.

Yamada, Tadashi, and Tetsuji Yamada. *Estimation of a Simultaneous Model of Married Women's Labor Force Participation and Fertility in Urban Japan.* NBER Working Paper No. 1362. Cambridge, MA: NBER, 1984.

Yun, Myeong-Su. *Wage Differentials, Discrimination and Inequality: A Cautionary Note on Juhn, Murphy, and Pierce Decomposition Method.* IZA Discussion Paper No. 2937. Bonn, Germany: Institute for the Study of Labor, 2007.

Chapter 3

Unpaid Time Use by Gender and Family Structure

Rachel Connelly and Jean Kimmel

Why is time a valuable commodity? Some uses of time simply make us happy. We enjoy a walk in the park on a sunny day or a conversation with a friend. Most people particularly enjoy time spent playing with children, although this time may be subject to diminishing marginal returns (Connelly and Kimmel 2013; Oster 2013). Nevertheless, not all time is devoted to immediate gratification. A substantial portion of our time is spent in activities where the primary purpose is to produce income or a final consumption commodity. While most of us do not enjoy doing our laundry, we do enjoy having clean clothing.

Each of us trades time between activities that generate utility directly (often called leisure) and activities that are undertaken for their outcome (often called work or labor). This distinction defines the traditional labor market model known as the labor/leisure trade-off. Unfortunately, the model is difficult to test because researchers rarely have information about time spent outside of paid employment. A newly available, large nationally representative survey data set allows us to do a better job distinguishing among categories of leisure. Time devoted to paid work can be a source of direct utility, although recent research relying on newly available subjective well-being data reinforces the traditional labor economics assumption that it is the outcome of this time (earned income) that generates utility, rather than the paid work time itself.

In a family context, the fact that time is useful for ends beyond direct consumption creates the potential to trade time across family members or across support networks of other individuals—that is, beyond immediate family members. A recent stay in the hospital highlighted this point. What do friends do when one is in the hospital? They visit, producing the enjoyment of a shared conversation, and they bring food, usually homemade food. What are we giving each other when we bring a casserole to the home of friends in need? We are giving our time, and this gift of time reveals the depth of our caring, as time may be more valuable than money in many situations.

The ability of family members to share responsibilities by trading time with each other was formalized by Gary Becker's (1981) model of family life. According to this model, one member can specialize in market work while another specializes in home production. There is no direct utility involved in either of these activities in the Becker model; instead, each activity is undertaken for the purpose of increasing the total amount of "stuff" a family can consume.

This model can be expanded to include many commodities, each of which is produced with some time input (Becker 1965). In Becker's expanded time use model, there is no *a priori* expectation that one person in the household will engage in all of the home production. Even so, we may observe specialization within household production activities. One spouse may specialize in cooking, while the other spouse specializes in cleaning. The potential for family members to trade time uses among themselves is a second reason to study unpaid time use.

We expect that more total time will be devoted to home production in homes with a stay-at-home spouse. If that person is the wife, she performs the bulk of this unpaid work. In families in which both spouses are employed full-time, we expect less total home production time and a more even distribution of those chores among members. What about single-parent households? The theory does not predict whether they will perform more or less home production than coupled households; the answer will depend on relative labor/leisure preferences as well as the pair's relative productivities in market work and unpaid work, and income differences.

Modern time use research in the United States dates to 1965, with the Americans' Use of Time Study (AUTS) Project. AUTS was part of a 12-country Multinational Time-Budget Research Project masterminded by Alexander Szalai. Since then, small-scale time use surveys have been conducted in the United States in 1975, 1985, 1995, and

2000. Many European countries, as well as Australia and New Zealand, launched much larger national time diary surveys in the 1990s, permitting researchers to look at finer categories of time use and more targeted subgroups in the population. During this period, there was a call for a similar survey collection effort in the United States.

After years of planning and testing, the U.S. Bureau of Labor Statistics initiated the annual American Time Use Survey (ATUS) in 2003 using a subsample of the outgoing rotation group from the Current Population Survey (CPS), a nationally representative sample. The ATUS provides large samples, making it possible to describe detailed time use patterns for various demographic groups, while also stratifying results by age, education, family structure, employment status, and even day of the week.

In this chapter, we begin by summarizing the extensive evidence concerning changes in time use across the past 50 years of American life. Then, relying on our own analyses of data from the 2010 ATUS, we focus on three issues: (1) differences in time use by gender and family structure (including marital status and the presence of children in the household); (2) a reexamination of gender differences in total work (i.e., paid work plus unpaid labor in the home); and (3) an examination of gender differences in how we feel while engaged in various activities, using the newly available data regarding subjective well-being. In our investigation of both time use and subjective well-being, we present statistical comparisons of time use in finely defined uses of time. In particular, we note gender differences in developmental child caregiving time as distinct from caregiving time spent in physical care of children.

A BRIEF HISTORICAL PORTRAIT OF THE EVOLUTION OF TIME USE PATTERNS

Our ability to observe the evolution of time use patterns in the United States is due to the hard work of a number of time use researchers. We have already mentioned Alexander Szalai's Multinational Time-Budget Research Project in 1965. Data were also collected in time diary form in separate surveys in the years 1975, 1985, 1992, 1995, 1998–1999, and 2000. These data, along with the 1965 data and the current American Time Use Survey, have been assembled and harmonized in the American Heritage Time Use Study (AHTUS). An excellent summary of the multiple time diary data sets can be found in the article by Aguiar, Hurst, and Karabarbounis (2012).

Two fundamental societal shifts in time use dominated the landscape from 1965 to 2010. The first was the "gender revolution" of the late 20th century, in which married women with children increased their employment hours substantially. This increase in employment hours was accompanied by a large decrease in housework and a smaller decrease in leisure time. Their husbands' home production increased, but not enough to counter the decrease in women's household production hours or to achieve gender parity in housework hours.

Surprisingly, the second historical shift resulted from the development of improved-quality, affordable television sets and an expansion of programming. National network television news expanded in the late 1960s and color television sets replaced black-and-white TVs during the early 1970s. Television watching increased from 10 hours per week in 1965 (among the working-age population, 18–65 years) to 15 hours per week in 1975 and then to 16 hours per week in 2005.

Television watching continues to command a very high share of leisure time in the United States (40 percent)—higher than in many European countries, but lower than in Japan (45 percent of free time). Cross-sectional evidence on TV watching in 1965 suggests that individuals increased their time spent watching TV through a reduction in reading newspapers, listening to the radio, watching movies, pursuing hobbies, and sleeping. By our calculation, on average, men watch more TV than women—20 hours per week for men ages 25 to 64 in 2010, compared to 16 hours for women.

Mothers' increased time in paid employment carried with it a concern that the cost of this market work time might be borne by their children. This change, it was feared, would come through reduced maternal time devoted to child caregiving. Happily, this concern has proved unfounded. While it is true that in any given year, mothers who are not employed spend more time on child caregiving than employed mothers, the total amount of time devoted to child caregiving for all mothers has increased over the years. An employed mother in 2000 reported spending as much time on primary child care as a non-employed mother in 1975 (Bianchi, Robinson, and Milkie 2006).

Other researchers also report an increase in child caregiving over this period for women. Using the AHTUS, Fisher et al. (2007) found that women's child caregiving time (for women between the ages of 19 and 65) doubled from 1965 to 2003. Bianchi et al. (2012) report that for all women aged 25 to 64, child caregiving hours per week increased from 10.5 in 1965 to 7.3 in 1975, 8.5 in 1985, 11.2 in 1995, 12.0 in 1998–1999, 13.9 in 2003–2004, and finally 13.7 in 2009–2010. It is unlikely that these results are artifacts of the ATUS data collection method as suggested by Fisher et al. Kimmel and Connelly (2007) and others show, by using the ATUS cross-sectionally, that mothers with the highest wages report both the most hours of paid work and the most hours of child caregiving. High-wage women are more likely to be in the labor market and to have more hours of employment than lower-wage women but without contracting the number of hours they also spend in child care.

The concurrent increase in women's employment and the decrease in unpaid work—excluding child care—were not evenly spread out over this 50-year period. Women's employment hours increased slowly from 1965 to 1985, then rose sharply from 1985 to 1992, and have been mostly steady since then. This statement is based on data that include all women aged 19 to 65 whose employment is defined broadly as encompassing employment hours, education, training, commuting, and applying for jobs and classes (Fisher et al. 2007).

Unpaid work for these same women began falling much earlier, with large declines observed from 1965 to 1975 and again from 1985 to 1992. From 1992 to 2003, the decline was quite small (Fisher et al. 2007). Many have speculated on the cause of the decline in unpaid work. Bianchi et al. (2000) offer a nice treatment of the sociology theory. The economic theory focuses on women's increased wages— both their absolute wages and their wages relative to men (Bianchi et al. 2000). The relative timing of the two decreases in unpaid work among women provides preliminary evidence that declining demand for time at home (caused by lower fertility levels and changing family structure) are part of the cause of the increase in women's labor hours as we moved from the 1960s into the 1970s and 1980s.

Advances in household technology may also have played a role in the reduction of time devoted to unpaid work in the home. Robinson (2011), citing data from the 1965 cross-sectional analysis, argues that advances in household technology led mostly to increases in home outputs rather than to time reductions. However, the same may not be true for more recent technological changes in the home. Hamermesh (2007) attributes most of the decline in unpaid work time since 1965 to a decline in time spent preparing and cooking food. The proliferation of microwave ovens, as well as the increased availability of processed foods in the supermarket, are credited with a reduction in food preparation time. Bianchi et al. (2012) show that most of the decline for women involved "core housework"; by comparison, time spent in other areas of home production, such as household management and repairs, has remained stable.

What were American men doing during this period? The trends in men's paid and unpaid work time—excluding child caregiving time—were just the opposite of women's: their paid work hours declined and their unpaid work hours increased. As was noted for women, these trends were not smooth over the 50-year period. According to Fisher et al. (2007), the large decline in paid work hours for men aged 19 to 64 (with paid work defined very broadly as explained previously) came between 1965 and 1985. Since then, their paid work hours have held steady. Men's unpaid work hours, excluding child caregiving, increased during the same 1965 to 1985 time period and have remained relatively constant since then. Bianchi et al. (2012) report men's housework hours (for men aged 25 to 64) doubled from 1965 to 1985, from 4.9 hours per week to 9.8 hours. Since then, this amount of time has remained steady at approximately 10 hours.

The decline in women's unpaid work hours and the increase in men's unpaid work hours led to a reduction in the ratio of women's to men's housework hours from 1965 through 1998. In 1965, women's housework time was 6.1 times greater than men's; by 1985, this ratio had declined to 2.0. Since then, the ratio has remained fairly constant, as both men's and women's individual trends have remained flat.

Within the broader trends noted for unpaid work, child caregiving again appears to be an outlier. The increase in women's child caregiving hours has not been countered by a decline in men's child caregiving hours; in fact, the opposite is true. Men's child caregiving hours also increased over this period. In 1965, married fathers devoted an average of 2.6 hours per week to child caregiving (Bianchi et al. 2012). In 1975, men's child caregiving time remained essentially unchanged at 2.4 hours, and in 1985, it had risen just slightly to 3.0 hours per week. Between 1985 and 1995, however, married fathers' child caregiving increased to 4.5 hours per week, an increase of 1.5 hours, which occurred during the same period in which married mothers' child caregiving also saw its biggest increase of 2.7 hours.

For children of married parents, these increases mean that the caregiving time of parents rose by more than 4 hours per week between 1985 and 1995.

As sleep and personal care time increased only 1 hour over the period (Aguiar and Hurst 2007), any increase in paid work time and child caregiving time not countered by a decrease in home production time would imply a decrease in leisure. However, according to Fisher et al. (2007), the decline in paid work time for men and the decline in unpaid home production time for women dominate the total of paid work and unpaid work and child caregiving from 1965 to 1985 (called "total work" for these purposes).

"Total work" time declined for both sexes over this period (Fisher et al. 2007). The decline was steeper for men than women, especially between 1975 and 1985. Men's "total work" hours increased slightly from 1985 to 2003. Women's "total work" hours continued to decline slightly until 1993, but then increased somewhat thereafter. The "total work" hours of working-age men and women were almost the same in 1993 and 2000, leading to Burda, Hamermesh, and Weil's (2013) hypothesis of "gender iso-work" within any given society or large demographic group within the society. Later in this chapter, we reconsider the gender iso-work issue with 2010 evidence and find that the iso-work claim no longer holds when we control for family status.

Aguiar and Hurst (2007) document an increase in leisure from 1965 to 2003. Their focus, like that of Fisher et al. (2007), is the working-age population, which they define as people between the ages of 21 and 65, neither in school nor retired. However, Aguiar and Hurst found that this increase in leisure is largely concentrated among the group with low education levels. Using a measure of "core leisure" that includes watching TV, socializing, participating in or watching sports, reading, hobby time, and other entertainment time, Aguiar and Hurst find an increase of 5.6 hours per week for men and 3.7 hours for women. These estimates control for changing demographic structure of the population from 1965 to 2003.

Bittman and Wajcman (2000) examine time diary data collected from 1981 to 1992 for 10 developed countries and find that paid employment and having young children exert the largest influence in reducing women's leisure time. Bianchi, Wight, and Raley (2005) present leisure trends for mothers with at least one child younger than the age of 18 in the household. Excluding personal care time, leisure (they call it "free time") has declined by approximately 3 hours per week, from 34.8 hours in 1965 to 31.6 hours in 2003. These authors' measure for 2000 is 31.8 hours, showing substantial continuity between the ATUS data and the earlier data. Thus, while total per capita leisure may have been constant over the century, as argued by Ramey and Francis (2009), and the leisure of the average working-age person has increased (according to both Fisher et al. [2007] and Aguiar and Hurst [2007]), the leisure of mothers in the United States has declined slightly over the last 50 years as both paid work hours and child caregiving time have increased. These changes result in a growing feeling of time squeeze that Bittman and Wajcman (2000) find most likely to be reported by parents of young children.

DESCRIPTIVE ANALYSIS OF TIME USE IN 2010 BY GENDER

In this section, we present more extensive descriptive analysis of time use in American families with a focus on time *not* devoted to paid work. We begin our analysis by examining time in five broad categories of time use and then present more detailed information on time devoted to specific activities. Our focus is on how differences in family structure affect time use.

Despite a century of declining gender differences, especially due to the increase in women's labor force participation, men and women in the United States still differ substantially in how they use their time (Bianchi et al. 2012; Connelly and Kimmel 2010). Thus, for all of our empirical analyses, we stratify our analysis by gender.

Both marriage and the presence of children have been shown to be associated with substantive differences in adults' time use. Marriage or partnership can lead to time substitution, in the sense that one spouse can cook while the other watches the children. But marriage also may increase total time spent in certain activities, such that couples' time may appear to be complementary. For example, it may be more fun to go for a walk with one's spouse than alone. Hamermesh (2002) considers the advantages of couples' leisure coordination. Vernon (2012) finds that married couples spend more time on housework than the sum of the time of single men and single women. The increased total housework time may come from increased use of home-produced goods over market goods. A sit-down home-cooked meal instead of fast food consumed on the go is an example. Connelly and Kimmel (2009) report evidence of time complementarity for home production time for married couples with children younger than age 13.

Caring for young children is extremely time intensive, even when market child care is used to facilitate employment. Connelly and Kimmel (2009) report that, in the years 2003 to 2006, American mothers of children younger than the age of 6 spent 185 minutes on child caregiving on a typical weekday and 132 minutes on a typical weekend day. Although the time demands of children decrease as children age, the presence of children in the household still substantially changes the mix of time use activities.

In this descriptive exercise, our definition of families is purposely broad to acknowledge the diversity of living arrangements within the U.S. population. While most of the work on time use has focused on the working-age population, the elderly live within family structures as well and we are interested in how they use their time. Aguiar, Hurst, and Karabarbounis (2012) present a model of lifetime time use that predicts differential bundles of goods and time use across the life cycle.

We include individuals ages 18 to 84 in our analyses and consider four possible family structures: those coupled with dependent children present (dependent children are defined as those younger than 18 years of age), those coupled with no dependent children present, a single parent with dependent children present, and a single adult with no dependent children. Other adults may or may not be present in any of these four family structures. Twenty-four percent of Americans aged 18 to 84 live as couples (married or cohabiting) with children present. Thirty-five percent live as couples with no children present, 5 percent as single parents, and 36 percent as single adults with no children present. Table 3.1, Panel A, compares men and women in the four family categories.

Couples without children are considerably older. Those single individuals with no children are both a high percentage of people younger than age 30 and a high percentage of people age 60 years or older. Average years of education are similar across family groups, but couples with children present have the highest percentage of those with a college degree. Singles with children tend to be nonwhites and Hispanics relative to other family categories.

Employment status differs substantially across categories. Men in couples with children have the lowest rates of being "not employed," while women in couples with children have the highest rates of being employed "part-time."

Table 3.1 Selected Demographic Characteristics by Gender and Family Status

	Men				Women			
	Couples with Kids	Couples without Kids	Single with Kids	Single without Kids	Couples with Kids	Couples without Kids	Single with Kids	Single without Kids
Panel A: Full Sample, Aged 18–84								
Years of Education	14.4	13.7	13.3	13.3	14.5	13.6	13.3	13.3
Less than high school	8.4%	13.2%	13.9%	16.0%	7.7%	10.3%	14.1%	15.7%
High school graduate/some college	49.4%	53.4%	64.6%	58.3%	47.8%	60.7%	64.6%	58.9%
College graduate or more	42.2%	33.5%	21.5%	25.7%	44.4%	28.9%	21.3%	25.4%
Mean Age	40.9	57.7	40.7	46.7	37.8	56.9	36.5	55.9
Percentage younger than 30	8.7%	5.7%	10.8%	25.4%	14.9%	6.4%	25.8%	14.8%
Percentage older than 59	2.4%	49.2%	3.1%	27.0%	0.3%	44.9%	0.9%	48.0%
Nonwhite	14.8%	16.1%	23.1%	24.0%	13.9%	17.4%	31.5%	29.5%
Hispanic	15.2%	12.4%	18.5%	14.8%	15.2%	12.9%	18.9%	12.1%
Employment Status								
Full, 35+ hours	81.0%	48.4%	70.8%	46.5%	44.3%	39.9%	49.8%	34.6%
Part, 0–35 hours	5.9%	6.5%	3.9%	10.5%	20.6%	11.2%	12.9%	10.0%
Not employed	13.1%	45.1%	25.4%	43.1%	35.1%	49.0%	37.3%	55.4%
Sample size	1381	1085	130	1704	1485	1182	644	2151

Panel B: Working-Age Sample, Aged 25–64

Year of Education	14.0	14.0	13.0	13.7	14.4	14.2	13.3	14.3
Less than high school	10.3%	11.0%	9.6%	10.3%	8.0%	4.0%	12.6%	6.5%
High school graduate/ some college	51.4%	50.9%	75.1%	58.8%	48.3%	59.4%	65.6%	54.9%
College graduate or more	38.3%	38.1%	15.4%	30.9%	43.7%	36.6%	21.9%	38.7%
Mean Age	40.6	49.3	38.7	40.4	38.7	49.2	36.7	44.1
Percentage younger than 30	8.5%	8.2%	17.6%	26.5%	11.9%	8.8%	25.1%	20.9%
Nonwhite	15.1%	14.6%	24.1%	24.1%	15.2%	12.8%	34.0%	30.1%
Hispanic	19.4%	10.2%	26.8%	12.3%	12.9%	9.1%	22.4%	11.7%
Employment Status								
Full, 35+ hours	85.9%	77.1%	83.2%	69.4%	64.2%	76.1%	69.3%	70.6%
Part, 0–35 hours	7.3%	5.9%	5.0%	12.6%	28.6%	14.6%	18.9%	13.2%
Not employed	6.8%	17.0%	11.8%	18.1%	7.3%	9.3%	11.7%	16.2%
Sample size	1,255	619	106	941	1,023	617	427	910

Weighted averages, American Time Use Survey 2010.

Because retirement is so unevenly distributed across family types, Table 3.1, Panel B, shows a sample of individuals ages 25 to 64 to match the sample used by Bianchi et al. (2012). These individuals represent a population group much more likely to be employed— a factor that greatly affects time use. Panel B also shows substantial demographic differences across family status. Single men without children are much more likely to be younger than age 30 and more likely to be "not employed" than other men. For both men and women, couples with no children have the oldest mean age, suggesting that many are "empty-nesters." Women in this category have the highest probability of being employed full-time compared to the other family status categories.

AGGREGATE TIME USE BY FAMILY STATUS CATEGORY

Table 3.2 shows time use of men and women in five aggregate categories, stratified by the four family living arrangements. As before, we consider the full sample, 18 to 84 years of age, in Panel A and the working-age sample, 25 to 64 years of age alone, in Panel B.

These aggregate time use categories represent very different types of activities. Employment is mainly for the purpose of earning income. Many studies combine child caregiving with home production, but here we do not, following Reid's (1934) concept that home production is something one could pay someone else to do.

Kimmel and Connelly (2007) show that child caregiving and home production are quite different, with child caregiving being related positively to wages, while home production varies negatively with wages. We argue that child caregiving includes a substantial investment component (i.e., we engage in parental caregiving time today as an investment in our child's future well-being) and that this investment component is different from the immediacy of most home production outcomes. Guryan et al. (2008) show that the income and child caregiving are positively related, whereas the income gradients for both leisure and home production are negative. New information on subjective well-being shows that both men and women enjoy most aspects of child caregiving substantially more than most other home production activities (Connelly and Kimmel 2013).

Some leisure activities (such as exercise) have investment aspects, but most reflect current consumption and directly produce utility.

Table 3.2a Time Use per Day by Family Status, Full Sample, Aged 18–84, 2010

	Men				Women			
	Couples with Kids	Couples without Kids	Single with Kids	Single without Kids	Couples with Kids	Couples without Kids	Single with Kids	Single without Kids
Minutes of Time Use per Day of Men and Women								
Home production	132	167	125	127	228	233	187	165
Leisure	351	471	354	476	318	418	318	452
Child caregiving	64	2	59	2	117	2	105	3
Work	356	231	331	220	206	193	209	181
Other	538	570	571	615	571	595	621	638
Percentage of Time per Day of Men and Women								
Home production	9.1%	11.6%	8.7%	8.8%	15.9%	16.2%	13.0%	11.4%
Leisure	24.4%	32.7%	24.6%	33.0%	22.1%	29.0%	22.1%	31.4%
Child caregiving	4.4%	0.1%	4.1%	0.1%	8.1%	0.1%	7.3%	0.2%
Work	24.8%	16.0%	23.0%	15.3%	14.3%	13.4%	14.5%	12.6%
Other	37.3%	39.6%	39.6%	42.7%	39.7%	41.3%	43.2%	44.3%
Sample size	1,471	1,154	137	1,798	1,555	1,250	671	2,245

Weighted averages, American Time Use Survey 2010.

Table 3.2b Time Use per Day by Family Status, Working-Age Sample, Aged 25–64, 2010

	Men				Women			
	Couples with Kids	Couples without Kids	Single with Kids	Single without Kids	Couples with Kids	Couples without Kids	Single with Kids	Single without Kids
Minutes of Time Use per Day of Men and Women Aged 25–64								
Home production	131	154	125	135	228	224	188	163
Leisure	352	420	354	447	318	379	322	405
Child caregiving	65	3	59	2	113	2	91	4
Work	357	305	332	282	212	248	216	256
Other	535	557	569	575	570	587	623	613
Percentage of Time per Day of Men and Women Aged 25–64								
Home production	10.0%	12.0%	9.5%	10.4%	18.8%	18.4%	15.0%	12.8%
Leisure	26.9%	32.7%	26.9%	34.2%	26.2%	31.2%	25.7%	31.7%
Child caregiving	4.9%	0.2%	4.5%	0.1%	9.3%	0.2%	7.3%	0.3%
Work	27.3%	23.7%	25.3%	21.6%	17.4%	20.4%	17.3%	20.0%
Other	40.9%	43.4%	43.3%	44.0%	47.0%	48.2%	49.7%	48.0%
Sample size	1,434	743	134	1,164	1,489	871	608	1,212

Weighted averages, American Time Use Survey 2010.

TV watching makes up the largest part of leisure. It does not make us as happy as more active forms of leisure do, perhaps because we do more of it, or perhaps because we engage in it when we are more tired. TV watching requires no marginal expenditure and less mental energy than other forms of leisure. In our detailed analysis, we separate TV watching from other forms of leisure.

The final category, "Maintenance," comprises mostly sleep and personal care time, but also includes educational time. We think of the maintenance category as investment time, albeit mostly short-term investment.

Differences in time use across family categories are evident even after controlling for gender. The presence of children, of course, increases child caregiving time. The time devoted to child caregiving is drawn mainly from leisure and paid work time. Home production time is also somewhat higher for individuals with children compared to those without children, except for men in couples with children. Here, we see evidence of time substitution: men in couples with children spend somewhat less time on home production and more time on employment, while women in couples with children display the opposite time use pattern. The large amount of time for leisure for both coupled men and women without children is partly a result of including older Americans in the sample. However, Panel B shows that the higher leisure time in the couples-without-children category is still evident even when we limit the sample to a traditional working-age population.

Table 3.2 also allows us to examine differences in time use between men and women within the same family category. Men in each family category have more leisure and employment minutes and fewer home production and child caregiving minutes than women in the same family circumstances. The numbers in the table do not support the hypothesis of Burda, Hamermesh, and Weil (2013) that men and women in similar circumstances enjoy the same amount of leisure.

The time use of individuals without children living in couples and single individuals with no children has received less attention in the literature than the time use of families with children (Vernon [2010] is an exception). Considering individuals of all ages (Panel A), both men and women in couples without children spend more time in home production than their single counterparts. Childless single men and women spend that extra time in leisure, not in home production. These conclusions do not change when we limit the sample to individuals age 25 to 64 (Panel B).

HOME PRODUCTION TIME DISAGGREGATED

Just as we argued that our aggregate time use categories captured differences in the purpose of the time use, so we suspect that there are substantial differences in the nature of time within each of our aggregate categories. We divide home production time into five sub-categories based on known gender differences. This gives us evidence of differences in the average *process* utility (i.e., the utility one gets from the activity rather than its outcome).

Shopping is one such process. It includes shopping for groceries and other things. Housework, which includes laundry and interior cleaning, probably has the least amount of process utility. Food preparation is considered separately, as the average level of happiness is higher when engaged in this activity than most of the other home production activities. Lawn work, repairs, and vehicle maintenance includes work outdoors and can also have consumption value for some persons. It is also a category that is often attended to by men. "Other home production" is the residual category and includes household management, caring for other household adults, caring for non-household children and adults, and the time it takes to acquire household services.

Tables 3.3a and 3.3b shows differences in time use within the home production category across gender and family status. The expected gender differences come through loud and clear. Women in all family situations do more housework, more shopping, and less yard work/ repairs than men in the same family situation.

The largest gender difference in total minutes in home production is within the category of couples with children. In this category, women spend 96 minutes more each day on home production than men. Of those 96 minutes, 66 are devoted to extra housework, while men in the couples-with-children category do 24 minutes per day more lawn work/repairs than women in the same group.

We might expect women and men who are single with no children to spend similar amounts of time on home production chores, but this is not the case. Single women spend 37 more minutes on home production than single men, including 25 minutes in extra housework. People may substitute for their own efforts by paying someone else to perform the task or by simply reducing the consumption of goods that are home produced. As single women represent a larger percentage of older people and home production time tends to increase with

Table 3.3a   Minutes of Home Production Time per Day by Family Status, Full Sample, Aged 18–84, 2010

	Men				Women			
	Couples with Kids	Couples without Kids	Single with Kids	Single without Kids	Couples with Kids	Couples without Kids	Single with Kids	Single without Kids
Home Production	**132**	**167**	**125**	**127**	**228**	**233**	**187**	**165**
Shopping	31	34	26	29	49	45	41	34
Housework	19	16	29	22	85	73	61	47
Yard work/repairs	36	57	20	26	12	17	6	10
Cooking	18	18	26	14	48	42	40	27
Other home production	28	42	25	36	34	56	40	47
Sample size	1,471	1,154	137	1,798	1,555	1,250	671	2,245

Weighted averages, American Time Use Study 2010.

Table 3.3b   Percentage of Home Production Time by Family Status, Full Sample, Aged 18–84, 2010

	Men				Women			
	Couples with Kids	Couples without Kids	Single with Kids	Single without Kids	Couples with Kids	Couples without Kids	Single with Kids	Single without Kids
Home Production								
Shopping	23.2%	20.6%	21.0%	22.4%	21.5%	19.3%	21.9%	20.5%
Housework	14.6%	9.6%	22.8%	17.5%	37.2%	31.2%	32.4%	28.5%
Yard work/repairs	27.1%	34.2%	15.8%	20.8%	5.1%	7.2%	3.0%	6.2%
Cooking	13.7%	10.5%	20.5%	11.3%	21.1%	18.2%	21.4%	16.1%
Other home production	21.3%	25.0%	19.8%	28.1%	15.1%	24.1%	21.3%	28.7%
Sample size	1,471	1,154	137	1,798	1,555	1,250	671	2,245

Weighted averages, American Time Use Survey 2010.

age, we see more home production associated with being single and female. Couples without children collectively spend more time on yard work than any of the other groups. The increase in yard work time (also shopping) for couples without children may also be a function of being retired.

From these numbers, we can calculate the percentage of home production time spent on various activities. Men in couples with children spend less than 15 percent of their home production time on housework, while women in couples with children spend 37 percent of their home production time on housework. This is evidence of the substitution of wives' time for husbands' time within couples.

LEISURE TIME DISAGGREGATED

Tables 3.3c and 3.3d provide a disaggregation of leisure time. Television watching accounts for nearly 40 percent of all leisure time, except for women in couples with children, for whom this share is 34 percent. Time spent reading or on the computer is similar for men and women in the same family status categories. Gender differences are seen in exercise: men exercise more while women have more social time (except for single mothers and fathers, who devote the same amount of time to these activities). Perhaps exercise is social time for men.

Looking across family status categories by gender, no large differences emerge. We might have expected single persons without children to spend more time socializing but, surprisingly, it is those individuals with children who spend a larger percentage of their leisure time socializing. It may be that children's lives provide structure for adult socialization via enhanced integration into the community, more connection with religious institutions, and sporting events.

CHILD CAREGIVING TIME DISAGGREGATED

Researchers often distinguish between time devoted to child development and time devoted to the physical care of children. Developmental caregiving includes time spent reading to children, helping with homework, playing with children, talking and listening to children, and going to school conferences. Maintenance child caregiving includes physical care, organization and planning, attending

Table 3.3c Minutes of Leisure Time per Day by Family Status, Full Sample, Aged 18–84, 2010

	Men				Women			
	Couples with Kids	Couples without Kids	Single with Kids	Single without Kids	Couples with Kids	Couples without Kids	Single with Kids	Single without Kids
Leisure	**351**	**471**	**354**	**476**	**318**	**418**	**318**	**452**
TV	139	214	137	191	108	160	139	196
Reading/computer	21	43	18	56	27	46	21	51
Social	51	56	63	69	65	68	61	75
Exercise	25	22	22	31	12	14	6	12
Other	114	136	113	129	106	129	90	117
Sample size	1,471	1,154	137	1,798	1,555	1,250	671	2,245

Source: Weighted averages, American Time Use Survey 2010.

Table 3.3d Percentage of Leisure Time by Family Status, Full Sample, Aged 18–84, 2010

	Men				Women			
	Couples with Kids	Couples without Kids	Single with Kids	Single without Kids	Couples with Kids	Couples without Kids	Single with Kids	Single without Kids
Leisure								
TV	39.7%	45.4%	38.8%	40.1%	33.9%	38.2%	43.8%	43.4%
Reading/computer	5.9%	9.2%	5.2%	11.9%	8.4%	11.1%	6.7%	11.3%
Social	14.7%	11.8%	17.7%	14.5%	20.3%	16.4%	19.3%	16.7%
Exercise	7.1%	4.7%	6.3%	6.5%	3.9%	3.5%	1.8%	2.7%
Other	32.7%	28.8%	31.9%	27.0%	33.4%	30.9%	28.4%	26.0%
Sample size	1,471	1,154	137	1,798	1,555	1,250	671	2,245

Weighted averages, American Time Use Survey 2010.

Table 3.3e   Minutes of Child Caregiving Time per Day by Family Status, with Children Sample, Aged 18–84, 2010

	Men		Women	
	Couples with Kids	Single with Kids	Couples with Kids	Single with Kids
Child caregiving	64	59	117	105
Developmental	27	32	41	32
Physical	37	27	76	73
Sample size	1,471	137	1,555	671

(Weighted averages, American Time Use Survey 2010)

children's events, watching children, waiting for children, and obtaining medical care for children.

Previous research has shown that men's child caregiving is disproportionately devoted to developmental care. Tables 3.3e and 3.3f show that men devote at least 43 percent of their caregiving time to developmental activities, while women devote about one-third of their child caregiving time to these activities.

Tables 3.3e and 3.3f also show the distribution of child caregiving time by family status and gender. Women's division of time between developmental and physical care appears to be independent of whether a partner is present. Thus, single mothers scale back on both developmental care and physical care to account for the 12 fewer total minutes they spend on child caregiving. Single fathers also spend less time on child caregiving overall than married men but devote a larger share of this child caregiving time to developmental care.

Table 3.3f   Percentage of Child Caregiving Time by Family Status, with Children Sample, Aged 18–84, 2010

	Men		Women	
	Couples with Kids	Single with Kids	Couples with Kids	Single with Kids
Child caregiving				
Developmental	42.6%	54.6%	35.0%	30.6%
Physical	57.4%	45.4%	65.0%	69.4%
Sample size	1,471	137	1,555	671

Weighted averages, American Time Use Survey 2010.

One must refrain from generalizing too much from these results. These groups differ in the age and number of children and in average income and education. Each of these factors has been shown in other research to affect child caregiving time. Tables 3.3g and 3.3h give us a feel for differences in time spent in child caregiving, controlling for one of these factors—namely, the age of the youngest child. The results indicate that in families with very young children, more time is devoted to child caregiving overall by both fathers and mothers, with increases in both developmental and physical child caregiving. Single mothers devote a larger percentage of their time to physical care, controlling for the age of the youngest child, compared to coupled mothers, especially when the youngest child younger than age six. For all family status/gender groups, a large percentage of time is devoted to developmental care for younger children.

Table 3.3i shows the full range of time use activities of families with children differentiated by the age of the youngest child. In addition to increasing child caregiving time, the presence of a younger child is associated with reduced paid work time for women and single fathers, reduced leisure time for men and for women in couples, and reduced home production time for everyone except single fathers.

TIME USE REGRESSION EVIDENCE

Thus far, we have provided a descriptive glimpse of time use within American families. These descriptive discussions are limited, however, as we have not controlled adequately for systematic differences across individuals in age, education, number and age of children, or even day of the week or season when the time diary data was collected. In this section we present regression results with the samples stratified by gender, permitting us to control for multiple characteristics of the individual and his or her household simultaneously. Note, however, that the regression models that form the basis for the results discussed here are *ad hoc* in nature; in other words, they are not based on underlying theoretical models that would permit us to say something about causality. Nonetheless, they provide a means for delving deeper into time use choices by family status and gender.

We estimate time use equations separately for home production, child caregiving, leisure, and "total work" (home production, child caregiving, and paid market work). Each time use model is estimated

Table 3.3g   Minutes of Child Caregiving Time by Family Status and Age of Youngest Child, with Children Sample, Aged 18–84, 2010

	Men				Women			
	Couples with Youngest Child Older Than 5	Couples with Youngest Children 0–5	Couples with Youngest Child Older Than 5	Couples with Youngest Children 0–5	Couples with Youngest Child Older Than 5	Couples with Youngest Children 0–5	Couples with Youngest Child Older Than 5	Couples with Youngest Children 0–5
Child caregiving	41	88	37	101	67	175	64	142
Developmental	15	40	18	59	20	65	19	44
Maintenance	26	48	19	42	46	110	45	98
Sample size	759	712	94	43	798	757	385	286

(Weighted averages, American Time Use Survey 2010)

Table 3.3h Percentage of Child Caregiving Time by Family Status and Age of Youngest Child, with Children Sample, Aged 18–84, 2010

	Men				Women			
	Couples with Youngest Child Older Than 5	Couples with Youngest Children 0–5	Couples with Youngest Child Older Than 5	Couples with Youngest Children 0–5	Couples with Youngest Child Older Than 5	Couples with Youngest Children 0–5	Couples with Youngest Child Older Than 5	Couples with Youngest Children 0–5
Child caregiving								
Developmental	35.9%	45.9%	49.4%	58.3%	30.6%	37.0%	29.5%	31.1%
Maintenance	64.1%	54.1%	50.6%	41.7%	69.4%	63.0%	70.5%	68.9%
Sample Size	759	712	94	43	798	757	385	286

(Weighted averages, American Time Use Survey 2010)

91

Table 3.3i Time Use per Day by Family Status and Age of Youngest Child, with Children Sample, Aged 18–84, 2010

	Men				Women			
	Couples with Youngest Child Older Than 5	Couples with Youngest Children 0–5	Single with Youngest Child Older Than 5	Single with Youngest Children 0–5	Couples with Youngest Child Older Than 5	Couples with Youngest Children 0–5	Single with Youngest Child Older Than 5	Single with Youngest Children 0–5
Minutes of Time Use per Day								
Home production	146	116	116	142	241	214	202	174
Leisure	361	340	370	323	333	299	316	320
Child caregiving	41	88	37	101	67	175	64	142
Work	359	354	349	298	234	174	244	177
Other	533	542	567	577	565	579	614	628
Percentage of Time per Day								
Home production	10.1%	8.1%	8.1%	9.8%	16.7%	14.8%	14.0%	12.1%
Leisure	25.1%	23.6%	25.7%	22.5%	23.1%	20.8%	21.9%	22.2%
Child caregiving	2.9%	6.1%	2.6%	7.0%	4.6%	12.1%	4.4%	9.8%
Work	24.9%	24.6%	24.2%	20.7%	16.2%	12.1%	17.0%	12.3%
Other	37.0%	37.7%	39.4%	40.0%	39.2%	40.2%	42.7%	43.6%
Sample size	759	712	94	43	798	757	385	286

Weighted averages, American Time Use Survey 2010.

Table 3.4   Coefficients and Standard Errors for Family Status Indicators

	Men			Women		
	Couples No Kids	Single with Kids	Single No Kids	Couples No Kids	Single with Kids	Single No Kids
HH production	14.902	–13.561	–0.042	–34.617***	–29.798***	–61.802***
	(11.48)	(15.83)	(10.55)	(13.22)	(11.02)	(12.24)
Child caregiving		7.516			–1.726	
		(11.97)			(6.44)	
Leisure	30.366*	–10.581	72.741***	28.492**	–4.013	57.595***
	(15.67)	(29.91)	(14.88)	(13.69)	(13.03)	(13.21)

Standard errors in parentheses. * significant at 10%; ** significant at 5%; *** significant at 1%. Coefficients and standard errors are from OLS regressions separately by time use and gender. Other variables included in the regression were indicators of the presence of two or more children; the presence of a child younger than age six; age indicators in five-year intervals; indicators for high school dropouts and college graduates; indicators for nonwhite and Hispanic; diary collected in the three ~~summer months, diaries collected~~ on Friday, on Saturday, and on Sunday.
(American Time Use Survey data)

separately by gender and includes variables controlling for family status, the presence of children in the household, age, education, and specifics of the diary day.[1] We then use the estimated coefficients to construct predicted levels of leisure and "total work" (which combines home production, child caregiving, and paid market work).

Table 3.4 presents the ordinary least squares (OLS) coefficients and standard errors for the family status indicators that are of primary interest to this analysis.[2]

Couples-with-children is the reference category, so that reported coefficients can be interpreted as the number of minutes more (or less) that men or women not in the reference category spent on the same activity. We find substantial differences in minutes spent in home production of women by family status, whereas men in all four family status categories perform approximately the same number of minutes of home production. Coupled women in households with dependent children perform more unpaid work than women in other family structures. The biggest difference in time use by family status is for single females with no children, who perform 62 fewer minutes of unpaid home production than coupled women with children, while single women with children report 30 fewer minutes of home production than coupled women with children.

In terms of the other coefficients (results not shown, but available on request from the authors), we note that having younger children (younger than age six) and having two or more children does not affect the home production minutes of either men or women. The other demographic characteristics also do not matter in terms of home production minutes for men and women.

Looking to statistically significant differences across gender (these results come from Wald tests of coefficients across equations), home production time is greater for women than for men in couples with children, couples without children, and singles without children. Only single men with children and single women with children perform about the same number of minutes of home production.

For the analysis of child caregiving, we limited the sample to those persons in households with children younger than age 18, and to individuals who are younger than age 65. This makes it more likely that we are observing child care by parents rather than grandparents. Row 2 in Table 3.4 shows the family status coefficients and standard errors. When it comes to caregiving, being a single parent rather than a coupled parent makes no significant difference for either men or women.

The rest of the regression (results not shown, but available on request) indicates that child caregiving time is affected most by the age of the children and somewhat less by the number of children. Fewer minutes are devoted to child caregiving by older parents (ages 45 and older), both males and females, most likely because their children are older. The most substantive difference by gender is the increase in child caregiving minutes reported by mothers and fathers with children younger than the age of six. Mothers report 70 more minutes of child caregiving daily when their youngest child is younger than six, while fathers increase their caregiving by 38 minutes. Having two or more children increases mothers' time spent on caregiving by 12 minutes and fathers' time by 10 minutes.

Row 3 of Table 3.4 records the coefficients and standard errors for the family status indicators from models of leisure time. We find that for both men and women, life without children increases the amount of leisure. Men in couples without children have 30 minutes more leisure per day than men in couples with children, while women in couples without children have 28 more minutes of leisure.

Single men and women have significantly more leisure time than those in couples—approximately 30 minutes for women and 40 minutes for men. Added together, these data make for 72 minutes of extra leisure per day for single men relative to couples with children and 58 minutes of extra leisure per day for single women compared to women in couples with children.

The extra time for caregiving by men seems to come from leisure time, as men with a child younger than age six have 24 fewer minutes of leisure. Having a young child does not significantly reduce coupled women's leisure time more than it already is reduced by having any dependent children (coefficients not shown).

PREDICTING TIME USE PATTERNS

We can use the full set of regression coefficients to produce predicted total minutes per day for individuals with specific sets of characteristics to examine differences by gender and family status more concretely. In each case, we construct the predicted minutes based on the following characteristics: a high school graduate or some college, weekday and not summer diary, and white and not Hispanic. For ease of exposition (and possibly amusement), we provide names for our hypothetical individuals. Monica and Chandler are married, aged 37, with two children, one younger than 6. Rachel and Ross are also 37, single parents with two children, one younger than 6. These couples are joined by Phoebe and Joey, single, no children, aged 27; Bertha and Jack, currently single, no dependent children, aged 77 (a widow and a widower); and Kay and Arnold, married, no dependent children, aged 57 (empty-nesters). All their predicted minutes are shown in Table 3.5.

Looking first at coupled individuals aged 37 with two children, one younger than the age of 6, Monica is predicted to have 164 home production minutes and Chandler is predicted to have 97 home production minutes. Single-parent Rachel is predicted to have 134 minutes of home production and Ross is predicted to have 83 minutes of home production. Phoebe and Joey, 10 years younger, single, and with no children, each do 98 minutes of home production, similar in level to Ross and Chandler, but much less than Monica and Rachel.

Clearly, age matters quite a bit in home production time, although we cannot tell whether this is purely generational or possibly a function of owning a home. Bertha and Jack are 77, single with no

Table 3.5   Predicted Minutes per Day

		Predicted Home Production Minutes	Predicted Child Caregiving Minutes	Predicted Leisure Minutes	Predicted "Total Work" Minutes
Coupled parents with 2 children, one younger than age 6, age 37	Monica	164	147	233	658
	Chandler	97	98	277	625
Single parents with 2 children, one younger than age 6, age 37	Rachel	134	145	229	652
Single, no dependent children, age 27	Ross	83	105	266	615
	Phoebe	98		345	457
Single, no dependent children, age 77	Joey	98		399	472
	Bertha	147		511	282
Coupled, no dependent children, age 57	Jack	140		597	218
	Kay	185		296	568
	Arnold	126		331	542

Predicted minutes using the OLS regression described in note to Table 3.4.

dependent children. Their predicted home production minutes are 147 and 140, respectively, which is two-thirds of an hour more each day than the home production minutes of Phoebe and Joey. Finally, for coupled Kay and Arnold, age 57, with no dependent children, Kay is predicted to spend 185 minutes on home production, while Arnold is predicted to spend 126 minutes on this activity. The sum of their minutes is higher than that for any of the other pairs, reinforcing for us the notion that home production is not a zero-sum game. While there is clearly substitution going on between married partners Kay and Arnold and Monica and Chandler, there is also a choice regarding total home production minutes.

Turning to predicted child caregiving minutes, Monica is predicted to engage in 147 total child caregiving minutes, while Chandler is predicted to do 98 minutes of child caregiving. Rachel (the single mother) is predicted to have nearly the same number of child caregiving minutes as Monica, and Ross (the single father) is predicted to have more child caregiving minutes than Chandler, but substantively fewer minutes than Monica or Rachel. The data for both Rachel and Ross indicate that the children suffer a reduction in total child caregiving minutes when there is only one parent in the household. In results not presented in these tables, we found that the gender differences in predicted child caregiving minutes arise from gender differences in physical child caregiving rather than differences in development child caregiving.

Column 3 of Table 3.5 reports the predicted leisure minutes of our 10 hypothetical individuals. Our interest in leisure differences across genders and family types is heightened by Burda, Hamermesh, and Weil's (2013) claim of "iso-work." Their hypothesis of iso-work states that as per capita income grows in non-Catholic countries, men's and women's "total work" hours (where "total work" includes employment, home production, and child caregiving) converge.

Here we consider "iso-leisure" as well, given that leisure is the main source of direct utility. We think iso-leisure is a better measure of equality than iso-work, but Table 3.5 includes both (total work is reported in column 4).

In Table 3.2, it is apparent that average leisure minutes are higher for men than women across each family status category, both for the full sample and for the working-age sample. Table 3.5 supports these findings even after we control for demographic differences. In every pair, the man has more leisure minutes than the woman. Arnold and Kay are the closest to each other in terms of leisure minutes per day, yet still Arnold enjoys 35 more minutes of leisure than does Kay.

The total work in column 4 uses the same definition of "total work" as developed by Burda, Hamermesh, and Weil (2013): home production time plus child caregiving time plus paid employment time. Using the same regression specification, we estimated time in employment and calculated predicted minutes for each of our 10 hypothetical people. We then summed the predicted values for these three time uses (twice in the case of those with no dependent children). The minutes of "total work" for the man and the woman in each pair are more similar than they were for leisure (because women sleep more and we all have only 24 hours in a day), but in four out of the five pairs, the woman is predicted to have higher "total work" time than the man. Over the last 50 years, men and women have been moving closer to each other in their time use patterns, as our literature review showed, but Table 3.5 hardly confirms that trend. It is premature to declare that we have achieved equality in either "total work" time or in leisure.

HOW DO WE FEEL WHILE ENGAGED IN UNPAID ACTIVITIES?

One reason to study gender differences in time use is the implication of these differences for overall well-being. According to an Organization for Economic and Cooperative development (OECD 2013) report, overall well-being includes economic well-being (as proxied by income), health status, and subjective well-being. Simply knowing differences in time use across individuals is not sufficient information to glean an understanding of overall well-being. As was described in the previous section, Bertha (single, no dependent children, age 77) and Monica (coupled, two dependent children, age 37) have very different combinations of time uses, yet we cannot determine which one's time choices generate the greatest utility. We might also want to compare Chandler to Monica. Chandler has more employment time than Monica, but perhaps he does not dislike that employment time as much as Monica dislikes hers. We have long understood that we get varying amounts of utility (or disutility) from different uses of our time, but as researchers we did not have the data necessary to consider these differences.[3]

This situation changed in 2010, when the ATUS survey instrument incorporated measures of "experienced emotions" (also known as "subjective well-being"), permitting us to consider overall well-being more directly.[4] "Experienced emotions" is Kahneman's term for the emotions one feels while engaged in an activity. Kahneman and Krueger (2006) make the case for using the one-day recall time diary apparatus to also collect information concerning time-specific experienced emotions.

Following their recommendation, a subsample of ATUS respondents in 2010 were asked to report how they were feeling during three randomly selected activities reported during their diary day. Their feelings were reported using a scale of 0 to 6 (with 6 indicating a strong emotion and 0 indicating no emotion) along six dimensions: happy, sad, meaningful, in pain, tired, and stressed. In this section, we present the subjective well-being (SWB) averages for the same 13 activities we highlighted earlier: shopping, housework, yard work repairs, other home production, cooking, TV watching, reading/using the computer, social, exercise, other leisure, developmental child caregiving, physical child caregiving, and paid work. SWB questions were not asked about sleeping or personal care activities. We discuss the correlations across SWB measures by gender, then consider gender comparisons in SWB, and finally fine-tune these comparisons with a focus on differences by marital status, work status, and the presence of children in the household.[5]

Table 3.6 provides a quick look at the correlations across SWB measures by gender and allays any concern that one or more of the measures may be redundant (i.e., not provide unique information about

Table 3.6   Correlation of SWB Scores for the Same Activities

	Meaningful	Happy	Sad	Tired	Pain	Stressed
Men						
Meaningful	1					
Happy	0.4253	1				
Sad	−0.1132	−0.2583	1			
Tired	−0.0898	−0.1867	0.2607	1		
Pain	−0.0167	−0.1332	0.3355	0.3337	1	
Stressed	−0.0765	−0.3047	0.4452	0.3172	0.2661	1
Women						
Meaningful	1					
Happy	0.4353	1				
Sad	−0.1061	−0.3455	1			
Tired	−0.1016	−0.2075	0.2467	1		
Pain	−0.0346	−0.2	0.3538	0.3477	1	
Stressed	−0.0864	−0.3666	0.4081	0.3795	0.3259	1

Weighted by activity weights.

well-being). For example, *a priori*, one might expect happy to be the opposite of sad (implying a high correlation coefficient across the two), but this is not the case. The two emotions actually appear to be quite independent of each other. For men, the correlation coefficient of happy to sad is −0.26; for women, the coefficient is −0.34. As expected, though, the four negative SWB measures are more correlated with one another than with the positive measures, and the same is true for the positive measures. For both men and women, the greatest correlations are seen with happy and meaningful (0.42 and 0.44, respectively) and sad and stressed (0.44 and 0.41).

Table 3.7 provides average happy, tired, and stressed scores by detailed activity category and then overall averages (across the 13 activities). Women report being significantly happier, but also report being more tired and more stressed. In individual activities, women's happiness scores are significantly higher than men's in shopping, housework, yard work/repairs, exercise, and other leisure. Men's happiness scores are higher than women's when engaged in developmental child caregiving. Women are more stressed than men when shopping (even though they are happier), doing yard work/repairs, during social activities, during developmental child caregiving, and during employment time.

Table 3.8 shows the rank ordering of activities for men and women in terms of happiness. Developmental child care receives the highest score on happiness from both men and women. Leisure activities rank higher than home production activities. Employment, housework, and home production receive the lowest happiness scores from both men and women, with employment being ranked the lowest for women and housework the lowest for men, implying that both our own and our spouse's total work is not satisfactory. In other words, we do not like what we are doing when it comes to "total work." Cooking is the one category of home production that makes us happier than some leisure activities. TV watching ranks fairly low on the happiness scale for both men and women. Not surprisingly, shopping appears higher in women's rankings than men's, but physical child caregiving is the second-highest-ranked activity for men and the sixth-highest-ranked activity for women.

There is a lot to be learned from these SWB measures, but for ease of exposition, we limit further analysis of the SWB to coupled men and women with at least one child younger than age six. As we suspect that how we feel about unpaid activities depends in part on how

Table 3.7 Average SWB Responses by Activity and Gender, 2010

	Average Happy			Average Tired			Average Stressed		
	Men	Women	Significant Difference by Sex	Men	Women	Significant Difference by Sex	Men	Women	Significant Difference by Sex
Shopping	4.114	4.346	*	1.786	2.110	**	1.367	1.614	*
Housework	3.342	4.016	***	2.068	2.557	**	1.380	1.458	
Yard work repairs	4.181	4.686	*	2.345	2.838		0.917	1.320	***
Other home production	3.872	4.093		2.027	2.430	***	1.234	1.657	
Cooking	4.359	4.524		1.733	2.415	***	1.081	1.160	
TV watching	4.264	4.202		2.285	2.507	**	1.149	1.012	
Reading/computer	4.329	4.339		1.689	2.120	**	1.016	0.856	
Social	4.635	4.818		1.732	2.363	***	0.962	1.216	*
Exercise	4.530	4.941	**	2.056	2.224		0.923	0.914	
Other leisure	4.592	4.770	**	1.867	2.124	***	1.083	1.065	
Developmental CC	5.470	5.179	**	1.999	2.392		0.769	1.212	**
Physical CC	4.826	4.634		2.015	2.531	***	1.237	1.339	
Employment	3.928	3.908		2.243	2.635	***	2.240	2.739	***
Total	4.206	4.318	**	2.081	2.429	***	1.493	1.640	***

Full sample, aged 18–84, weighted by activity weights.

Table 3.8   Rank Ordering of Average Activity Happiness Scores of Men and Women in the Full Sample

Women's Happiness Rank	Men's Happiness Rank	
1	1	Developmental CC
2	5	Exercise
3	3	Social
4	4	Other leisure
5	9	Yard work repairs
6	2	Physical CC
7	6	Cooking
8	10	Shopping
9	7	Reading/computer
10	8	TV watching
11	12	Other Home Production
12	13	Housework
13	11	Employment

much time individuals are spending in paid activities within the couple, we further limit this analysis to full-time employed men and to women who have a full-time employed husband. We also focus on the coefficients that are statistically significant. Specifically, we compare those individuals in couples with children where the wife is not employed to those individuals in a couple with children where the wife is employed on a full-time basis.

Table 3.9 shows that "not employed" coupled mothers of preschoolers report higher happiness scores overall (4.7 versus 4.3) than full-time employed coupled mothers of preschoolers. Members of the former group also report higher happiness scores for cooking, TV watching, reading/using the computer, and physical child caregiving.

There are fewer statistically significant differences for the tired and stressed attributes. Coupled, "not employed" mothers of preschoolers report a lower tired score for cooking (2.5 versus 3.5), but a higher average tired score for shopping (2.6 versus 1.9). When it comes to stress, "not employed" mothers report a higher SWB stress measure for developmental child caregiving (1.1 versus 0.4) but lower stress for physical caregiving (0.8 versus 1.8).

Coupled men with a preschooler are less happy in all reported activities (4.3 versus 4.6) and are more tired (2.5 versus 2.1) and more stressed (1.7 versus 1.3) when their wives are employed full-time. Few of our selected 13 activities are statistically significantly different,

Table 3.9a Average Happy, Tired, and Stressed Scores, by Time Use Activity, Gender, and Wife's Employment Status, Women in Couples with Full-Time Employed Husbands and at Least One Child Younger Than Age Six

	Average Happy		Average Tired		Average Stressed		Number of Observations	
	Mothers, Not Employed	Mothers, Full-Time Employed	Mothers, Not Employed	Mothers, Full-Time Employed	Mothers, Not Employed	Mothers, Full-Time Employed	Mothers, Not Employed	Mothers, Full-Time Employed
Shopping	4.531	4.693	2.602	1.863*	1.844	1.557	76	66
Housework	3.569	3.218	3.460	3.220	1.941	2.040	51	26
Yard work/repairs	Too small		Too small		Too small		6	3
Other home production	3.556	3.597	2.619	3.103	1.493	2.118	48	29
Cooking	4.465	3.744*	2.564	3.449**	1.377	1.956	73	48
TV watching	5.158	3.763*	2.932	3.425	1.028	0.836	30	35
Reading/computer	5.362	4.537*	3.339	3.992	0.337	0.658	13	17
Social	5.081	5.278	2.527	1.818	0.773	1.003	42	31
Exercise	4.845	5.686	2.315	3.199	0.783	0.211	14	10
Other leisure	5.193	4.807*	1.957	2.293	1.010	1.192	114	118
Developmental child care	5.171	5.292	2.386	2.267	1.114	0.380**	47	31
Maintenance child care	5.048	4.565**	2.673	3.257	0.804	1.793***	158	123
Employment	na	4.320	na	2.721	Na	2.230	Na	43
Total	4.702	4.380**	2.556	2.796	1.313	1.580*		

Note: Full sample, aged 18–84, weighted by activity weights, weighted t-tests. *Significant at 10%; **significant at 5%; ***significant at 1%. (American Time Use Survey)

Table 3.9b Average Happy, Tired, and Stressed Scores, by Time Use Activity, Gender, and Wife's Employment Status, Full-Time Employed Men with at Least One Child Younger Than Age Six

	Average Happy		Average Tired		Average Stressed		Number of Observations	
	Mothers, Not Employed	Mothers, Full-Time Employed	Mothers, Not Employed	Mothers, Full-Time Employed	Mothers, Not Employed	Mothers, Full-Time Employed	Mothers, Not Employed	Mothers, Full-Time Employed
Shopping	3.130	4.742***	2.488	2.436	2.499	1.267**	46	67
Housework	Too small		Too small		Too small		6	6
Yard work/repairs	Too small		Too small		Too small		7	18
Other home production	4.405	3.710	2.495	2.229	1.223	0.938	25	19
Cooking	4.513	4.350	2.360	1.698	1.235	0.854	15	26
TV watching	4.627	5.024	1.797	2.930*	0.347	1.014**	43	48
Reading/computer	4.788	4.732	4.030	2.514	1.598	0.950	12	10
Social	4.912	5.406	1.397	1.245	0.510	0.376	36	31
Exercise	5.441	5.387	1.817	1.410	0.386	0.988	21	20
Other leisure	4.716	5.039	1.788	2.269	1.231	0.557	136	124
Developmental child care	5.814	5.318	1.664	2.757*	0.255	1.193	40	27
Maintenance child care	4.844	4.581	1.769	2.421	0.942	2.476*	57	109
Employment	4.357	3.747**	2.343	2.642	1.855	2.230	65	77
Total	4.616	4.298**	2.127	2.469*	1.297	1.713**		

Note: Full sample, aged 18–84, weighted by activity weights, weighted t-tests. *Significant at 10%; **significant at 5%; ***significant at 1%. (American Time Use Survey)

however, partly because the sample sizes are small. Interestingly, those men with wives employed on a full-time basis report higher happiness scores for shopping (4.7 versus 3.1), but lower happiness scores during their own paid work (3.7 versus 4.4). Additionally, fathers whose wives work full-time report greater tiredness and stress while watching TV, and more tiredness during developmental child caregiving (2.8 versus 1.7).

Overall, we conclude that couples with a young child and a full-time employed wife are under considerable time pressure, as seen from their much lower minutes of leisure in the previous section and the SWB score differentials for both men and women in the couple (less happy, more tired, and more stressed). It is no wonder, then, that there is pressure from husbands and wives for the wife to "opt out." Analysis (not shown here) of those mothers and fathers with only school-aged children indicate that these differences in direct utility measures disappear as the child becomes older.

DISCUSSION AND CONCLUSION

In this chapter, we presented a broad overview of family time use with a focus on unpaid activities. We reviewed the evidence regarding the evolution of family time use patterns across the previous several decades and presented regression evidence that permits us to speak to the question of whether men's and women's time usage grows more similar—a concept leading to the iso-work and iso-leisure hypotheses. Finally, we described newly available evidence concerning how we feel while engaged in our chosen activities.

Our empirical analysis looks at differences across family status, with family status categorized four ways: coupled with dependent children, coupled without dependent children, single with dependent children, and single without dependent children. We looked broadly at the adult population aged 18 to 84 so as to include the time use experience of older Americans. However, we also presented descriptive analysis just for the working-age population aged 25 to 64 to facilitate comparison of our findings with the growing body of U.S. time use research. We found that family status is associated with substantively different allocations for men and women. In particular, single women with no dependent children perform the least amount of home production and have the most leisure. Single men also enjoy substantially more leisure than their coupled counterparts. These results persist even when we limit the sample to the working-age population.

Our analysis reveals that substantive gender differences in time use remained in place in 2010, leading us to conclude that recent reports of gender time use convergence are, at a minimum, premature.[6] There is no question that men's and women's time use has become more similar over the last 50 years. If these trends in time usage were to continue, eventually men's and women's time use would become identical. However, there is no reason to expect these time trends to be linear; in fact, the historical evidence shows that there has been almost no change in the 1990s and 2000s.

Burda, Hamermesh, and Weil (2013) report that we have reached convergence in "total work," but our examination of 2010 U.S. data does not indicate the existence of gender iso-work or iso-leisure within a given family status. In all five male/female composite pairs examined here, men had at least 30 additional minutes of leisure per day. Only the time use patterns of 27-year-old singletons with no children are suggestive of gender iso-work. In each of the four other family status pairs, women's "total work" time exceeded men's. We also found gender differences in happiness, tired, and stressed emotions experienced during daily activities. Compared to men, women report somewhat greater happiness, but also considerably more tiredness (in nearly every activity); moreover, in many activities, women report greater stress than men. We found that women report strong negative emotions 25 percent of the time compared to 22 percent for men. Even in child caregiving—an activity that both men and women agree makes them very happy—women report a stronger negative emotion than positive emotion 19 percent of the time, compared with 10 percent for men. These differences provide evidence that there are real differences in overall well-being by gender.

We disagree with the contention that time use convergence has already happened (or is inevitable). Our data are more consistent with the view of Coontz (2013), who argues that the gender revolution has stalled. Why it has stalled leads us to the same familiar debate as to why the gender wage gap remains. One side argues that women's preferences for caregiving drive these results. They may also arise as a rational response within the couple because "someone has to watch the children." The other side points to structural barriers in the labor market, the United States' family-based income tax system, and the lack of public provision of employment-facilitating child care both for preschoolers and after-school care as factors leading to failure to achieve time use convergence.

In the debate over gendered time use, motherhood wage gaps have become more economically important (Waldfogel 1998). Our findings show no statistical difference between child caregiving for mothers who are part of a couple versus single mothers. Similarly, men's and women's leisure time differs more according to the presence of dependent children in the home than by "marital" status.[7]

The time use data presented in this chapter allow us to see the effect of dependent children on men's and women's time use. For men, both employment time and child caregiving time increase (the latter from zero), and these two increases in time use are achieved at the cost of reduced leisure. For women, employment hours are unchanged except by the presence of children younger than age six.[8] Women in couples increase their home production hours in the presence of children, while single mothers do not. Both groups of women, of course, spend substantial time on child caregiving, and the cumulative effect is a reduction in their leisure. The effect of dependent children is particularly strong for couples with children younger than the age of six when both parents are employed full-time. We also saw that average happiness levels are lower in this scenario, while average stress and tiredness levels are higher.

Even though the total number of years spent with very young children may be limited, women are making decisions before, during, and after that time that have long-term consequences for gender equity in both wages and time use. These decisions, in fact, may be the main reason gender convergence has stalled. Bianchi et al. (2012) argue that the child caregiving time differential is now the more important source of gender inequality. This claim is consistent with the evidence that home production hours have been declining for women (while increasing somewhat for men), but child caregiving hours have been increasing for both men and women. Occupational segregation in the paid workforce remains, in part, because women anticipate a number of years of reduced work hours or less travel and perhaps less pressure.

Sheryl Sandberg, the outspoken chief operating officer of Facebook, has argued that professional women have a tendency to "lean out" of the labor market long before they ever have children. She used her 2010 Ted speech and subsequent Barnard College commencement speech, given in May 2011, to urge young women to "lean in" and to "sit at the table."[9] Sandberg acknowledges that the extreme time demands of young children continue to cause many women to withdraw from the labor market when their children are young and that some may find it difficult to return. Sandberg's solution is to make one's partner "a true partner" in child caregiving and home production and for the woman to have achieved a job worthy of her return following childbirth. Neither of these "prerequisites" may be as easy to meet as Sandberg seems to imply.

Hewlett (2007) and others have written about the need to create more "on ramps" to facilitate the return to paid work. Anne-Marie Slaughter, the former Director of Policy Planning at the U.S. State Department, who authored an article titled "Why Women Still Can't Have It All" that appeared in *The Atlantic* in 2012, is less optimistic that full equality in the workplace is possible for women. According to Slaughter, "having a supportive mate may well be a necessary condition if women are to have it all, but it is not sufficient." She finds the extreme time demands of high-level positions and the lack of control over the location and timing of one's work time to be substantial barriers keeping women from "having it all." Similarly, Selmi (2007) argues that women will never become full partners in the workplace until men become full partners in the home.

For women, the labor market effects of motherhood may persist long after the children are grown. An extensive literature on the motherhood wage gap (i.e., the gap in wages between mothers and female non-mothers) estimates this gap to be approximately 5 percent for one child and even greater for mothers with two or more children.[10] Hersch (2009) analyzed ATUS data (linked to CPS files) and showed that more housework hours are associated with lower wages. Schober (2012), using longitudinal data from the United Kingdom and Germany, reports that when women withdraw from the labor market upon the birth of a baby, they increase both their housework and their child caregiving time. Upon their return to the labor market, these newly acquired time use habits prove difficult to alter. Controlling for current hours of employment, women who experience motherhood-related career interruptions continue to do more of the housework and child caregiving than women who did not withdraw temporarily from the labor market. Grunow, Schulz, and Blossfeld (2012) show that even when couples initially share housework fairly equally, their workloads gradually grow more unequal, especially after the birth of a child.

With labor force participation rates for married women with young children being high (though not as high as they were 10 years ago), divorce rates higher than they were in the 1970s, fertility rates low, and employment rates increasing for older persons, the total number of years that the average woman will spend in the labor market is substantial. We need to think carefully about how smart labor market policies and business practices might ease that short-term crunch time in women's and men's lives around the birth and youth of their children. With improvements in such policies and practices, we may one day achieve true gender iso-leisure, accompanied by a reduction in the family wage gap.

NOTES

1. The complete listing of right-hand-side dummy variables is as follows: children younger than age six, two or more children, diary day controls (Monday through Thursday is the single excluded category); Friday, Saturday, Sunday, nonwhite, Hispanic, summer diary day, multiple age categories (with age 35–59 as an excluded category), education categories (less than a high school education, high school graduate or some college as the excluded category, college graduate or more), and four household status variables (coupled with children is the excluded category; coupled without children, single with children, and single without children).

2. Full regression results are available from the authors.

3. F. Thomas Juster, "Preferences for Work and Leisure," in *Time, Goods, and Well-Being*, edited by Juster F. Thomas and Frank P. Stafford (Ann Arbor, MI: University of Michigan Press), 335–351. Juster considered these issues in his time diary data collection project of 1985, but his measure of well-being is a general activity judgment rather than the emotions attached to a specific time use (how happy you are while at your job versus how happy you were yesterday during the four hours you were at the office). Likewise, many surveys (including the General Social Survey) ask life satisfaction questions, but these global measures are also quite different from the experienced-emotions questions of the ATUS.

4. According to the Bureau of Labor Statistics (as reported March 26, 2013, at http://www.bls.gov/tus/wbnotice.htm), there was an error in the subjective well-being sampling scheme that

excluded the final reported activity on individuals' diary days from selection into the subjective well-being sample. Thus, some activities may be under-sampled in the subjective well-being data.

5. Connelly and Kimmel's (2013) paper *If You're Happy* extends this descriptive analysis with two different methodologies designed to incorporate five measures of SWB, leaving "meaningful" aside. Following Alan Krueger, "Are We Having More Fun Yet? Categorizing and Evaluating Changes in Time Allocation," *Brookings Papers on Economic Activity* 2 (2007): 193–215, we use both cluster analysis (which categorizes activities that are similar in these five dimensions) and the U-index (which measures the percentage of time spent in unpleasant activities, where "unpleasant" is defined as a stronger negative emotion than the score for "happy").

6. A recent Pew Research Center report is careful to point out that convergence has not yet been achieved. However, by using the phrase "are converging" in the first paragraph, the authors convey (intended or not) a sense that this convergence is just a matter of time; Kim Parker and Wendy Wang, "Modern Parenthood," Pew Research Center, Pew Social Demographic Trends (March 14, 2013), http://www.pewsocialtrends.org/2013/03/14/modern-parenthood-roles-of-moms-and-dads-converge-as-they-balance-work-and-family/. See also Michael Burda, Daniel Hamermesh, and Philippe Weil, *Total Work, Gender and Social Norms,* National Bureau of Economic Research Working Paper No. 13000 (NBER, Cambridge, MA2007), 239–261; Fisher et al. 2007, 1–33. http://www.nber.org/papers/w13000.

7. Leisure time of single parents with children is not statistically different from that of coupled parents. Single men and women with no dependent children do have statistically more leisure time than coupled men and women with no dependent children.

8. Regression results for employment are not shown. They are available from the authors.

9. Sheryl Sandberg, "Why We Have Too Few Women Leaders?" Ted talk, December 10, 2010, http://www.ted.com/talks/sheryl_sandberg_why_we_have_too_few_women_leaders.html.

10. See, for example, Catalina Amuedo-Dorantes and Jean Kimmel, "The Motherhood Wage Gap for Women in the United States: The Importance of College and Fertility Delay," *Review of Economics of the Household* 3, no. 1 (2005): 17–48; Deborah J. Anderson, Melissa Blinder, and Kate Krause, "The Motherhood Wage Penalty Revisited: Experience, Heterogeneity, Work Effort, and Work-Schedule Flexibility,"

Industrial and Labor Relations Review 56, no. 2 (2003): 273–94; and Jane Waldfogel, "The Effect of Children on Women's Wages," *American Sociological Review* 62, no. 2 (1997): 209–217.

REFERENCES

Aguiar, Mark, and Erik Hurst. "Measuring Trends in Leisure: The Allocation of Time over Five Decades." *Quarterly Journal of Economics* 122, no. 3 (2007): 969–1006.

Aguiar, Mark, Erik Hurst, and Loukas Karabarbounis. "Recent Developments in the Economics of Time Use." *Annual Review of Economics* 4 (2012): 373–397.

Becker, Gary. "A Theory of the Allocation of Time." *Economic Journal* 75, no. 299 (1965): 493–515.

Becker, Gary. *A Treatise on the Family.* Cambridge, MA: Harvard University Press, 1981.

Bianchi, Suzanne, John Robinson, and Melissa Milkie. *Changing Rhythms of American Family Life.* New York: Russell Sage Foundation, 2006.

Bianchi, Suzanne, Vanessa Wight, and Sara Raley. "Maternal Employment and Family Caregiving: Rethinking Time with Children in the ATUS." Paper presented at the ATUS Early Results Conference, Bethesda, MD, December 2005.

Bianchi, Suzanne, Melissa A. Milkie, Liana Sayer, and John P. Robinson. "Is Anyone Doing the Housework: Trends in the Gender Division of Household Labor." *Social Forces* 79, no. 1 (2000): 191–228.

Bianchi, Suzanne, Liana Sayer, Melissa A. Milkie, and John P. Robinson. "Housework: Who Did, Does, or Will Do It, and How Much Does It Matter?" *Social Forces* 91, no. 1 (2012): 55–63.

Bittman, Michael, and Judy Wajcman. "The Rush Hour: The Character of Leisure Time and Gender Equity." *Social Forces* 79, no. 1 (2000): 165–195.

Burda, Michael, Daniel Hamermesh, and Philippe Weil. "Total Work and Gender: Facts and Possible Explanations." *Journal of Population Economics* 26, no. 1 (2013): 239–261.

Connelly, Rachel, and Jean Kimmel. "Spousal Influences on Parents' Non-market Time Choices." *Review of the Economics of the Household* 7, no. 4 (2009): 378.

Connelly, Rachel, and Jean Kimmel. *The Role of Caregiving in Mothers' Time Use: Recent Evidence from the New American Time Use Survey.* Kalamazoo, MI: W.E. Upjohn Institute, 2010.

Connelly, Rachel, and Jean Kimmel. *If You're Happy and You Know It, Clap Your Hands: How Do We Really Feel about Caregiving?* IZA Working Paper no. 7531. Bonn, Germany: Institute for the Study of Labor, 2013.

Coontz, Stephanie. "Why Gender Equality Stalled?" *New York Times* (February 16, 2013). http://www.nytimes.com/2013/02/17/opinion/sunday/why-gender-equality-stalled.html?pagewanted=all&_r=0.

Fisher, Kimberly, Muriel Egerton, Jonathan I. Gershuny, and John P. Robinson. "Gender Convergence in the American Heritage Time Use Study (AHTUS)." *Social Indicators Research* 82 (2007): 1–33.

Grunow, Daniela, Florian Schulz, and Hans-Peter Blossfeld. "What Determines Change in the Division of Housework over the Course of Marriage?" *International Sociology* 27, no. 3 (2012): 289–307.

Guryan, Jonathan, Erik Hurst, and Melissa Kearney. "Parental Education and Parental Time with Children." *Journal of Economic Perspectives* 22, no. 3 (2008): 36.

Hamermesh, Daniel. "Timing, Togetherness, and Time Windfalls." *Journal of Population Economics* 15, no. 4 (2002): 601–623.

Hamermesh, Daniel. "Time to Eat: Household Production under Increasing Income Inequality." *American Journal of Agricultural Economics* 89, no. 4 (2007): 852–863.

Hersch, Joni. "Home Production and Wages: Evidence from the American Time Use Survey." *Review of Economics of the Household* 7, no. 2 (2009): 159–178.

Hewlett, Sylvia Ann. *Off Ramps and On-Ramps: Keeping Talented Women on the Road to Success.* Boston, MA: Harvard Business School Press, 2007.

Kahneman, Daniel, and Alan Krueger. "Developments in the Measurement of Subjective Well-Being." *Journal of Economic Perspectives* 20, no. 1 (2006): 3–24.

Kimmel, Jean, and Rachel Connelly. "Determinants of Mother's Time Choices in the United States: Caregiving, Leisure, Home Production, and Paid Work." *Journal of Human Resources* 42, no. 3 (2007): 654, 668.

Organization for Economic and Cooperative Development (OECD). *OECD Guidelines on Measuring Subjective Well-Being.* Paris: OECD, 2013.

Oster, Emily. "Why You Shouldn't Work Less, Even If You Prefer Spending Time with Your Family." *Slate* (January 8, 2013). http://www.slate.com/articles/double_x/doublex/2013/01/work_life_crunch_why_you_shouldn_t_spend_fewer_hours_at_work.html.

Ramey, Valerie, and Neville Francis. "A Century of Work and Leisure." *American Economic Journal: Macroeconomics* 1, no. 2 (2009): 189–224.

Reid, Margaret. *Economics of Household Production.* New York, NY: John Wiley, 1934.

Robinson, John P. "IT, TV and Time Displacement: What Alexander Szalai Anticipated but Couldn't Know." *Social Indicators Research* 101 (2011): 198–199.

Schober, Pia. "Time to Care (Longer): Maternal Labor Market Interruptions and the Gender Division of Domestic Work." Working paper presented at the Population Association of America Meeting, San Francisco, CA, May 2012.

Selmi, Michael. "The Work-Family Conflict: An Essay on Employers, Men and Responsibility." *University of Saint Thomas Law Journal* 4 (2007): 573–595.

Slaughter, Anne-Marie. "Why Women Still Can't Have It All." *The Atlantic* (June 13, 2012). http://www.theatlantic.com/magazine/archive/2012/07/why-women-still-cant-have-it-all/309020/.

Vernon, Victoria. "Marriage: For Love, for Money . . . and for Time?" *Review of Economics of the Household* 8, no. 4 (2010): 433–457.

Waldfogel, Jane. "Understanding the 'Family Gap' in Pay for Women with Children." *Journal of Economic Perspectives* 12, no. 1 (1998): 137–156.

Chapter 4

Families and the Economics of Flexible Workplaces

Karine Moe

The American workforce in 2012 looked strikingly different from that in 1970. Women now make up nearly half of the labor force and, in almost half of American households, all adults work. Almost two-thirds (62 percent) of families with children younger than age 18 have either a single employed parent or two employed parents (United States Bureau of Labor Statistics, Table 4, 2010; United States Bureau of Labor Statistics, Women in the Labor Force, 2010). The dual-earner couple has overtaken the breadwinner-homemaker model. Yet all the domestic work of the "second shift" still needs doing. Dinner needs to be cooked; laundry has to be done; and grandma needs a ride to the doctor.

These changes in how Americans spend their time have led to inevitable conflicts between work and home. According to the 2008 National Study of the Changing Workforce (NSCW), more than 40 percent of employees indicate their work and family lives interfere with each other. Parents feel particularly time crunched, with roughly three-fourths of parents reporting not having enough time with their children (Tang and Wadsworth 2010). These reports are not restricted to mothers. For example, the percentage of fathers in dual-earner couples with children younger than age 18 who reported work-family conflicts rose from 35 percent in 1977 to 60 percent in 2008 (Aumann, Galinsky, and Matos 2011). These feelings of conflict range across non-parents as well. In the NSCW data, roughly 60 percent of employees who are either married or living with a partner indicate not having enough time with their spouses or partners, while roughly the same fraction of all employees report not having enough time for themselves (Tang and Wadsworth 2010).

In response to these time pressures, many workers express a desire for more flexible workplaces. The discussion about increased workplace flexibility has gained national recognition. In 2010, the White House sponsored a Forum on Workplace Flexibility, which gathered participants from business, government agencies, advocates, researchers, union leaders, and employees. This push from the White House led to a series of other of conferences, including a National Dialogue on Workplace Flexibility, which was sponsored by the U.S. Department of Labor's Women's Bureau, and the Sloan Foundation and Georgetown Law Center's Workplace Flexibility 2010 program.

Moe and Shandy (2010), in an analysis of college-educated women in the United States, found that flexibility ranked high among the characteristics that women valued in their jobs. In a 2008 Aspen Institute survey, MBA students (both male and female) at 15 business schools ranked "work-life balance" as the third most important factor when choosing a job, after "challenging responsibilities" and "compensation" (Aspen Institute Center for Business Education 2008). Almost all (87 percent) of the wage-earning and salaried employees surveyed in the 2008 NSCW report that having the flexibility to balance their work and personal lives would rank as either "extremely" or "very" important if they were to look for a new job.

Access to flexible work policies ranges widely across firms, and within firms, the policies can range across occupations. Even when these policies exist "on the books," the culture within firms can heavily penalize workers who choose to take advantage of flexible work options. Indeed, some researchers attribute significant portions of the gender wage gap to women's use of flexible work opportunities (Goldin and Katz 2011). This chapter contributes to our understanding of how families affect markets through their increasing demand for flexible workplace policies.

The chapter begins by documenting the trends that have led to this increased demand for flexible workplaces. Families operate under conditions vastly different from those faced by prior generations. In addition, as the likelihood that an adult in the family can dedicate his or her time fully to managing the household declines, we see an increasing pressure on employers to provide more flexibility in how the work gets done.

We can define flexibility in many different ways, and the following section describes the basic categories of flexible workplace policies and explains how flexibility coincides and differs from family-friendly policies. Next, the chapter details the state of provision of flexible work policies in the United States, including who has access to and who actually takes advantage of these offerings. The chapter then provides an economic model of flexible work policy provision, which treats flexible policies as an amenity. Using this model as a framework, we explore how firms explicitly and implicitly penalize workers who choose the amenity, and then describe the limited existing evidence on the economic costs and benefits to firms of providing flexible workplaces. The chapter closes with a discussion of why, given the possibility of net benefits, firms should increase their provision of flexible work policies, and how such provision, by improving conditions for families, can also improve firm productivity and profitability.

CHANGING DEMOGRAPHICS, CHANGING FAMILY STRUCTURE

Workers, and by extension, families, today sit at the crossroads of some important demographic shifts. Over the past 40 years, women's education levels have jumped dramatically. In 1970, only 11.2 percent of women in the labor force (as compared to 15.7 percent of men) had a college degree or higher. By 2009, the women had surpassed men, in that 36 percent of the female labor force held a college degree or higher, as compared to only 33 percent of men. The number of women with graduate degrees has also grown dramatically. Nearly half of all new entrants to law and medical schools are now female, and women account for almost 80 percent of entering veterinary classes. While the number of women enrolled in business schools lags behind the number enrolled in other professional programs, even in MBA programs women now account for nearly one-third of enrollments (Moe and Shandy 2010).

These increased education levels have opened the doors to women in the labor force. All women, and, in particular, women with children have notably increased their labor force participation in recent decades. In 1975, 47.4 percent of mothers with children younger than age

18 participated in the labor force. By 2009, that share had risen to 71.6 percent. If we restrict ourselves to mothers with children only between the ages 6 and 17, the participation rate rises to 78.2 percent (Bureau of Labor Statistics 2010).

These changes have led to greater engagement in market employment for families. In 1967, roughly two-thirds of children lived in families where one parent worked full-time, while the other parent was at home full-time. By 2009, about two-thirds of children lived in households where all parents worked. Children increasingly live in single-parent households, and the number of children in working-parent households includes both children living in two-parent households, with two working parents, and children in single-parent households, where that single parent works (Fox et al. 2011).

The structure of families changed dramatically during this same time period. The U.S. divorce rate skyrocketed in the 1960s and 1970s, going from a rate of 2.2 divorces per 1,000 population in 1962 to 4.4 divorces per 1,000 population in 1973, and 5.3 divorces per 1,000 population in 1979 (National Center for Health Statistics 1983). While it has dropped since that time, the divorce rate in the United States remains at a high level. It dropped slightly through the mid-1980s, leveling off at about 4.7 divorces per 1,000 population in the 1990s. The first decade of the 21st century has seen continuing declines in this rate, which was estimated at 3.6 divorces per 1,000 population in 2010 (National Vital Statistics System 2012).

In addition, nonmarital births have risen dramatically. While the divorce rates stabilized in the early 1980s, nonmarital births continued to rise well into the 1990s (Ellwood and Jencks 2006). With dramatic increases in both divorce rates and nonmarital births, the two-parent family no longer accounts for the majority of family households (Lofquist, Lugalia, O'Connell, and Feliz 2012).

Because single parents typically cannot rely on a second income earner, an increase in the number of single-female-headed households has led to an increase in women's labor force participation. Indeed, single mothers fueled much of the increase in overall women's labor force participation during the 1990s (DiCecio, Engemann, Owyang, and Wheeler 2008).

This movement of women into the workforce has, in turn, translated into increases in overall family work hours. In 1969, married couples of prime working age (ages 25–54) worked 56 hours per week, on average. By 2000, that number had jumped to 67 hours per week, with the increase mostly driven by women's entry into the labor market (Moe and Shandy 2010).

Increasing life expectancies have led to another demographic shift in the past 50 years. According to the Centers for Disease Control and Prevention, people who were born in 1940 can expect to live about a dozen years longer than those who were born in 1910 (Arias 2011). These longer life spans imply that families will encounter the requirements of elder care for longer periods of time. As women delay childbearing to older ages, they are more likely to find themselves part of the "sandwich generation"—that is, those adults who must balance work along with caring for both children and elderly parents. The average age at first birth in 2007 was 25 years, up from 21 years in 1970. Also, in 1970 only 4 percent of first births were to women in their thirties, while in 2007 that share had increased to 22 percent (U.S. Department of Commerce 2011).

These demographic shifts of increased education, single parenthood, and work engagement for women, along with increased life expectancies, have created a perfect storm, of sorts, where families increasingly feel pressed for time (Moe and Shandy 2010). The problem facing families is that as the number of joint hours of work has risen, the tasks at home have not gone away. The second shift, referring to the work families must do to maintain their households outside of paid employment, persists (Hochschild and Machung 1989).

Interestingly, the time that families spend on household tasks has not changed dramatically since the early 1900s. Technology has certainly increased the speed with which families can do laundry, cook meals, or wash dishes. Families, however, seem to compensate for the increased speed by increasing standards. For example, although washers and dryers certainly diminish the time spent per load of laundry, people today have higher standards for clean clothing. Consequently, laundry is done more often. Vacuum cleaners increase the efficiency of cleaning carpets, but time spent vacuuming has grown along with the size of houses (Stratton 2003).

A critical element of the two-parent, single-breadwinner model of family structure was the at-home parent (usually the mother), who managed the home front by taking care of household duties and the children. With the new dual-earner and single-parent models, there is no longer a parent to fill this full-time role. Given that the work still needs to be done, families face several options. They can outsource some of the work—by hiring housecleaning help, for example.

Outsourcing is expensive, however, and many families cannot afford the luxury of a housekeeper. In addition, even outsourcing requires management, and that takes time. Families can also squeeze some tasks into their evening and weekend hours, thus impinging on leisure time they could have spent as a family. Moreover, they can lower their standards, such as by buying prepared foods that are not as healthy but help get dinner on the table. Nevertheless, some tasks cannot be outsourced and some must be accomplished during the weekday, such as waiting to let the plumber in to fix the leaking toilet.

These mundane, but critical tasks pale in comparison to the importance families place on caring for their children, however. With parents working outside the home, someone must take care of the children. Child care put an enormous stress on working parents. Good-quality and affordable child care can be challenging, if not impossible, to secure. Many families find they must use more than one childcare provider. The inflexible hours of most daycare centers can also put stress on parents whose employers may expect their employees to be able to work late on little notice. In addition, most daycare providers will not allow sick children to attend their programs, so parents feel stress when they have to miss work to care for a sick child.

Pavalko and Henderson (2006) argue that care of elderly relatives may put even more stress on families. Unlike child care, which is relatively predictable in that it is needed most heavily in infancy, but diminishes as the child gets older, care of ill or elderly relatives is more unpredictable, with care needs that may be sporadic or long term. If both mom and dad are working, who is going to take care of grandpa, especially as issues pop up sporadically? With the aging of the U.S. population as the 21st century moves on, we can expect that these pressures faced by the sandwich generation will only increase.

Without an adult at home to maintain and sustain the household, last-minute problems—such as a child waking up with a fever, grandma breaking her hip, or the water heater voiding all over the basement—loom large in the lives of working families. Some workers are lucky and can get the flexibility they need to manage. Unfortunately, many others are not so lucky, and such problems can lead to pay reduction or job loss. These frustrations have led many workers to desire more flexible work arrangements. In this way, families can affect markets by demanding flexibility at work. The following section describes the myriad forms that flexibility can take in the marketplace.

DEFINING FLEXIBILITY

While the technicalities of flexible work options vary considerably, in general flexibility is a way to define the circumstances under which work gets done. Flexibility could mean flexible start and end times, the ability to take time off during the day if needed, compressed work weeks, reduced hours, part-year employment, telecommuting, paid leave to care for a sick child or elderly parent, or parenting leave. Flexibility does not necessarily equate to part-time work. Flexible employers may require the equivalent of full-time hours, but allow that work to be done off-site or during nonstandard work hours. Note that "family-friendly" and "flexible" are not necessarily synonymous. For example, many would classify teaching at the K–12 level as a flexible occupation, yet it can be quite challenging for teachers to get time off during the workday. Most teachers have little flexibility during the workday, yet the occupation as a whole is considered family-friendly, in that the teachers are typically off from work when children are off from school.

Flextime, often defined as the ability to control the start and end times of the workday, can be set, wherein the employee is allowed to choose the start and quit times, but once the choice is made, the employee must stick with that choice. Some workplaces allow employees to alter their start and quit times on a daily basis, as needs arise. Flextime can also include compressed work weeks, where an employee will work, for example, 10 hours per day for 4 days, instead of the typical 8 hours per day on Monday through Friday. These types of arrangements are sometimes made seasonally, where an employer will set "summer hours" that allow workers to add hours on Monday through Thursday, and then work only until noon on Fridays.

Instead of determining time of work, flexible work locations allow employees to work at off-site locations—in other words, away from the employer-provided workplace. Off-site work might be done while traveling, in client locations, hotels, planes, or airports, for example. Alternatively, the employee may be able to work from home, either occasionally or on a regular basis. This last type of flexibility is often called telecommuting.

Employees also value the flexibility to take time off during regular work hours to attend to personal and family concerns. Sometimes this type of time off can be planned, as in the case of vacations, doctor appointments, parent-teacher conferences, or parental leave. These planned days or weeks off may be paid or unpaid. While 12 weeks of parental leave is guaranteed under the Family Medical Leave Act (FMLA) for employees of firms with more than 50 employees, the law does not mandate that such leave be paid time off. The ability to take unplanned time off as the need arises constitutes a different kind of flexibility. Reasons for taking unplanned time off could include personal sickness or the need to care for a sick child or elderly parent. These unplanned types of absences could range from a few hours to a few days.

The opportunity to reduce work hours represents another type of flexibility. Some employees choose to reduce their hours of work, but continue to work throughout the year. Sometimes the reduction keeps the worker in the full-time range of employment, but at other times the reduction could place the worker in a part-time status. A different type of hours reduction would be seasonal. In this case, the employee works regular full-time weekly hours, but only for several months of the year. Job sharing represents another means of reducing hours for workers.

Allowing workers to flex over the course of their careers is yet another category of flexibility. In this scenario, workers could flex in and out of the workforce depending on their life circumstances. One of the concerns, addressed later in this chapter, of moving to a part-time status is that the employee will be Mommy (or Daddy) Tracked. In such cases, once workers choose to reduce hours or responsibilities to allow for more personal time, they are unable to get back on their desired career track (Mason and Ekman 2007). Firms that allow flexibility over the course of a career set up sabbatical policies and allow workers to reduce work responsibilities temporarily.

Cali Ressler and Jodi Thompson (2008) coined the term "Results-Only Work Environments" (ROWE) to describe a more radical view of workplace flexibility. In a ROWE company, employers evaluate the results or performance, as opposed to the presence, of employees. ROWE employees work whenever and wherever they want, with the expectation that the work gets done. Obviously, this level of flexibility is feasible only for certain types of jobs. Early adopters of ROWE typically offer the option at their corporate headquarters, but not at their distribution or service centers.

WHO USES FLEXIBLE WORK OPTIONS?

Tang and Wadsworth (2010) document the access to workplace flexibility of U.S. employees, using the data collected from the 2008 National Study of the Changing Workforce. The Families and Work

Institute, with support from the Alfred P. Sloan Foundation, conducted the 2008 NSCW, a nationally representative survey of 3,502 households. Sample weighting was done relative to the U.S. population using data from the 2007 March Current Population Survey. For further technical information about the survey, see Tang and Wadsworth (2010). Unless otherwise noted, the data from this section come from that report.

While 36 percent of employees report that they enjoy "a lot" or "complete" control over their time at work, 39 percent have either "some" or "very little" control and 25 percent "no" control over their work time. Interestingly, while only 1 in 3 workers has "a lot" or "complete" control, 50 percent of employees report having enough schedule flexibility to manage their work and family obligations.

Control over work schedules varies by gender, education, occupation, and industry. Unsurprisingly, more highly educated and managerial or professional workers report higher levels of control over work schedule than other types of workers. Women are more likely than men to have higher levels of control, and service industry workers realize slightly more work schedule flexibility than goods-producing employees.

Forty-four percent of workers report having access to the type of flextime that allows employees to alter their start and end times of work, but such a policy typically requires the workers to commit to a particular fixed schedule. Interestingly, according to the 2007 National Study of Employers, 79 percent of employers allow at least some workers to change their start and quitting times periodically, but that number drops to only 37 percent when asked about "all" or "most" employees (Council of Economic Advisers [CEA] 2010). A likely explanation for this disparity lies in the wording of the survey question. Perhaps the employer allows only a small fraction of workers that flexibility, or perhaps there is a cultural distinction between an employer's policy and the implementation of that policy by lower-level supervisors. Men are more likely than women to report having access to this traditional form flextime, as do better-educated workers, professionals, managers, and service industry workers. Of the 44 percent of workers who have access to flextime, almost 80 percent indicate that they use it to meet their needs. Of the 56 percent of workers who do not have access to flextime, approximately two-thirds indicate a desire for it. A large majority (84 percent) of the U.S. employees surveyed indicated that they could alter their start and end times on short notice.

Nearly 35 percent of employees can access compressed work weeks, and these workers are more likely to be highly educated managerial or professional employees. Not quite half of those employees with access to compressed work weeks actually use them, with men taking advantage of the availability more often than women. Among those who do not have access to the possibility of a compressed work week, younger workers and those with more care responsibilities (either for children or for elderly relatives) are more likely to desire it.

Most employees work at a fixed location away from home, but almost one in five wage-earning or salaried employees works at multiple locations away from home. Most of these employees report working either at changing client locations or on the road. Only 3 percent report that they work primarily from home. Even those who work primarily at a fixed location may want the flexibility to work occasionally from home. Almost half of workers who are not allowed to work at home report wanting the option to work occasionally from this location. Nearly one in six workers is allowed the flexibility to work some paid hours at home. These workers are more likely to be college educated, managerial or professional, and older than the age of 30. In addition, men are more likely than women to have the option of working occasionally from home. Roughly two-thirds of those who have the option of working some hours at home have opted to do so.

About one in six employees works part-time in his or her primary job, and about two-thirds of part-time workers indicate that they are part-time by choice. Unlike in the other types of flexibility discussed so far, women are more likely than men to work part-time, as are high school dropouts and workers outside of managerial or professional occupations. Part-time workers are more likely to indicate that they are part-time by choice if they are women, hold college degrees, or work in managerial and professional occupations.

Only one-third of employees indicate that it is either "very" or "somewhat" difficult to take unscheduled time off during the workday to attend to personal or family reasons. Workers with college degrees or those in managerial or professional occupations are more likely to have at least five paid work days off per year for personal illness. Slightly fewer than 40 percent of all wage-earning and salaried workers have to choose between coming to work ill or taking a pay cut, and these workers are more likely to be young and have young children.

More-educated parents and those in managerial or professional occupations are also more likely to have paid time off to care for sick children. It is far less likely for employees to have access to paid time off to care for elderly relatives. Only 31 percent of those who provide elder care report taking time off, with about half taking a few hours at a time and the other half taking a leave of absence. The majority of poor working parents have no paid leave (vacation, sick, or personal days), and only 23 percent of employees in the bottom income quartile have paid sick days, as compared to close to 70 percent of workers in the top quartile (Levin-Epstein 2006).

While the FMLA covers only 72 percent of the workforce, a large majority of private-sector employees receive unpaid family leave. Among those surveyed who had children younger than the age of six and who were employed when their child was born, 83 percent report taking time off; only 3 percent were not allowed to take any time off. Women take more leave than do men—15 weeks versus 5 weeks, respectively. Slightly more than half of the fathers report taking off one week, while almost half of mothers report taking off more than 10 weeks. Slightly more than one-third of those who took time off following the birth or adoption of a child report that they received full pay, while almost half received no pay. In addition, women were approximately half as likely to receive full pay as men, but about as likely to receive no pay as men.

Access to flexible work options seems to be related more to education and occupational status than to actual need for such flexibility. We see that across the different types of flexible work arrangements, more highly educated workers, especially those in professional or managerial occupations, enjoy greater access to flexibility (Bond and Galinsky, 2006; Bond and Galinsky, 2011). Since we can consider flexibility work opportunities as a component of a worker's overall compensation, it is unsurprising that more highly educated workers, who enjoy higher levels of compensation overall, would also enjoy broader access to work place flexibility. It may be that the nature of low-wage jobs makes it more expensive for firms to provide flexibility (CEA 2010). For example, flexibility may be costly for firms that rely on production workers to keep the line running or on service workers to provide round-the-clock coverage (Corporate Voices for Working Families 2006).

Finally, women are more likely than men to avail themselves of reduced time and parental leave options. These reductions in work time lead to pay penalties and may contribute in large part to the gap in wages by gender. The following section derives a model of wage determination and workplace flexibility that can be used to understand the connections between take-up of flexibility policies and the gender wage gap.

AN ECONOMIC MODEL OF FLEXIBLE WORKPLACE PROVISION

The gender gap in education and wages has narrowed substantially over the past 30 years, and has all but disappeared among young, unmarried, childless workers. At around age 30, however, the wage gap reemerges, now primarily between mothers and non-mothers (Waldfogel 1998). This gap can be explained in part by labor supply choices of mothers that are family friendly yet costly, such as job interruptions and the use of flexible work options. A model of compensating differentials can help us to understand how women's demand for flexible work options may contribute to the gender wage gap.

Compensating differentials theories model wage differences across jobs that require similar levels of skill, but differ in the desirability of working conditions. For example, window washers who work on skyscrapers are typically paid a higher wage, or compensating differential, for the danger associated with their job. Compensating differentials also arise with positive nonwage job characteristics, in which case the employee may be willing to take a pay cut in exchange for the desirable job characteristic. Amenities (or corrections for the disamenities) are costly to firms, so firms choose the wage-amenity pair that maximizes profits. Likewise, instead of choosing to maximize wages, workers maximize utility, which is a function of wages and nonwage amenities.

Goldin and Katz (2011) outline an economic framework of compensating differentials to model the provision of an amenity, such as workplace flexibility. This model makes predictions as to how changes in the demand for workplace flexibility, as well as changes in the cost to firms of provision of such flexibility, affect the use of flexible work options and the gender wage gap.

The model assumes that there are two types of jobs: flexible jobs that are associated with the amenity and inflexible jobs that do not have the amenity. Suppose the flexible jobs pay ΔW less than the inflexible jobs (where ΔW is a small decrement in wages or salary).

Assume firms are heterogeneous in the cost of provision of the amenity. Under this model, some firms can provide flexible workplace policies at low cost, while others face higher costs. In such a scenario, firms that can provide the amenity for less than ΔW will offer the amenity, while other firms will not.

On the demand side of the market for the amenity (or the supply side of the labor market), suppose all workers value income but are heterogeneous in their taste for the amenity. Therefore, some workers highly value flexibility and are willing to take a cut in salary equal to ΔW (the compensating differential) in exchange for this amenity. Workers who place less value on the amenity will choose the inflexible job with the higher salary.

If demand for flexible work exceeds the supply, then firms can lower the wage that they pay to workers who want the amenity, thereby increasing the wage differential, ΔW. Conversely, an excess supply of flexible jobs will cause the wage differential to fall. Thus, equilibrium in this market occurs when the demand for the amenity equals its supply. The model implies that people who are more willing to pay for workplace flexibility will earn less than those who do not value the amenity.

The equilibrium can be shifted by changes in either the demand or the supply of the amenity. First consider a labor supply shift. If the labor supply of workers who value the amenity increases, then the wage differential will increase to offset the greater demand for the amenity. In this case, the wage differential increases, as does the number of workers who work in flexible jobs. Alternatively, suppose that the cost of providing the flexible work amenity falls. (One could also think of this as a reduction in the comparative productivity of the less flexible workplace.) In this case, more firms are willing to supply the amenity at the given wage differential. This excess supply decreases the wage differential as well as increases the number of workers in the flexible jobs. Thus, the model predicts that as technology improves—lowering the cost of telecommuting, for example—the number of workers, both male and female, should increase.

To use this model to explain the gender wage gap, Goldin and Katz (2011) assume that there are two types of workers, men and women, and that women are willing to pay more for the amenity of flexible work than are men. In this case, if at all values of ΔW women demand more of the amenity than men, then the model predicts that men will forgo the amenity, which they do not value highly, and earn higher

salaries than women. It also follows that if men increase their valua-
tion of workplace flexibility, we should expect a decrease in the gender
wage gap. The following section explores empirical evidence for the
existence of the compensating differential related to workplace
flexibility.

PENALTIES OF USE

While many firms offer flexible work policies, workers can be hesitant
to use them for fear that their careers will suffer. Multiple surveys
have found that even when employers offer flexibility, unspoken rules
prevent employees from taking advantage of these opportunities. For
example, the 2002 National Study of the Changing Workforce by the
Families and Work Institute found that 43 percent of employed
parents believed taking on a flexible schedule would harm their
chances of job advancement (Galinsky, Bond, and Hill 2004). A nationally representative survey of highly educated women conducted by
the Center for Work-Life Policy found that only 4 out of 10 women
whose companies offered telecommuting policies felt they could
actually take them. Women, even at the senior level, reported fears of
facing stigma should they choose to go part-time. Slightly more than
one-third of women doctors, lawyers, and businesswomen reported
difficulties in moving to a part-time position, and three-fourths of
women in the financial sector attested to serious barriers to taking a
part-time position, even when those opportunities might be technically "on the books" (Hewlett, Luce, Shiller, and Southwell 2005)

    As noted previously, highly educated workers have greater access
to flexible work arrangements. At the highest levels of corporate leadership, 91 percent of women report they have flexibility to alter their
work schedules if needed for personal reasons. Even so, only 24 percent believe that they can turn down an opportunity at work for family reasons without harming their career trajectories. Moreover, only
15 percent report that they could use any type of flexible leave policy
without harming their careers (Catalyst, 2003).

    It appears that many of these fears may be well founded. Goldin
and Katz (2011) analyzed the gender pay differences in occupations
at the high end of the earnings scale that require advanced degrees
(law, medicine, corporate & financial, veterinary, dental). Looking at
the top 87 occupations by male income, they found that "[a]fter
accounting for potential experience, hours worked, weeks worked,

and other observable factors, the remaining difference between men and women by occupation is largely due to the penalties imposed on women for greater job interruption and their need for more flexibility" (64). These findings suggest that women with advanced degrees are more likely to choose jobs that allow greater flexibility and suffer pay penalties as a consequence.

Goldin and Katz (2011) conclude that, while women earn less than men in all occupations, the differential is highest in the business occupations and lowest in the technology occupations. They posit that, given its relative youth, the technology industry may be better structured to handle a workforce that demands work flexibility. The health occupations are mixed on this front, with those characterized by high fractions of self-employed workers having the highest differentials. If self-employed workers have less flexibility in terms of hours that they must be available to clients, then it would make sense that the penalties for flexibility for them would be greater.

Bertrand, Goldin, and Katz (2010) corroborate the high differential among business occupations. They report that while male and female MBAs begin their careers with very similar wages, their earnings quickly diverge and the fraction of female MBAs who are employed falls substantially. These authors suggest that a significant portion of this wage gap can be attributed to gender differences in weekly hours worked and job interruptions. They also find that presence of children is a significant contributor to the shorter work hours and greater career discontinuity among female MBAs. The model of compensating differentials implies that given these outcomes, either business sectors have higher costs when they provide flexible workplaces or male MBAs value workplace flexibility considerably less than female MBAs, or both.

Thus, many employees who tap into flexible workplace policies suffer penalties with respect to wages and advancement. Of course, these employees may also have families to support. In such a case, parents and other caregivers who opt to use flexible work options are likely to be forced to choose between providing time and economic resources to their families.

If the costs to employers of providing these options negatively affect the bottom line, then we would expect firms to pass those costs along to the employees or to not provide the options at all. Next, we examine the evidence on the costs and benefits to firms that offer flexible workplace policies.

ECONOMIC COSTS AND BENEFITS OF FLEXIBILITY TO FIRMS

The compensating differentials framework models flexible work policies as amenities, which are costly to employers. Costs of such policies might include higher fixed costs or productivity declines. For example, when a firm offers a paid parenting leave, the worker is paid for work that someone else must accomplish. Even unpaid leaves are costly, in that overhead costs, such as rent, lighting, and administrative support, must be spread over fewer revenue-generating employees.

If the employee values the amenity more than the cost of its provision, then these flexible workplace practices can be a cost-effective way to attract and retain workers. Research has revealed that many employees clearly do value such flexible options. The 2008 National Study of the Changing Workforce, for example, found that workers in more flexible workplaces have higher job satisfaction, higher levels of job engagement, better health, and higher likelihood of staying with their current employer (Matos and Galinsky 2011).

Unfortunately, data on the costs of flexible work policies are quite limited and mostly anecdotal (CEA 2010). Even within a single firm, the cost of providing these types of policies varies considerably across employees. Anderson et al. (2011), in a case study of a law firm, find that the cost of a paid parenting leave policy varied considerably within the firm based on the employee's classification and the timing of the leave. Yet, in the 2008 National Study of Employers, cost was the most frequently listed obstacle to providing flexible work opportunities, followed by potential productivity declines. Firms in this study also cited difficulties associated with supervision and administrative hassles, among other challenges (Galinsky, Bond, and Sakai 2008).

On the flip side, productivity increases can work to offset these types of costs. For example, many employers that have instituted such policies report lower turnover, increased ability to attract high-quality employees, lower absenteeism, and increased productivity. Thus, while the model of compensating differentials treats workplace flexibility as a costly amenity, it is important that firms recognize the *net* cost of such provision. In some cases, the productivity gains could be high enough to completely offset the costs.

Increasing retention presents a significant cost savings to employers. When an employee separates from a firm, the employer must incur significant replacement costs. Recruiting can include direct costs, such as advertising for the position, search firm fees, relocation expenses, and signing or referral bonuses, as well as the indirect costs associated with the time devoted to interviewing. Departing workers take with them any accumulated firm-specific human capital. Thus, new employees need training, which generates additional costs, and the employer must take into account the opportunity costs placed on those employees who must cover the tasks of the departed worker until the replacement is settled in place.

Of course, the costs depend on the type of worker and the labor market for that occupation, but research indicates that replacement costs run about 150 percent of a worker's annual salary. Estimates for hourly workers are lower, but still account for between 50 percent and 70 percent of the hourly worker's annual pay (Levine-Epstein 2006). When multiplied across the number of workers exiting firms and the number of firms, these costs become sizable. The MetLife Mature Market Institute, for example, estimates that the cost to U.S. employers of replacing workers who leave the workplace for caregiving responsibilities totals more than $6.5 billion per year.

Flexible work policies can increase worker satisfaction, thereby leading to higher retention rates (CEA 2010). Research also reveals that firms that provide maternity leave benefits enjoy higher retention rates (Baum 2003). Waldfogel (1998) documents that, after controlling for preexisting differences, more than two-thirds of young women with formal maternity leave coverage returned to their employers, compared to fewer than half of those women without such coverage.

If flexible work policies can assist firms in retaining workers, then the cost of providing such policies may be more than outweighed by the reduction in costs associated with attrition. Unfortunately, research relating flexible workplace policies to reduced turnover is somewhat limited. Most of the research to date has been in the nature of case studies. Baughman et al. (2003), for example, surveyed 120 employers in upstate New York and found that offering flexible sick leave and childcare assistance led to measurable reductions in turnover. The Sloan Work and Family Research Network has sponsored a number of Workplace Flexibility Case Studies. A Sloan Family Research Network-sponsored study of the Detroit Regional Chambers found that after instituting flexible work schedules, retention rose from 75 percent to 90 percent, with turnover rates falling significantly below those in other organizations in southeast Michigan (Giglio 2005a). One health insurance provider, Aetna, reports annual voluntary turnover among its work-at-home employees of roughly 2 to 3 percent, as compared to company-wide turnover of 8 percent (Humer 2013).

Reduced absenteeism is another possible benefit to firms with flexible work policies. Unscheduled absenteeism generates substantial costs to firms and creates uncertainty about important factors such as workforce size and composition (CEA 2010). Studies show that workers report that flexible work arrangements reduce absenteeism by reducing employee stress related to balancing work and family commitments (McGuire, Flatley, Kenney, and Brasher 2010). Evidence also supports a link between better health and flexible work policies (Corporate Voices for Working Families 2006; Grzywacz, et al., 2007). Given that absenteeism is often related to health, flexible workplace practices can reduce absenteeism by improving worker health, which has the additional benefit of boosting productivity. Likewise, policies such as telecommuting can reduce absenteeism during weather-related emergencies. For example, the Executive Office of the President (EOP) estimates that 60 percent of EOP employees were able to log in remotely during the lengthy snow shutdown in Washington, D.C., in February 2010, saving the federal government approximately $30 million per day.

Some firms use flexible work practices, such as telecommuting, to save significant money on real estate costs. For example, in part to avoid having to build additional office space at its headquarters, General Mills has moved entire business units to virtual offices, wherein there is no expectation that employees will be working in the office at any time. While workers in these business units can use a desk when they are "on-site," they are not allocated specific office space. Since 1995, when it expanded its telework program, IBM has reduced its office space by 78 million square feet, with a cost saving in the United States alone of $100 million per year. The ratio of space to employee is now 8:1, up from 1:1 in the early 1990s. These changes have also reduced energy consumption by more than $20 million per year (Caldow 2009). Similarly, Aetna reports savings on real estate generated by telecommuting to be in the vicinity of $78 million per year (Humer 2013).

Once again, while the research is generally limited to case studies, evidence does suggest that flexible work policies can increase worker productivity (CEA 2010). As an example, a case study of the Hennepin County Human Services and Public Health Department (HSPHD) found that after expanding workplace flexibility in 2009, the department enjoyed improved productivity, with a decline in wait times for cases to be processed as well as higher levels of customer service (Kerrigan 2011). The Sloan Work and Family Research Network conducted other case study research that led to similar findings. For example, Cisco Systems estimates that teleworking saved the company almost $200 million in increased productivity (Giglio 2005b).

Of course, a significant means of increasing productivity lies in a firm's ability to attract and retain highly productive workers. Given that flexibility is so highly valued, employers are able to use flexible work practices as a lure in hiring. In describing the benefits of implementing a Results-Only Work Environment, the telework manager of the Hennepin County HSPHD reported that because money is so tight, all job postings mention that the office practices ROWE and describe what that means. The county has found that even in the face of restricted budgets, it has been able to hire high-quality workers based on the promise of a flexible work environment. It even reports hiring highly trained workers from other counties who were willing to take pay cuts to work in the ROWE in Hennepin County (Kerrigan 2011). This case study corroborates the findings of Baughman et al. (2003), who report that employers offering flexible scheduling policies are able to pay lower entry-level wages than their competitors.

The current state of the evidence indicates that employees who enjoy access to flexible work policies are happier, healthier, more productive, and more loyal to their employers. Reduced absenteeism, increased retention, and greater productivity clearly reduce costs to firms. Flexible options such as telecommuting can allow firms to save substantial money on real estate as well as to tap into worker productivity outside the office.

Given these benefits, the question remains as to why more employers do not provide flexible work policies. Clearly, the cost of provision varies by the type of employer, and some employers may find that the costs exceed the benefits. Those employers that stand to gain the most from provision of this amenity should be the first to do so. Therefore, the available evidence may overstate the net economic benefits to the average employer. For many employers, however, imperfect information may be leading management to make suboptimal decisions about these policies. Further research on the links between flexible policies and firm profits, conducted on a large scale as opposed to case studies, will help alleviate these asymmetric information problems.

The evidence regarding increases in worker productivity, retention, and cost savings continues to mount, and over the course of the past decade, greater numbers of firms have begun increasing their flexible work provisions (A Better Balance, 2010). Thus it was a shocking move against the tide, when, in early 2013, Yahoo chief executive officer Marissa Meyer abolished the company's work-at-home policy. Yahoo's human resources department announced the new rules, citing the need to improve collaboration and innovation. The following week, similarly beleaguered Best Buy announced a roll-back of its popular ROWE. These highly publicized changes led to a firestorm of debate on the trade-offs between higher productivity and retention, along with reduced real estate costs, and the potential losses in innovation.

CONCLUSION

This chapter contributes to our understanding of how families affect markets by viewing this issue through the lens of flexible workplace provision. The conditions under which families work have changed significantly in the past 50 years. Women's labor force participation rose throughout the 1900s, and women now represent half the U.S. workforce. The old model of breadwinner-homemaker seems to have fallen by the wayside. Instead, we find that in almost two-thirds of families with children younger than the age of 18, all of the adults work (Bureau of Labor Statistics 2010). Families are increasingly unlikely to have a parent out of the workforce to manage the home. In addition, the rise of single-parent families means that greater numbers of workers have sole responsibility for sustaining their children.

With rigid work expectations and no adults at home to run the household, small problems, like a leaking roof that needs immediate repair or a child who needs to see an orthodontist who offers only daytime appointments, can turn into major stressors for families. In two-parent families, parents must negotiate over who would suffer least by taking time from work. Single-parent households typically fare even worse, with no partner to help make those types of trade-offs.

Some workers are lucky and can get the flexibility they need to manage. Unfortunately, many are not so lucky, and such problems can lead to pay reduction or job loss. These frustrations have led many workers to desire more flexible work arrangements. In this way, families can affect markets by demanding flexibility at work.

In response to the time pressures imposed by their work-family conflicts, workers, both mothers and fathers, have begun to put pressure on employers to allow for more flexible work environments. While some believe that flexible work policies have arisen to meet the needs of women, in reality men are just as likely as women to avail themselves of telecommuting. Indeed, the need for flexibility is a family issue, not a women's issue.

Many firms, in response to these worker demands, have structured some type of flexible work opportunities for some employees. These options range from flexible start and end times to telecommuting to compressed work weeks.

Unfortunately, the workers who need such flexibility the most may not necessarily have access to these types of options, as flexible work options are highly correlated with education and occupational status. Moreover, even workers who technically have access to such amenities may fear reprisals and penalties and, therefore, may not avail themselves of those opportunities.

To create flexible work environments that serve the needs of workers and, by extension, their families, as well as employers, we need the culture at work to change. This cultural change would require us to shift away from a "face-time" mentality, where employers and employees believe that the only way to prove they are working is to be present at work, to one that takes as a default that work can be done, and done well, in off-hours and non-office locations. At the time of this writing, the highly publicized and debated decisions by Yahoo and Best Buy, among others, to cut back on their telecommuting options are still in play. It remains to be seen whether workers will vote with their feet and quit jobs that do not offer workplace flexibility. These two companies, in particular, are struggling to maintain their market positions. In fact, these changes might actually be part of a strategy to downsize workforces without increasing layoffs and severance packages. Also, despite the media coverage to these high-profile policy terminations, the overall number of companies offering telecommuting policies continues to grow (Humer 2013).

Employers also need to be more flexible in their thinking across the course of a person's career. For many employees, the "make it or break it" years of their careers coincide almost exactly with childbearing. Allowing workers to flex in and out, either by reducing hours or by taking a sabbatical, depending on their life circumstances, would create a win-win situation for firms and families alike. Workers could then adjust their work intensity, and employers could retain highly valued employees.

Enacting such a cultural shift will take time and effort. Employers must be convinced that providing flexibility will lead to an improvement in the bottom line. New research on the links between flexible policies and firm profits, conducted on a large scale as opposed to the current body of work that focuses primarily on case studies, would go a long way toward accomplishing that goal. Additional funding for such research is critical, but in the end, families can alter the way that work gets done in the United States by increasing the demand for flexible workplace policies

REFERENCES

Anderson, Donna, Kathryn Birkeland, and Lisa Giddings. *Is It Profitable to Offer Paid Leave: A Case Study.* Working paper. La Crosse, WI: University of Wisconsin-La Crosse, 2011.

Arias, Elizabeth. "United States Life Tables, 2007." *National Vital Statistics Reports* 59, no. 9 (2011).

Aspen Institute Center for Business Education. "Where Will They Lead: MBA Student Attitudes about Business and Society." 2008. http://www.aspeninstitute.org/sites/default/files/content/docs/bsp/SAS_PRINT_FINAL.PDF.

Aumann, Kerstin, Ellen Galinsky, and Kenneth Matos. "The New Male Mystique." Families and Work Institute, 2011. http://familiesandwork.org/site/research/reports/main.html.

Baughman, Reagan, Daniela DiNardi, and Douglas Holtz-Eakin. "Productivity and Wage Effects of 'Family-Friendly' Fringe Benefits." *International Journal of Manpower* 24, no. 3 (2003): 247–259.

Baum, Charles. "The Effects of Maternity Leave Legislation on Mother's Labor Supply after Childbirth." *Southern Economic Journal* 69, no. 4 (2003): 772–799.

Bertrand, Marianne, Claudia Goldin, and Lawrence F. Katz. "Dynamics of the Gender Gap for Young Professionals in the Corporate and Financial Sectors." *American Economic Journal: Applied Economics* 2, no. 3 (2010): 228–255. doi: 10.1257/app.2.3.228.

A Better Balance. "The Business Case for Workplace Flexibility." 2010. http://abetterbalance.org/web/images/stories/Documents/fairness/factsheets/BC-2010-A_Better_Balance.pdf.

Bond, James T., and Ellen Galinsky. "What Workplace Flexibility Is Available to Entry-Level, Hourly Employees?" Research Brief No. 3. Families and Work Institute, 2006. http://familiesandwork.org/site/research/reports/main.html.

Bond, James T., and Ellen Galinsky. "Workplace Flexibility and Low-Wage Employees." Families and Work Institute, 2011. http://www.familiesandwork.org/site/research/reports/WorkFlexAndLowWageEmployees.pdf.

Bureau of Labor Statistics. "Table 4: Families with Own Children: Employment Status of Parents by Age of Youngest Child and Family Type, 2009–10 Annual Averages." (n.d.). http://www.bls.gov/news.release/famee.t04.htm.

Bureau of Labor Statistics. *Women in the Labor Force: A Databook*. Report 1026. Washington, DC: Bureau of Labor Statistics, 2010.

Caldow, Janet. "Working outside the Box: A Study of the Growing Momentum in Telework." Institute for Electronic Government, IBM Corporation, 2009. http://www-01.ibm.com/industries/government/ieg/pdf/working_outside_the_box.pdf.

Catalyst. *Women in Corporate Leadership: 2003*. New York, NY: Catalyst, 2003.

Corporate Voices for Working Families. "Cole Engineering Becomes Business Champion for Workplace Flexibility." Corporate Voices for Working Families, Washington DC, 2006. http://www.coleengineering.com/employment/Workplace_Flexibility_Award.pdf

Council of Economic Advisers (CEA), Executive Office of the President. *Work-Life Balance and the Economics of Workplace Flexibility*. Washington, DC: White House, 2010.

DiCecio, Riccardo, Kristie Engemann, Michael Owyang, and Christopher Wheeler. "Changing Trends in the Labor Force: A Survey." *Federal Reserve Bank of St. Louis Review* 90, no. 1 (2008): 47–62.

Ellwood, David T., and Christopher Jencks. "The Spread of Single-Parent Families in the United States since 1960." In *The Future of the Family*, edited by Daniel Patrick Moynihan, Timothy Smeeding, and Lee Rainwater, 25–65. New York, NY: Russell Sage, 2006.

Fox, Liana E., Wen-Jui Han, Christopher Ruhm, and Jane Waldfogel. *Time for Children: Trends in the Employment Patterns of Parents, 1967-2009*. NBER Working Paper No. 17135. Cambridge, MA: NBER, 2011.

Galinsky, Ellen, James T. Bond, and E. Jeffrey Hill. *When Work Works: A Status Report on Workplace Flexibility.* New York, New York: Families and Work Institute, 2004.

Galinsky, Ellen, James T. Bond, and Kelly Sakai. *National Study of Employers.* New York, New York: Families and Work Institute, 2008.

Giglio, Ken. "Workplace Flexibility Case Study: The Detroit Regional Chamber's Flexible Work Schedules." Sloan Work and Family Research Network, 2005a. http://wfnetwork.bc.edu/pdfs/detroit_regional_chamber.pdf.

Giglio, Ken. "Workplace Flexibility Case Study: Cisco Systems and Telework." Sloan Work and Family Research Network, 2005b. http://workfamily.sas.upenn.edu/static/casestudy#cisco.

Goldin, Claudia, and Lawrence F. Katz. "The Cost of Workplace Flexibility for High-Powered Professionals." *Annals of the American Academy of Political and Social Science* 638 (2011): 45–67. doi: 10.1177/0002716211414398.

Grzywacz, Joseph G., Patrick R. Casey, and Fiona A. Jones. "The Effects of Workplace Flexibility on Health Behaviors: A Cross-Sectional and Longitudinal Analysis." *Journal of Occupational and Environmental Medicine* 49, no. 12 (2007): 1302–1309.

Hewlett, Sylvia Ann, Carolyn Buck Luce, Peggy Shiller, and Sandra Southwell. "The Hidden Brain Drain: Off-Ramps and On-Ramps in Women's Careers." *Harvard Business Review Research Report.* Boston, MA: Harvard Business Publishing, March 2005.

Hochschild, Arlie Russell, with Anne Machung. *The Second Shift: Working Parents and the Revolution at Home.* New York, NY: Viking Press, 1989.

Humer, Caroline. "In Telecommuting Debate, Aetna Sticks by Big At-Home Workforce." *Reuters* (2013). http://www.reuters.com/article/2013/03/01/us-yahoo-telecommuting-aetna-idUSBRE92006820130301.

Kerrigan, Heather. "ROWE Rollout Successes and Challenges." *Governing* (2011). http://www.governing.com/topics/public-workforce/rowe-rollout-successes-challenges-hennepin-minnesota.html.

Levin-Epstein, Jodie. *Getting Punched: The Job and Family Clock.* Washington, DC: Center for Law and Social Policy, 2006.

Lofquist, Daphne, Terry Lugalia, Martin O'Connell, and Sarah Feliz. *Households and Families: 2010.* 2010 Census Briefs, C2010BR-14. Washington, DC: U.S. Census Bureau, 2012.

Mason, Mary Ann, and Eve Mason Ekman. *Mothers on the Fast Track: How a New Generation Can Balance Family and Careers.* New York, NY: Oxford University Press, 2007.

Matos, Kenneth, and Ellen Galinsky. *Workplace Flexibility in the United States: A Status Report.* New York, New York: Families and Work Institute, 2011.

McGuire, Jean Flatley, Kaitlyn Kenney, and Phyllis Brasher. "Flexible Work Arrangements: The Fact Sheet." *The Scholarly Commons,* Georgetown University Law Center (2010). http://scholarship .law.georgetown.edu/legal/13.

Moe, Karine S., and Dianna Shandy. *Glass Ceilings and 100-Hour Couples: What the Opt out Phenomenon Can Teach Us about Work and Family.* Athens, GA: University of Georgia Press, 2010.

National Center for Health Statistics, U.S. Department of Health and Human Services. *Monthly Vital Statistics Report: Advance Report of Final Divorce Statistics* 32, no. 3 (1983): supplement.

National Vital Statistics System. "National Marriage and Divorce Rate Trends." 2012. http://www.cdc.gov/nchs/nvss/marriage _divorce_tables.htm.

Pavalko, Eliza K., and Kathryn A. Henderson. "Combining Care Work and Paid Work: Do Workplace Policies Make a Difference?" *Research on Aging* 28, no. 3 (2006): 359–374.

Ressler, Cali, and Jody Thompson. *Why Work Sucks and How to Fix It: No Schedules, No Meetings, No Joke—The Simple Change That Can Make Your Job Terrific.* New York, NY: Portfolio, 2008.

Stratton, Leslie. "Gains from Trade and Specialization: The Division of Work in Married Couple Households." In *Women, Family, and Work: Writings on the Economics of Gender,* edited by Karine S. Moe, 67–83. Oxford, UK: Blackwell, 2003.

Tang, Chiung-Ya, and Shelley MacDermid Wadsworth. "Time and Workplace Flexibility." Families and Work Institute, 2010. http:// familiesandwork.org/site/research/reports/main.html.

U.S. Department of Commerce, Economics and Statistics Administration and Executive Office of the President, Office of Management and Budget. "Women in America: Indicators of Social and Economic Well-Being." 2011. http://www.whitehouse .gov/administration/eop/cwg/data-on-women.

Waldfogel, Jane. "Understanding the 'Family Gap' in Pay for Women with Children." *Journal of Economic Perspectives* 12, no. 1 (1998): 137–156.

Chapter 5

Changing Technologies of Household Production: Causes and Effects

Joyce P. Jacobsen

One of the most interesting topics in the area of economics of family and household is how changes in household technology have affected both household production—the production of goods and services by household members for consumption by household members—and market production—the production of goods and services by paid labor, meant for sale. These changes have also apparently led to profound changes in consumption patterns as well as changes in time use, including women's increased participation in market production. Less obviously, but even more profoundly, they have apparently led to significant changes in our most fundamental choices regarding who we live with and how we live.

Most, if not all, of us alive today and reading this chapter can likely not remember a time when electricity did not power our homes and multiple home appliances run off that power. As of 2012, when I was typing these words (on my home computer, rather than pen them or typewrite them on a manual typewriter), the modern kitchen was a marvel of capital investment. In addition, many homes in the industrialized world harbor modern laundry facilities, as well as garage door openers, vacuum cleaners, and Internet access.

Yet many home activities remain fundamentally the same: we still prepare food and consume it—albeit with more store-bought prepared ingredients; tend to personal hygiene; store our possessions;

interact with family members and friends; sleep; and clean our abodes. In many ways, our homes function much as they did 200 years ago, though clearly much greater changes become notable as we go further back in human development, including the absence of fixed residences and few, if any, personal possessions. An alternative viewpoint, then, might be that very little has changed about fundamental human existence and needs: it is all about quantity and quality rather than fundamental changes in what we consume.

Similarly, while women are now much more likely to work outside the home and have many fewer children than in the past, it is also notable that much of what women do in the market often emulates their traditional home-based activities, such as preparing food, cleaning, and tending to children. In addition, while we are much less likely in most middle-class societies to have live-in servants, we procure a wide range of household services from multiple vendors, including gardening services, housecleaning, and child care. Thus, while the labor intensity of any one home activity is often lower, overall we still devote much time to household maintenance, both in our individual homes and economy-wide, and we often invest more in terms of time and money per child raised to adulthood.

This chapter considers several interrelated questions. First, from a historical viewpoint, what actually happened as various technologies were developed and adopted, and what spurred their development in the first place? In particular, was women's increased market work participation enabled in large part through the development of household technologies, or did the technologies develop in response to increased demand in the market sector for female labor? Second, how much has technology "liberated" us from the tyranny of home production, as opposed to being marshaled to produce yet more at home? Third, how much has household technology changed not only our time use patterns and our division of work between market and home production, but also the very structure of our households—such fundamental matters as who, when, and whether we marry, whether we stay married, where we live, and how many children we have? Fourth, has technological change in household production made us better off? Fifth, given that much of the world has not yet undergone the full household technology revolution, what can we expect to happen in the developing world over the near future, and will responses to technological change mirror those changes seen earlier in the now-industrialized world? And finally (addressed in a short speculative section), which additional changes may occur in the future in the industrialized world as household technology continues to evolve?

While these questions can be addressed using recent economic research, the answers are not uncontroversial. In this chapter I marshal the most recent evidence available as well as consider older but still relevant sources. However, further research may overturn the statements made herein, as this area of study is still young and contested.

IS NECESSITY THE MOTHER OF INVENTION?

An interesting question about technological innovation in general is how much it is the product of inspired individuals, working essentially from internal motivation, and how much it is stimulated by external forces, such as increased incomes in society and changing opportunity costs of time. The answer is likely twofold, in that we could always have used various innovations, such as antibiotics, but general scientific knowledge had to progress to a certain level, as well as individual insight occur, for the product to be invented. The subsequent rapidity of dissemination of innovation, however, appears to depend both on the price of the product and the degree of its desirability, as well as the ability of dissemination channels to produce and distribute items quickly, and the degree to which the innovation depends on additional infrastructure, such as electrification. In the case of household production, it appears that much of the innovation in this area, and the introduction of capital equipment into household production, had to wait for the second industrial revolution, which is characterized in part by the introduction of widespread electrification at the end of the 19th century. This is not surprising, as earlier forms of harnessed energy, such as coal and gas, while utilized for specific household purposes such as home heating and powering of stoves, were not as suited to other types of purposes like refrigeration.

Take a particular case of a particular household appliance—the washing machine. For generations before its invention, women obviously could have envisioned that having a machine that washed clothes automatically would be a big time and effort saver. Actually using a washing machine in one's house, however, would depend on the availability of electricity and running water, having enough space to store it, and having the funds to purchase and maintain it.

In addition, for many persons, sending laundry out for commercial laundering, or having a servant do the laundry, could be a more cost-efficient way of dealing with clothes. Also, those with fewer clothes and sheets to launder would have less incentive to invest in such an appliance. Moreover, if cleanliness standards are lower, then one also washes less often and has less incentive to buy such a machine. Consequently, even today many households do not own a clothes washer due to one or more of these reasons.

Notably, there was no single inventor of the clothes washer, and multiple competing models have always existed. Washing machines predate the invention of electric-powered washing machines by more than 100 years, as patents were issued for them as early as 1691 (Stanley 1995, 301). Washing machines could be turned by crank or powered by running water or steam, for instance. However, the first electric-powered washing machine appears to date from 1904 ("Electric Washing Machine" 1904), and certainly could not have been much earlier, given that electric power was not available. Central electrical power stations were first available in the late 19th century—1881 in Surrey, the United Kingdom, and 1882 in New York (McNeil 1990, 360-68).

While much early use of electricity was in production, in factories and offices, home electrification spread fairly rapidly in the United States. By 1920, one-third of homes were electrified; by 1930, more than two-thirds had electricity (although only 10 percent of farm homes); by 1960, almost all were electrified (Vanek 1978, 363). Similarly, by 1940, 70 percent of homes had indoor running water (17 percent of farm homes and 93 percent of urban homes); by 1970, 90 percent of rural homes had indoor running water (363). Thus the infrastructure necessary for households to be able to utilize household appliances such as dishwashers, refrigerators, freezers, clothes dryers, and vacuums was widely available prior to World War II and became ubiquitous in the postwar era. Similar to the story of the clothes washer, these other appliances also developed from early hand-powered prototypes into versions driven by electricity and hooked up to household water sources in the case of those that needed water to run. Bathroom appliances dependent on running water, such as the flush toilet and showerhead, also became standard household equipment during the first half of the 20th century.

Once electrification became standard, later waves of household appliances, particularly smaller non-built-in ones, disseminated much more quickly. For example, the microwave oven rose from adoption by 13 percent of married-couple households in 1978 to 81 percent a decade later in 1987 (Oropesa 1993), and then to 25 percent of all households by 1987. Thus, for later appliances, it may be that their invention came in response to the desire of households for yet more reduction of time and effort in household production. However, even in the case of the microwave oven, it was first necessary that the physics of microwaves be understood and harnessed. The Radarange was already commercially available by 1947, but it took another two decades for a home version to become available, and even then it was at prices that few could afford ($495 in 1967 dollars). Until the prices of microwave ovens dropped much further, households might well have appreciated having such a product, but were unable to afford it.

Thus both the timing of the invention and adoption of these technologies and their dependence on the networks of electricity and running water appear consistent with the same story—namely, that their appearance made it possible for people to spend less time in household production, in particular women. It may be that one of the explanations for the increased participation of women in paid work is that these technologies were invented. Whether or not this was the case we will examine in the next section.

HOW MUCH LIBERATION HAS OCCURRED?

Overall, U.S. investment in household durable goods more than tripled over the course of the 20th century as a percentage of GDP, and the stock of such appliances doubled (Greenwood, Seshadri, and Yorukoglu 2005, 111). Given all of this investment in household capital, has there been corresponding liberation of people from time spent in household production? Note this implies that most people find household tasks onerous and that they prefer other uses of their time to household production. It also implies that quality improvements in household production are minimal, that clear standards for household cleanliness and appropriate meals can be stated and followed, and that the nature of household production has not altered over time. All of these assumptions may well not be true.

The simplest way to answer this question would be to look at time use patterns to see what has happened as appliances have been increasingly used and electricity and running water become widely available. This would include looking in particular at whether people shift time out of household production and into other time use, including market work and leisure. Unfortunately, this evidence is not systematically available, particularly for older periods. Thus researchers have considered a range of phenomena, including more limited time-use studies of how long households with various appliances spend on household chores and whether women have increased their market work time as such appliances have become increasingly available. Indeed, one of the most interesting recent debates in the economics and sociological literatures has been over whether changes in household technology are responsible—and if so, to what degree— for the rise in female labor force participation that occurred in developed countries during the 20th century.

Figure 5.1 shows the patterns over the past 210 years in women's and men's labor force participation, as well as women's percentage of the labor force. While women's participation rises over the full period, the most notable change occurs in the post-World War II period. This rise coexists with a drop in men's participation, with the net effect being that women increase as a share of the labor force up

Figure 5.1   (1800–1860 from Weiss (1986): 657–59; 1870–1970 from U.S. Bureau of the Census (1976): Series D13; 1980–2010 from Council of Economic Advisors (2012): 365.)

to 47 percent by 2010 (U.S. Bureau of the Census, 1976; Council of Economic Advisors, 2012).

In addition, it is particularly notable that the growth in female labor supply that began during the second half of the 20th century and continues up to the present came from married women with children. Single women were already mostly working. For instance, in 1960 single (never-married) women had a 59 percent labor force participation rate, which rose to 65 percent by 2010. By comparison, the married women's labor force participation rate rose from 32 percent in 1960 to 69 percent by 2010, surpassing the single women's rate. In particular, married women with school-age children (children ages 6 through 17) rose from 39 percent to 77 percent participation rate over this period, and even those married women with preschool-age children saw their rate rise from 19 percent to 64 percent over this period. (U.S. Bureau of the Census 2004, 376–377; U.S. Bureau of Labor Statistics 2011, 12, 16).

Many economists and other social scientists have tried to ascertain what the most important causes are of this rise. As usual, economic theory can provide a guide as to what might be relevant factors—particularly through use of the concepts of substitution (in both production and consumption) and income effects—but cannot say definitively whether particular factors have actually caused the increase. The various factors can be divided into demand-side and supply-side factors.

Demand-side factors increase the wage that women can earn, thereby influencing individual labor-supply decisions. The factors that appear to be most important for causing increased female labor force participation are the overall increase in labor demand over the 20th century along with rises in labor demand in specific industrial and occupational sectors, albeit with fluctuations around the long-term upward trend. Given that labor demand is derived from the demand for goods and services, as the volume of traded goods rises, more labor is needed to produce these goods and services. Technological innovations also lead to increased labor demand as production becomes more efficient, leading to increased output (i.e., productivity) per worker. Demand for particular types of labor has fallen—in particular, demand for unskilled farm labor (where other inputs, such as farm machinery, pesticides, and irrigation systems, have substituted for workers) and demand for manufacturing labor (where capital substitution has occurred, as well as growth in demand for manufactured goods being outstripped by growth in demand for services). Meanwhile, demand for other types of labor has been growing—in particular, demand for occupations in which women have generally made up a larger share of the workforce, such as medical care, teaching, and office-related work. In addition, shifts in demand for goods and services and the relatively great complementarity between capital and skilled labor (as opposed to between capital and unskilled labor, or skilled and unskilled labor), along with the high degree of substitution of capital for unskilled labor, have increased the labor demand for skilled workers. As women have received more formal education, including career-oriented education, the consequent rise in their potential wage has made it more profitable for them to enter into market work (Black and Juhn 2000).

Indeed, wages for women have risen substantially in both absolute and relative terms over this period. Most notably, median annual incomes for women rose from 61 cents per dollar earned by men in 1960 to 77 cents in 2011 for year-round full-time workers (U.S. Bureau of the Census Current Population Reports No. 132, Table 43; No. 243, Table A-4).

When wages rise, the straightforward way for an individual to profit from the rise is to work, leading one to predict an increase in women's labor force participation, which is exactly what has happened. While some women who are currently working might reduce their hours due to the increase in wages, they will nevertheless remain employed and part of the labor force, so the net change in female labor force participation is positive. Indeed, it appears that real wage growth can explain most of the female labor force participation rise from 1950 to 1980 (e.g., Smith and Ward 1985).

In addition to these demand-side factors operating through the wage to cause movements along the female labor supply curve, three types of supply-side economic factors could shift the female labor supply to the right: changes in the technology used in nonmarket production; changes in family structure (including changing patterns of marriage, divorce, and childbearing and childrearing); and falling earnings for men, translating into less family income available for married women. We will consider the first of these three causes in most depth herein, as it relates to the main topic of this chapter.

Changes in the technology of nonmarket production include the increased availability of market-produced substitutes for nonmarket goods and the increased productivity of nonmarket labor, particularly housework (rather than child care). More market substitutes have become available for nonmarket production and at reduced prices. This has the effect of increasing labor supply (i.e., the supply of market labor) as the efficiency of market production has increased—in other words, the purchasing power of one's earnings has increased.

But consider the effect of changes in production efficiency on a household's production possibility frontier for a couple where one person does only nonmarket work and the other does only market work. Under the realistic presumption that both market and nonmarket products are normal goods, when potential income rises, more of both will be consumed. Then economic theory does not tell us whether increased efficiency in either form of production will lead to more or less time spent in the relatively less efficient form of production. Because the substitution and income effects move in opposite directions, we do not know the exact net result for the good that becomes relatively more expensive. If market efficiency increases (e.g., if the wage rises for both family members), the substitution and income effects of this wage change cause an unambiguous increase in consumption of market goods, but nonmarket production may go either down or up depending on whether the substitution effect is greater than the income effect. Therefore we also cannot tell if the person who had before done only nonmarket work will now participate in at least some market work. Similarly, if nonmarket efficiency increases, there will be an unambiguous increase in consumption of nonmarket products, but market goods can either decrease or increase, and we cannot tell whether the nonmarket producer will now participate in market work.

Thus, productivity gains in household production may or may not translate into less time spent in household production. After all, as the cost of producing housework, and of producing higher-quality housework, decreases, households might well demand more of it. Indeed, Ramey (2009) concludes that while there was a decline in women's housework hours from 1900 to 1965 of 6 hours per week, this fall was balanced by a rise in housework by other persons.

In evaluating what has happened, it appears that many supposedly timesaving innovations were widely adopted in the first half to two-thirds of the 20th century with no apparent significant reduction of nonmarket time (Cowan 1983; Robinson and Milkie 1997). For instance, Manning (1968) compares time spent on preparing meals by families with and without various cooking appliances (mixers, electric skillets, pressure cookers, freezers, and dishwashers) and finds that the families with the appliances basically spend the same or more time in meal preparation. While this could be due to either a direct effect or a sample selection effect (families who spend more time on preparing meals may also be more likely to purchase these appliances, perhaps because they enjoy spending time cooking), in either case there is no direct evidence of liberation. More broadly, Bose and Berano (1983) consider four types of household technologies: utilities, appliances, convenience and prepackaged foods, and private-sector market services (85) and conclude that none of them truly saved, or freed up, household labor (although these authors do suggest that utilities saved physical exertion).

It is, of course, quite possible that the families who own these appliances are creating greater value of household production, as they both invest more capital and invest either the same amount of time or more time in meal preparation, clothing maintenance, and other household chores. For example, Mokyr (2000) argues that better understanding of the causes and transmission of infectious diseases in the early part of the 20th century increased housewives' attention to home hygiene. Vanek (1974), in examining a set of approximately 20 studies of time spent in housework from 1920 through 1960, finds a remarkably stable number of hours spent on housework by women who did not work also outside the home, from approximately 48 to 56 hours per week. This is barely any change from 1900, when the average household spent an estimated 58 hours per week on housework (Lebergott 1993, Table 8.1). The composition of housework has changed over time, however, with less time spent on food preparation and cleanup and more time spent on shopping and family managerial tasks (Vanek 1974).

A different take on the lack of change in housework hours is that, at least for women who do not engage in market work, housework expands to fill available time, involving either less efficient production methods or achievement of higher normative standards on matters such as home cleanliness, elaborateness of meal preparation, and proportion of homemade objects. These adjustable standards, in turn, keep women inefficiently occupied in the home, reducing their market work.

Various commentators who have analyzed the reading material meant for a female readership (such as housekeeping magazines) propound these views that much housework is "make-work" and that social standards for housework are overly strict and highly adjustable. For instance, anthropologist Margolis (1984) argues that home-related periodicals emphasize activities in the home that have visible results, such as home decoration. She believes that the purpose of this emphasis is to validate the importance of housework, thereby supporting the inefficient housework system. However, Margolis concludes that there is, in addition, an opposite tendency for the prescriptive literature on mothering and housekeeping practices to support the increased demand for women's labor. Margolis (1976) also analyzes a sample of 200 hints taken from 70 "Hints from Heloise" columns published in January through March 1975. She concluded that 38 percent of these hints were needlessly time-consuming, 40 percent were neutral with regard to time use but were often superfluous activities, and only 8 percent were actually time-saving ways of performing useful chores. Certainly, modern upscale housekeeping magazines, such as *Martha Stewart Living*, rarely, if ever, emphasize time-saving aspects of their household suggestions, instead focusing on the beauty and handmade aspects of the suggested crafts and recipes.

Similarly, Fox (1990) studied ads for household appliances over a 70-year time span in the prominent women's magazine *Ladies Home Journal*, measuring the percentage of advertisements that extolled the household appliances' labor-saving character. While in 1909–1910, 21 percent of the ads stressed labor-saving, that percentage dropped to 13 percent in 1919–1920 and 1929–1930; rose to 19 percent in 1939–1940 and to 20 percent in 1949–1950; and then fell to between 5 and 6 percent in both 1969–1970 and 1979–1980. She concludes: "More *Journal* ads featured directives about housework than descriptions of the product; they emphasized work performance far more frequently than liberation from housework, and they also promoted service to family ... advertiser's [sic] efforts to create a market for household appliances and other means of domestic labor involved promotion of an ideology about housework that reinforced women's dedication to it" (25).

However, the story appears to change over the second half of the 20th century. During this period, more systematic time use data become available. For the United States, American Time Use Survey data, available annually since 2003, can be linked up with older data from decadal studies (1965, 1975, 1985) to characterize the changes in time use over the past 46 years. Over this span, there appears to be declines in both women's time spent in household production and

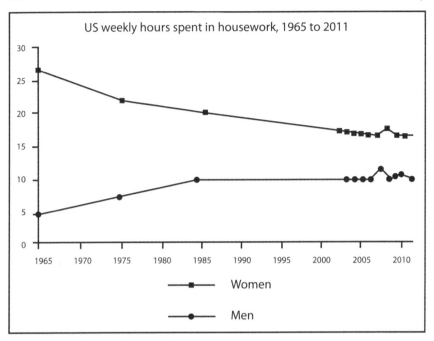

Figure 5.2   (1965–1985 from Robinson (1988); 2003–2011 from U.S. Bureau of Labor Statistics, American Time Use Survey.)

total time spent in household production. As shown in Figure 5.2, the drop in women's average weekly hours devoted to household production from 1965 to 2011, going from 27 hours to 15, is not offset by the rise in men's hours, from 5 to 10. Thus women spend more time doing housework than do men, but men are increasing their share of total housework, even as the total amount of housework per household is falling.

What happens with the freed-up time? Much of the freed-up time for women appears to be going into paid work, though some of it is spent in increased child care (Connelly and Kimmel 2010). In addition, more time appears to be available for leisure, both over the total life cycle and even during prime working years: between 1965 and 1985, total productive time (in both market and nonmarket activities) declined by 7 hours for employed women and 4 hours for employed men, implying that leisure time has actually increased for both women and men (Robinson and Godbey 1997, 108).

There are other possible causes of these changes besides liberating household technology. In particular, it has been disputed as to whether the increased and lower-cost availability of household utilities and durables goods is responsible for much, if any, of the rise in women's labor supply, with researchers coming down on both sides of the argument.

An influential paper, "Engines of Liberation," by Jeremy Greenwood and colleagues (2005), put forth the argument that household technology adoption is responsible for approximately 55 percent of the increase in female labor force participation over the 20th century, and that rising relative wages for women are responsible for only approximately 20 percent of this increase. While the authors acknowledge interaction effects, they argue that without the availability of liberating household technology, rising wages alone would not have been sufficient to draw women out of the household.

Jones, Manuelli, and McGrattan (2003) disagree. They analyze the 1950–1990 period and conclude that changes in household production have had almost no impact and that the changes in the relative wages explain both the rise in married women's market work and the simultaneous lack of change in work hours for men and single women. Particularly for the earlier part of this period, Greenwood et al.'s work, which also emphasizes the slowness of market hours adjustment to the new state of household technology, seems consistent with this story; the disagreement is more about the later part of the century.

In addition, numerous other changes occurred during this period that might affect female labor supply directly. Medical technology that has made it easier for women to control timing of childbirth, as well as reducing the difficulty of childbirth and making it easier to raise young children, are key additional technological advances that occurred during the 20th century. Albanesi and Olivetti (2007) argue that these medical advances, including the development and declining cost of infant formula, were key in freeing up women's time for market work. Goldin and Katz (2002) discuss a later transformative medical technology—namely, the invention of the birth control pill, which was approved for prescription by the U.S. Food and Drug Administration in 1960—as a crucial factor enabling college-educated women to continue their education and careers. Moreover, in part as a consequence of these technological changes, large demographic changes have occurred, all of which tend to increase female labor supply: later or no marriage, increased divorce rates, fewer children later in life, and smaller household sizes.

However, additional recent evidence indicates that the latter half to one-third of the 20th century did see time freed up from the household sector by labor-saving technology. Cavalcanti and Tavares (2008) find a relationship between the decrease in home appliance prices in Organization for Economic and Cooperative Development (OECD) countries from 1975 to 1999 and the increase in female labor force participation. For the United States, Coen-Pirani, León, and Lugauer (2010) argue that the increase in married women's labor force participation during the 1960s is related to increased appliance ownership (specifically freezers, washers, and dryers). The earlier half of the 20th century displays little evidence of such a direct effect. Cardia (2010), for example, tested the Greenwood et al. hypothesis for the period of 1940 to 1950, using U.S. Census data that include information on presence of indoor plumbing and refrigerators. She found some effect of indoor plumbing, but not of refrigeration, on differences in female labor force participation across states in 1940, and some evidence of increased female participation in the clerical sector.

So has there been liberation? The current assessment appears to be yes. If a person chooses not to spend more than a minimal amount of time in household production, it is now possible, with the aid of household appliances, to do so. This minimal amount may be in the range of 1 to 2 hours per day in total person-hours for a two- to three-person household observing reasonable cleanliness standards of a middle-class level.

However, many households still choose to spend more time in household production, perhaps because they enjoy aspects of it or because they hold themselves to a higher standard. In addition, to the extent that they must work to purchase market substitutes for non-market production, such as prepared food and manufactured clothing, on top of paying a house mortgage, a car loan, and schooling expenses, "liberation" may not be the first term that comes to mind to many two-worker households struggling to pay their bills.

HOW HAVE HOUSEHOLDS CHANGED?

The demographic changes that have occurred during the 20th century in industrialized countries are nothing short of revolutionary. In particular, the tremendous drop in women's lifetime fertility, combined with remarkable lifespan lengthening, have meant for the first time in human existence that adult women spend a large proportion of their life not directly engaged in pregnancy, childbirth, and childrearing.

Figure 5.3   (1800–1970 from U.S. Bureau of the Census (1976): Series B5 and B6; 1971–2011 from National Center for Health Statistics, Vital Statistics Reports.)

Figure 5.3 shows the precipitous long-run decline over the past 210 years in the U.S. birth rate, dropping from 57 births per 1,000 persons in 1800 to 13 per 1,000 persons in 2011. The post-World War II Baby Boom (and a subsequent early 1990s echoing boomlet) interrupts the long-run downward trend and help explain why mothers in the 1950s and 1960s might still have had high levels of household production related to those larger families.

Similarly, the long-run rise in age at first marriage is disrupted during this period, even as recent numbers have seen median age at first marriage reach recorded highs. In 1900, the median age at first marriage was 26 for men and 22 for women; in 2011, it was 29 for men and 27 for women (U.S. Bureau of the Census 2011b).

One net effect of increased lifespans, the higher age at first marriage, the higher divorce rate, and the lower birth rate has been the creation of a large number of smaller households. In 1960, the average household size was 3.3 persons; as of 2011, it was 2.6 persons. In 1960, 13 percent of households consisted of single persons; as of

2011, 27 percent of households met this criteria (U.S. Bureau of the Census 2011a).

While there are likely economies of scale in household production, it is also the case that households with larger numbers of dependents imply more work for the middle-aged adults housed therein. Also, childless households have very different types and degrees of household activities. These household composition changes, in turn, imply changes in household production, including potentially modified social standards of what constitutes reasonable housekeeping. Thus some reduction of housework can have come from the combined force of smaller households, in particular fewer children and more singles. Conversely, in olden times, economies of scale were obtained in other ways, particularly for unmarried persons, such as more group living (rooming houses, taking in boarders) and smaller house sizes.

While that changes in household composition can certainly cause changes in market-nonmarket work patterns, a perhaps more interesting question is how changes in household technology might have led in part to those changes in household composition. A chain of causality might be as follows: more efficient household technology, combined with rising market wages, induces women to enter the labor force. Working women are more likely to delay marriage and childbearing and to have fewer children. They may also be more likely to divorce rather than stay in an unsatisfying marriage, and not to remarry if they see less material gain from marriage, thereby leading to higher rates of single-person households at all points in the lifecycle.

Greenwood and Guner (2008) make a stronger argument regarding how changes in household production technology have affected the very nature of marriage. While traditional marriage implied more specialization of women into household production and men into market production, modern times reduce the economic incentive to marry so as to gain materially from specialization and exchange within marriage. Thus there might be both less marriage in general and more marriage occurring for love and emotional or companionable compatibility rather than for economic grounds. Greenwood et al. (2012) go further in developing a unified model to explain changes in marriage, divorce, educational attainment (particularly of women), and married women's labor force participation. They also emphasize the increased amount of assortative mating by education level, where men and women are increasingly likely to marry people with relatively similar earning potential.

Stevenson and Wolfers (2007) point out another mechanism by which changes in household production technology and availability of market substitutes have affected the gains from marriage. Some of these changes have reduced the need for people to develop skills that are useful in household production. For example, the availability of commercial canned goods means that households need not do their own canning. To the extent that male and female children used to be trained in different household production skills—or girls trained in household production skills while boys were trained in labor market-relevant skills—they would arrive at marriageable age having very different sets of skills. In the case of girls, those skills were often useful only within the context of household production. Now children are trained more similarly, including being more likely to spend their adolescence in secondary education and school-related extracurricular activities. One wonders if the feminist revolution was effected in large part by mothers, whether consciously or not, simply not training their daughters in the skills necessary to reenact their own household-centered lives. Both the gains from marriage and the decision of whom to marry, therefore, have been affected. For one thing, both men and women may look for high market earners rather than the relatively rare potential spouse who has high household production ability. This preference ties in with the increase in assortative mating by earnings potential that Greenwood et al. (2012) note: everyone would like to marry a high earner, but only other high earners are able to close the deal.

Fernández, Fogli, and Olivetti (2002) analyze another mechanism by which household technology could have had an effect, again related to the increase in married women's labor supply, but this time through alteration of men's marriage preferences. More men in recent generations have experienced a family model in which their mother was educated and worked for pay. Thus, if men are inclined to marry women who are in many ways like their own mothers, they will be less likely to look for marriage partners who want to specialize in household production. This may not occur solely because men want to marry women like their mothers, but also because both men and women are accustomed from their childhood experiences to be in households where both parents work. Such households may have less household production and less time spent with parents in the home, but also more store-bought goods and services as well as higher money incomes. These latter factors may be increasingly viewed as desirable as people become accustomed to them.

Thus, once the economy starts down a new track wherein more people both work outside the home and purchase market substitutes for formerly home-produced goods and services, preferences evolve to make this path even more likely over time. Again, other factors, such as changes in medical technology (as discussed previously) and many other factors that tend to lead to increased female labor supply, could also have contributed to these fundamental demographic changes. Nevertheless, the mechanism of changing household technology is especially intriguing and these stories plausible of how it could have contributed to demographic changes.

ARE WE BETTER OFF FOR IT?

The issue of unforeseen changes in household composition coming as a consequence of household technology changes makes one less sure that technological changes are a clear gain. Even if household structures had remained unchanged, it is unclear that increased potential household (and/or market) production makes all household members unambiguously better off. To the extent that household structures are also affected, it may be even more likely that the unforeseen consequences of changing household technology could be, on average, negative. Let us consider how this could be the case.

In the case where household structures are static, whether household members spend more or less time in household production, it is still the case that the technology has made the household better off in total because of their increased production possibilities (including the possibility of having more time spent in leisure). Nonetheless, even if the household is made better off in total, the allocation of improvement between household members may or may not end up improving gender equity. For instance, in situations where women can increase production through their labor but do not have control over the increased product's distribution, it is not clear if their well-being is improved. In general, increased market work by women is likely to be associated with increased power, as it should improve women's bargaining positions within marriage due to better fallback positions.

However, better bargaining power positions do not automatically mean that one is better off. Perhaps more power, career advancement, and money are accompanied by more stress. Indeed, happiness research—a growing field in the social sciences—has led to some interesting findings. In particular, rising living standards do not automatically translate into improved happiness. For example, Stevenson and Wolfers (2009) look at changes in men's and women's self-reported happiness from 1972 to 2006 and find that women are now less happy both in absolute terms and relative to men. They argue that the myriad of demographic and work changes that have occurred over this period have overall disadvantaged women relative to men.

What about the children? Some indicators show declining well-being of children, while others show improvement. In the United States, children are now more likely to live in poverty than are older persons (age 65 and older). As incomes have risen in the United States and many other countries, there have been increased rates of childhood obesity (and adult obesity), with studies showing between a tripling and quadrupling of these rates since the 1960s (National Center for Health Statistics 2012). In contrast, infant and child mortality rates have fallen drastically, contributing substantially to increased lifespans. These increases in total lifespan, including higher value per year of life (often measured by disability-adjusted life-years), are significant. But many aspects of children's well-being are more challenging to measure, such as whether they are better or worse off in divorced families compared to intact families. Certainly, children in single-parent families tend to have lower levels of household resources per person. Thus, if technology changes have contributed to more single-parent families, this may be a net negative for children. The causal links between female labor force participation, demographic changes, and changes in well-being are not well established, however, and they need not be either stable or irreversible.

Given that household technology changes either have been accompanied by or have caused household composition changes, it is difficult to evaluate how much better off these changes have made people. One approach may be to ask people how much they are willing to give up to achieve various other goals—for instance, would they be willing to give up a dishwasher in exchange for a dependable spouse who would wash dishes by hand.

WHAT IS HAPPENING NOW IN DEVELOPING COUNTRIES?

It is clear from looking at worldwide adoption rates of household technology that invention is not a sufficient precondition for adoption.

Many countries lag well behind the United States and other industrialized countries in percentage of households owning various appliances. Clearly, income level is a more important factor as well as infrastructure development.

It has become relatively easy to access country-level data through household surveys and other (often industry) sources regarding the extent of connectivity and provision of water and electricity, along with the adoption of technologies that utilize this infrastructure, such as phones and household appliances.

Running water for the urban population in particular is mostly a given at this point in time, with 78 percent of the worldwide rural population and 96 percent of the urban population using improved water sources (modification from naturally occurring sources) as of 2008 (World Bank 2011), but there are notable variations in water provision for rural populations across regions and low rates of improvement for the rural population persist in low-income countries. Meanwhile, 65 percent of the worldwide rural population and 94 percent of the urban population had electricity available as of 2009 (International Energy Agency 2010).

Information on household use of electrified appliances for a number of lower-income countries is available through the Demographic and Health Surveys program. Information is available for urban and rural areas as well as an overall percentage of electrified households, and for the percentage of households (again by urban and rural areas as well as overall) that own a radio, a television, a phone (here meaning with a landline rather than a mobile phone), and a refrigerator. In general, rates of appliance ownership are lower than electrification rates (based on the view that electrification is a necessary precondition), but not always: it is possible to have a battery-powered appliance (particularly a radio or television), or to have access to television or radio through another household or location. Interestingly, the rates of television access are high—higher in many cases than for radio access, perhaps because households now find televisions to be more of a necessity than radios. Landlines are not particularly common, and their installation may lag further behind now that mobile phones provide a substitute product. Refrigerators are less common than televisions or radios in general, but more common than landline phones.

Data from the Socio-Economic Database for Latin America and the Caribbean can be used to track a broader group of household appliances including refrigerators, washers, and air conditioners. These data show relatively high rates of appliance availability, although washing machines and air conditioners are much less frequently found than refrigerators. The more middle-class and urbanized the country, the more household appliance acquisition looks like that found in U.S. middle-class households. Indeed, female labor force participation has been rising in such countries as well—and family sizes dropping. Thus a similar demographic transition appears to be occurring in currently industrializing countries—or parts of countries—where household technology has now become common.

In many low-income countries, particularly in rural areas, women continue to spend long hours every day collecting water and/or fuel. Time use studies from these countries often reveal results that hearken back to discussions of household production in the United States from the 19th century. For example, Schreiner (1999, 65) mentions "up to six hours per day" spent on fuel and water collection by women in her study in Bamshela, South Africa. Thus it appears that one way to free up women's time both for more productive uses and for leisure would be to reduce the time spent on those activities. Yet again, however, it turns out not to be straightforward how providing better access to fuel and water, or more efficient appliances that utilize fuel and water (in particular cooking appliances), affects time use.

Innovations to reduce the amount of time spent in procuring usable water abound, but generally relate to reducing the distance to the water source (e.g., digging a local well or bringing water closer by pipe or other means), improving its potability, increasing its quantity, and reducing the amount of physical effort necessary to get it (e.g., pumping technology). To date, the number of studies that have been able to find a measurable outcome related to improved access to water remains small; the two main focuses have been whether time is freed up for more market participation by women and whether there is better participation of children in schooling.

One issue is whether reducing distance to the water source actually reduces the amount of time allocated to water collection. Again, as the cost of collection decreases, it is possible that households decide to allocate more rather than less time to water collection and usage, at least in an intermediate range where water is not available at the turn of a faucet in one's house, but is made closer at hand than previously. A study by Ilahi and Grimard (2000), using data from Pakistan, reveals that greater distance to a water source does increase the time spent in water collection for women and decrease their participation in income-generating activities. However, in households with "private water technology" (as opposed to public infrastructure outside the home), women spend the freed-up time on leisure rather than on market work. Menon (2009), using 1995–1996 household data from Nepal, focuses on the predictability of water rather than distance to source, and finds that household members, including women, are less likely to work in agriculture if rainfall in their area is less predictable, implying that improving water source predictability would increase agricultural activities.

Several other studies find little effect on off-farm work for women, including the study conducted by Koolwal and van der Walle (2010), using data from countries in several regions (sub-Saharan Africa, South Asia, and Middle East-North Africa). This was also the case in earlier studies carried out by Lokshin and Yemtsov (2005) for rural Georgia between 1998 and 2001 (no effect on women's wage employment) and by Costa et al. (2009) for rural Ghana.

However, these studies do find other measurable effects. Koolwal and van der Walle (2010) note that both boys' and girls' enrollments in school rise as the time spent collecting water falls. They also find some improvements in children's health in data from Yemen and Malawi. Lokshin and Yemtsov (2005) find a significant reduction in the incidence of water-borne diseases due to the improvements in water supply. Costa et al. (2009) find a reduced time burden on women, but with no increase in the time spent on paid work.

While a number of potential substitutes for traditional fuel sources used for cooking and lighting (mainly wood) exist, including solar power, rechargeable or long-lasting batteries, and propane, electricity can serve as a substitute as well as being usable in many other ways. Thus, we might expect electricity to have perhaps a more significant effect on women's market labor than does water, because not only does it free up time spent getting fuel, but it also may be complementary to other market-related activities.

Indeed, Costa et al. (2009) find that in rural Ghana, unlike for improved water supply, improved electricity availability increases the time spent in remunerated activities. Similarly, Dinkelman (2010) reports that in South Africa, women's employment rates increased significantly (by about 9.5 percentage points) in electrified areas; men's employment was not significantly affected. Grogan and Sadanand (2009) find a similar effect for rural Guatemala, with electrification associated with women spending more time in market work and having increased earnings.

In contrast to these rather sizable effects of improved electricity service, simply improving fuel efficiency by creating more efficient cooking stoves has not been very successful to date. Otsyina and Rosenberg (1999) mention how the rate of adoption of improved stoves (less wood needed, less smoke produced) in the area they studied in rural Tanzania was quite low. They stress the problems in disseminating the technical knowledge necessary to construct and utilize the stoves, pointing out that transmission of this knowledge is related to gender roles: the women (who would be the primary users of the stoves) were not used to attending technical workshops and were not out and around in the world as much as the men to learn new things. Indeed, more successful adoption of improved cook stoves in Kenya was achieved due to more attention paid to dissemination and training (International Centre for Research on Women 2010, 14).

However, the issue of what is done with freed-up labor time, if indeed time is freed up at all, still looms in the back of planners' minds. For countries with apparent excess labor, the advantage of labor-saving devices may not be obvious, and neoclassical economists' views regarding increased productivity leading to higher demand for labor may not be sufficiently enticing. Indeed, one reason we do not see larger paid work effects from improved water supply may be that there are no paid work opportunities for the women to step into, particularly in rural areas. Hessler's profile of former Peace Corps member Rajeev Goyal, who successfully developed a pipe-and-pump water delivery system for Namje, a remote Nepalese village, mentions Goyal's concern with "what Namje women would do now that they no longer spent six hours a day hauling water" (Hessler 2010, 106). In this case, the women started a women's co-op and made hats for export (which Goyal sold), but after a while this plan fell through. Without sufficient human and physical capital available that is complementary to paid work, it is not clear that the time can be rechanneled into remunerated work. Thus the secondary development issue is how to develop such outlets once the necessary infrastructure of water and electricity delivery, along with more efficient household technology, is laid down.

WHAT WILL HAPPEN NEXT?

The most unsatisfying part of an economics essay is always the part where the author tries to predict what will happen next. Economists are notoriously bad at prediction (and only slightly better at explanation after the fact). Thus this section should be viewed as pure speculation.

For those countries discussed in the preceding section, as urbanization continues to increase and incomes rise, it is likely that they will complete the technological transition to levels similar to those found in the industrialized world. Nevertheless, they are more likely to model European levels of appliance usage (smaller kitchens, including smaller stoves and refrigerators; smaller washers and less use of clothes dryers) than the U.S. levels of appliance usage, given the likely rising costs of energy and greater space constraints in urban areas.

For those countries already experiencing practically 100 percent supply of home electricity, running water, and refrigeration, it appears that in many ways the technological revolution of mechanizing household production so as to reduce labor hours and effort in home production has run its course. Anyone who has perused the Williams-Sonoma catalog knows that the types of mechanized appliances now offered to customers are either increasingly specialized tools (panini presses; espresso makers) or minor variants on existing concepts (countertop convection ovens; single-serving coffee machines). Other appliances actually signal a rejection of time-saving (and often less costly) market substitutes for more labor-intensive home production methods (home baby food makers, juicers).

This trend may in part reflect the fact that people are not so interested in being liberated from home production as they are in being liberated from the backbreaking, repetitive aspects of household production. Far fewer modern households choose to eschew hot running water and electricity in favor of pumping well water, burning candles to read by, and gathering firewood. The modern middle-class household gets to choose how to manage its household production, rather than having to do it as a matter of life or death. Also, to the extent that household production can serve as an outlet for creative expression, choosing to make one's own clothing and bake one's own bread moves into the realm of leisure activity and out of the realm of necessity. In particular, for retired persons as well as persons who choose to reduce their market hours, household production can become the wanted rather than the dreaded.

At the same time, many traditional household activities are passing out of the realm of active knowledge transmission from parent to child and into the realm of book learning. It is a rare parent nowadays who instructs their child in sewing and home canning. It is unlikely that these skills will be widely revived.

Meanwhile, other household skills, particularly the ability to manage household finances, including making large investment decisions (saving for retirement, for children's education; purchasing a second home or a time-share), have become more salient. Households that master personal finance skills will likely outperform households that do not in terms of maximizing lifetime consumption paths.

Any additional revolution in home technology awaits the invention of more fully roboticized home production. While isolated technologies, such as the Roomba robot vacuum cleaners, have become more common, full-scale robotization of additional routine home activities appears unlikely without the development of multipurpose robots that can essentially manipulate objects more similarly to humans as well as self-perambulate about the house. It is unlikely that such technologies will be introduced anytime soon, as current labor prices will still make servants and maid services a more cost-effective means of factor substitution for the foreseeable future.

Thus the fundamental dilemma—that everyone would like to have a "wife" to do things around the house—remains unsolved. Until the inventions of robotic housekeepers, self-cleaning houses, and self-cooking dinners come to fruition, the issues of how to do housework and who will do it remain part of the human condition.

REFERENCES

Albanesi, Stefania, and Claudia Olivetti. *Gender Roles and Technological Progress.* National Bureau of Economic Research Working Paper No. 13179. Cambridge, MA: NBER, June 2007.

Black, Sandra E., and Chinhui Juhn. "The Rise of Female Professionals: Are Women Responding to Skill Demand?" *American Economic Review* 90 (2000): 450–455.

Bose, Christine E., and Philip L. Berano. "Household Technologies: Burden or Blessing?" In *The Technological Woman: Interfacing with Tomorrow,* edited by Jan Zimmerman, 83–93. New York: Praeger, 1983.

Cardia, Emanuela. *Household Technology: Was It the Engine of Liberation?* Working paper. Montreal, Canada: Universite de Montreal and CIREQ, 2010.

Cavalcanti, Tiago V. de V., and José Tavares. "Assessing the 'Engines of Liberation': Home Appliances and Female Labor Force Participation." *Review of Economics and Statistics* 90 (2008): 81–88.

Coen-Pirani, Daniele, Alexis León, and Steven Lugauer. "The Effect of Household Appliances on Female Labor Force Participation: Evidence from Microdata." *Labour Economics* 17 (2010): 503–513.

Connelly, Rachel, and Jean Kimmel. *The Time Use of Mothers in the United States at the Beginning of the 21st Century.* Kalamazoo, MI: Upjohn, 2010.

Costa, Joana, Degol Hailu, Elydia Silva, and Raquel Tsukada. "The Implications of Water and Electricity Supply for the Time Allocation of Women in Rural Ghana." International Policy Centre for Inclusive Growth (Brasilia), 2009. http://hdl.handle.net/10419/71815.

Council of Economic Advisors. *Economic Report of the President.* Washington, DC: Government Printing Office, 2012.

Cowan, Ruth Schwartz. *More Work for Mother: The Ironies of Household Technology from the Open Hearth to the Microwave.* New York: Basic Books, 1983.

Demographic and Health Surveys Program. http://www.measuredhs.com/.

Dinkelman, Taryn. *The Effects of Rural Electrification on Employment: New Evidence from South Africa.* Princeton University Research Program in Development Studies Working Paper no. 272. Princeton, NJ: Princeton University, 2010.

"Electric Washing Machine the Latest. Housewives Can Do Washing in One-Third the Time." *Des Moines Daily Capitol* (November 12, 1904): 13.

Fernández, Raquel, Alessandra Fogli, and Claudia Olivetti. *Marrying Your Mom: Preference Transmission and Women's Labor and Education Choices.* National Bureau of Economic Research Working Paper No. 9234. Cambridge, MA: NBER, October 2002. http://www.nber.org/papers/w9234

Fox, Bonnie J. "Selling the Mechanized Household: 70 Years of Ads in *Ladies Home Journal.*" *Gender and Society* 4 (1990): 25–40.

Goldin, Claudia, and Lawrence F. Katz. "The Power of the Pill: Contraceptives and Women's Career and Marriage Decisions." *Journal of Political Economy* 110 (2002): 730–770.

Greenwood, Jeremy, and Nezih Guner. *Marriage and Divorce since World War II: Analyzing the Role of Technological Progress on the*

Formation of Households. IZA Discussion Paper No. 3313. Bonn, Germany: Institute for the Study of Labor, January 2008.

Greenwood, Jeremy, Nezih Guner, Georgi Kocharkov, and Cezar Santos. *Technology and the Changing Family: A Unified Model of Marriage, Divorce, Educational Attainment and Married Female Labor Force Participation.* National Bureau of Economic Research Working Paper No. 17735. Cambridge, MA: NBER, January 2012.

Greenwood, Jeremy, Ananth Seshadri, and Mehmet Yorukoglu. "Engines of Liberation." *Review of Economic Studies* 72 (2005): 109–133.

Grogan, Louise, and Asha Sadanand. *Electrification and the Household.* Working paper. Guelph, Canada: University of Guelph, 2009.

Hessler, Peter. "Village Voice." *The New Yorker* (December 20 and 27, 2010): 100–109.

Ilahi, Nadeem, and Franque Grimard. "Public Infrastructure and Private Costs: Water Supply and Time Allocation of Women in Rural Pakistan." *Economic Development and Cultural Change* 49 (2000): 45–75.

International Center for Research on Women. *Bridging the Gender Divide: How Technology Can Advance Women Economically.* Washington, DC: International Center for Research on Women, 2010.

International Energy Agency. *World Energy Outlook 2010.* Paris: International Energy Agency, 2010.

Jones, Larry E., Rodolfo E. Manuelli, and Ellen R. McGrattan. *Why Are Married Women Working So Much?* Federal Reserve Bank of Minneapolis Research Department Staff Report 317. Minneapolis, MN: Federal Reserve Bank of Minneapolis, June 2003.

Koolwal, Gayatri, and Dominique van der Walle. *Access to Water, Women's Work and Child Outcomes.* World Bank Policy Research Working Paper no. 5302. Washington, DC: World Bank, 2010.

Lebergott, Stanley. *Pursuing Happiness: American Consumers in the Twentieth Century.* Princeton, NJ: Princeton University Press, 1993.

Lokshin, Michael, and Ruslan Yemtsov. "Has Rural Infrastructure Rehabilitation in Georgia Helped the Poor?" *World Bank Economic Review* 19 (2005): 311–333.

Manning, S. *Time Use in Household Tasks by Indiana Families.* Purdue University Research Bulletin no. 837. Purdue, IN: Purdue University, 1968.

Margolis, Maxine. "In Hartford, Hannibal, and (New) Hampshire, Heloise Is Hardly Helpful." *Ms.* 4 (1976): 28–36.

Margolis, Maxine L. *Mothers and Such: Views of American Women and Why They Changed.* Berkeley, CA: University of California, 1984.

McNeil, Ian. *An Encyclopedia of the History of Technology.* London, UK: Routledge, 1990.

Menon, Nidhiya. "Rainfall Uncertainty and Occupational Choice in Agricultural Households of Rural Nepal." *Journal of Development Studies* 45 (2009): 864–888.

Mokyr, Joel. "Why 'More Work for Mother?' Knowledge and Household Behavior, 1870–1945." *Journal of Economic* History 60 (2000): 1–41.

National Center for Health Statistics. *Prevalence of Obesity in the United States 2009–10.* NCHS data brief. Atlanta, GA: Center for Disease Control, January 2012.

National Center for Health Statistics. *Vital Statistics Reports.* (Various years).

Oropesa, R. S. "Female Labor Force Participation and Time-Saving Household Technology: A Case Study of the Microwave from 1978 to 1989." *Journal of Consumer Research* 19 (1993): 567–579.

Otsyina, Joyce A., and Diana Rosenberg. "Rural Development and Women: What Are the Best Approaches to Communicating Information?" In *Gender and Technology,* edited by Caroline Sweetman, 45–55. Oxford, UK: Oxfam, 1999.

Ramey, Valerie A. "Time Spent in Home Production in the Twentieth-Century United States: New Estimates from Old Data." *Journal of Economic History* 69 (2009): 1–47.

Robinson, John P., and Geoffrey Godbey. *Time for Life: The Surprising Ways Americans Use Their Time.* University Park, PA: Pennsylvania State University, 1997.

Robinson, John P., and Melissa Milkie. "Dances with Dust Bunnies." *American Demographics* 19 (1997): 37–59.

Schreiner, Heather. "Rural Women, Development, and Telecommunications: A Pilot Programme in South Africa." In *Gender and Technology,* edited by Caroline Sweetman, 64–70. Oxford, UK: Oxfam, 1999.

Smith, James P., and Michael Ward. "Time-Series Growth in the Female Labor Force." *Journal of Labor Economics* 3 (1985): S59–S90.

Socio-Economic Database for Latin America and the Caribbean. http://sedlac.econo.unlp.edu.ar/eng/.

Stanley, Autumn. *Mothers and Daughters of Invention: Notes for a Revised History of Technology.* New Brunswick, NJ: Rutgers University Press, 1995.

Stevenson, Betsey, and Justin Wolfers. "Marriage and Divorce: Changes and Their Driving Forces." *Journal of Economic Perspectives* 21 (2007): 27–52.

Stevenson, Betsey, and Justin Wolfers. "The Paradox of Declining Female Happiness." *American Economic Journal: Economic Policy* 1 (2009): 190–225.

U.S. Bureau of the Census. *Historical Statistics of the United States.* Washington, DC: Government Printing Office, 1976.

U.S. Bureau of the Census. *Statistical Abstract of the United States.* Washington, DC: Government Printing Office, 2004.

U.S. Bureau of the Census. "America's Family and Living Arrangements." 2011a. http://www.census.gov/hhes/families/data/cps2011.html.

U.S. Bureau of the Census. "Estimated Median Age at First Marriage, by Sex: 1890 to the Present." 2011b. http://www.census.gov/population/socdemo/hh-fam/ms2.xls.

U.S. Bureau of the Census. *Current Population Reports*, Series P-60. (Various years).

U.S. Bureau of Labor Statistics. "American Time Use Survey." (Various years). http://www.bls.gov/tus/tables.htm.

U.S. Bureau of Labor Statistics. *Women in the Labor Force: A Databook.* Report 1034. Washington, DC: Bureau of Labor Statistics, 2011.

Vanek, Joann. "Time Spent in Housework." *Scientific American* 231 (1974): 116–120.

Vanek, Joann. "Household Technology and Social Status: Rising Living Standards and Status and Residence Differences in Housework." *Technology and Culture* 19 (1978): 361–375.

Weiss, Thomas. "Revised Estimates of the United States Workforce, 1800–1860." In *Long-Term Factors in American Economic Growth*, edited by Stanley L. Engerman and Robert E. Gallman, 641–676. Chicago, IL: University of Chicago Press, 1986.

World Bank. "World Development Indicators Database." 2011. http://data.worldbank.org/data-catalog/world-development-indicators.

Chapter 6

Nontraditional Families, Alternative Households

Lisa K. Jepsen

Social scientists investigate many types of households, including traditional married families, same-sex couples, cohabiting but unmarried opposite-sex couples, single parents, and polygamous households (Ferber [2003] provides a brief summary of polygamous families). Households produce workers for labor markets; they produce children as well. But households also consume goods and services such as housing and health care. The decision to form a household will depend on what the individuals (whoever they may be) expect to get out of the commitment. Over the past few decades, economists have had access to data that allow us to investigate whether the choices of households are influenced by sexual orientation. Differences in labor market outcomes by sexual orientation are well studied. Much less well studied are potential differences in consumption and personal health and well-being. Many of the studies examined in this chapter build on Gary Becker's theories of the household. Those theories generate different predictions for same-sex couples than they do for opposite-sex couples, whether formally married or simply cohabiting.

The organization of this chapter is complicated by the "Which came first—the chicken or the egg?" problem. I would like to distinguish household production decisions from household consumption decisions. If I could disentangle the two types of decisions, I could present first the inputs into the household production function, including the human capital and demographic traits that influence couple formation. I could then transition to the outputs of the household, including intra-household bargaining models, labor supplied (both within the household and to the external labor market), children, housing, and overall health and well-being. Unfortunately, I cannot clearly separate production from consumption because the data we use to study such decisions rarely allow us to distinguish between decisions made before versus after individuals form a household.

Because most studies of same-sex couples reference Becker's theories of marriage markets and specialization, this chapter begins with Becker's theories. Because data limitations greatly influence how we analyze nontraditional households, the second section discusses the most commonly used sources of data. Research on couple formation is then presented. It seems reasonable to assume that many human capital acquisition and labor supply decisions are influenced by the types of households in which individuals live or expect to live. Thus the couple formation section is followed by a discussion of intra-household bargaining models, human capital acquisition, and labor markets. The chapter concludes with topics concerned with the outputs of household production functions: children, housing, and overall health and well-being.

The number of states that offer legal marriage to same-sex couples is increasing. As more same-sex couples marry, economists will have greater opportunities to compare the households and families of homosexual couples to those of heterosexual couples. Consequently, this chapter offers a look at research in progress.

BECKER'S THEORIES

Gary Becker lays the foundation for the study of the economics of households in *A Treatise on the Family* (1991, enlarged edition). Treating a family or household as an economic unit opens the door to questions like "What is a family?" and consideration of which factors play a role in household formation and role specialization within established households. Becker (1991) uses the terms "household" and "family" interchangeably, but his theories apply to people living together who can make joint decisions.

Becker suggests that individuals select a mate in the same fashion as they select other goods—by maximizing utility. People want mates who are similar to them with respect to age, race, and education.

Becker classifies such traits as complements and predicts the matching of likes with likes, a process he calls positive assortative mating.

Once formed, households maximize household utility, which suggests that they may make different decisions than individuals would make. For example, if I were single, I would live close to the university where I work. But my husband and I work more than 60 miles apart, so I commute much farther than I would if I were maximizing my individual utility rather than my household utility. Because couples maximize household utility rather than individual utility, they may allocate more hours of one member to the labor market and more hours of the other member to home production.

Married, opposite-sex couples have the greatest incentives to specialize because the woman has the legal protections of marriage. She may have legal access to her husband's earnings if they divorce, which may increase her willingness to give up the acquisition of market-based human capital. Becker's key assumption underlying specialization is that an hour of women's household or market time is not a perfect substitute for an hour of men's time, even when both make the same investments in human capital. If women have a comparative advantage over men in the household sector, when they make the same investments in human capital, an efficient household with both sexes would allocate the time of women mainly to the household sector and the time of men mainly to the market sector (Becker 1991, 38).

Becker's models begin with the controversial assumption that women have a comparative advantage in raising children. The assumption is based on the biological advantages he sees that women have in bearing and caring for infants. Historically, women's life expectancies were short. Short life expectancies coupled with high fertility rates meant that women were pregnant, nursing young babies, or raising small children for most of their adult lives without access to day care, disposable diapers, or washing machines. In such settings, families where the woman stayed home and the man worked in the market likely created the best chances of success for the children. Ferber (2003) suggests that Becker's arguments exhibit circular reasoning: "For this essentially amounts to arguing that women spend more time in the household because men have a relative advantage in the labor market, and men have a relative advantage in the labor market because women spend more time in the household" (11).

Although Becker focuses on a traditional, nuclear family consisting of a husband as the head of household, his wife, and their children, he does discuss alternative family models and briefly mentions same-sex couples. Becker (1991) contends that "households with only men or only women are less efficient because they are unable to profit from the sexual division of comparative advantage" (38–39).

If we believe that specialization is based on gender, the incentives to specialize should be stronger for cohabiting (though unmarried) opposite-sex couples than for cohabiting same-sex couples, whereas the incentives for cohabiting (though unmarried) opposite-sex couples will be weaker than the incentives for married couples because the woman lacks the legal protections of marriage. Becker's theories of specialization also predict that husbands in formally married, opposite-sex couples will work more hours in the labor force and earn higher wages than their wives. Large differences between the earnings of men and women in opposite-sex couples are consistent with Becker's theories. The predictions for same-sex couples are much less clear.

AVAILABLE DATA

Empirical studies that consider sexual orientation are limited by the availability of data sets that identify sexual orientation, contain information about both heterosexuals and homosexuals, and include the typical labor market and demographic variables of interest to economists such as earnings or wages, education, age or work experience, race, gender, and occupation and industry. Three U.S. data sets are most commonly used: the decennial Census, the General Social Survey (GSS), and the National Health and Social Life Survey (NHSLS).

The U.S. Census Bureau classifies a household as a "family" if there is a head of household and at least one other person who selects one of the following categories: husband or wife, child (biological, adopted, or stepchild), brother or sister, father or mother, grandchild, parent-in-law, son- or daughter-in-law, or other relative. Nonfamily households include single people or people who live with a roomer, boarder, housemate, roommate, *unmarried partner*, or other nonrelative (Lofquist, Lugaila, O'Connell, and Feliz 2012). The option of "unmarried partner" first became available in the 1990 Census.

The U.S. Census Bureau provides statistics on households by family type from the decennial Census. Table 6.1 and Figure 6.1 show the percentages of "family" and "nonfamily" households for 1990, 2000, and 2010.

Table 6.1   Percentages of Households by Type

	1990	2000	2010
Family			
Married couples	55.1	51.7	48.4
Other	15.0	16.4	18.1
Nonfamily			
One person	24.6	25.8	26.7
Other	5.3	6.1	6.8

Sources: Hobbs and Stoops (2002), Figure 5-9; Lofquist et al. (2012), Table 3.

The Census classifies an unmarried-partner couple as either a family household or a nonfamily household depending on who else lives in the household. If a family member as described previously—most likely a child—lives with the unmarried couple, then the Census classifies the couple as a family. If no children or other family member lives with the unmarried couple, then the Census classifies the couple as a nonfamily household.

Two trends in the data are apparent. Married couples as a percentage of total U.S. households declined from 55 percent in 1990 to 48 percent in 2010. That said, they still account for roughly half of all

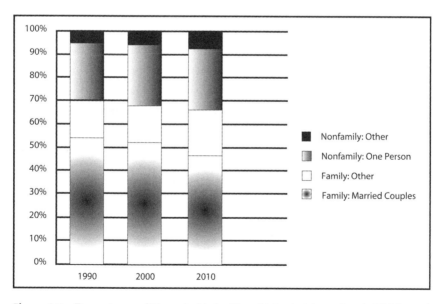

Figure 6.1   Percentages of Households by Type (Adapted from data in Hobbs and Stoops (2002), Figure 5-9; Lofquist et al. (2012), Table 3.)

households in the United States. Single-person households, often senior citizens, have increased from 15 percent of total households in 1990 to 18 percent in 2010.

Beginning with the 1990 decennial Census and continuing with the 2000 and 2010 Censuses, the category of "unmarried partner" has been an option for how someone is related to the head of household. Researchers use the genders of the head of household and the partner, along with the selection of "unmarried partner," to identify same-sex couples. For example, if the head of household is a woman and she lives with an unmarried partner who is also a woman, researchers typically label this household as a cohabiting lesbian couple. The same process works to identify a gay male cohabiting couple. If the head of household and the unmarried partner are of opposite genders, researchers identify the couple as a cohabiting but not legally married opposite-sex couple. Black et al. (2000) investigate possible misidentification of homosexuals in the Census, GSS, and NHSLS. They find consistency across all three data sets and do not find evidence of systemic misclassification provided that researchers do not use observations with allocated values.

A major advantage of using Census data is the large, nationally representative sample surveyed. Other data sets created by the Census Bureau that provide similar ways to identify cohabiting homosexuals include the Current Population Survey (CPS) and the American Community Survey (ACS), but the number of observations in them is smaller.

Future research will be limited by the change in Census procedures. Beginning with the 2010 Census, the government stopped distributing the "long form" to U.S. households. Thus, economists will no longer have individual-level data about age, education, race, and income for a sample of the almost 309 million people living in the United States (the 2010 population size according to www.census.gov). The American Community Survey (ACS) will fill some of this gap. The ACS surveys approximately 3 million households each year and includes questions about each individual's age, race, education, income, relationship to the head of household, and other questions from the decennial Census "long form."

Homosexuals living with their partners may not be choosing the unmarried partner designation, but could be selecting "roommate," instead. Consequently, the Census data likely undercount same-sex couples. That said, the couples who do identify as unmarried partners are probably the most likely to be "out" and, therefore, represent a useful sample from which to study economic outcomes and status. The greatest limitation of using Census data is the inability to identify sexual orientation at the individual level rather than the couple level.

Table 6.2 reports the percentage of U.S. households by type. Clearly, the percentage of married households is declining, whereas the percentage of people who live alone is increasing. The percentage of

Table 6.2   Households by Type Census Data

	1990	2000	2010
Total number of U.S. households	91,993,582	105,480,101	116,716,292
(% of total households)	100%	100%	100%
Single-person households	22,421,114	27,230,075	31,204,909
	24.4%	25.8%	26.7%
Husband-wife households	51,718,214	54,493,232	56,510,377
	56.2%	51.7%	48.4%
Unmarried partner households (all gender combinations)	3,225,626	5,475,768	7,744,711
	3.5%	5.2%	6.6%
Opposite-sex unmarried partner households	3,080,496	4,881,377	6,842,714
	3.3%	4.6%	5.9%
Same-sex male partner households*	81,343	301,026	425,279
	0.1%	0.3%	0.4%
Same-sex male unmarried partner households	N/A	N/A	265,470
Same-sex male spousal partner households	N/A	N/A	159,809
Same-sex female partner households*	63,787	293,365	476,718
	0.1%	0.3%	0.4%
Same-sex female unmarried partner households	N/A	N/A	287,150
Same-sex female spousal partner households	N/A	N/A	189,568

*In the 1990 and 2000 Censuses, same-sex couples who selected "spouse" rather than "unmarried partner" were reclassified as an "unmarried partner" household. No states had legalized same-sex marriages in either 1990 or 2000. In the 2010 Census, the two options are reported separately, which reflects the availability of legalized same-sex marriages in some states.

Sources: Adapted from data in Gates (2007); Hobbs (2005); Lofquist et al. (2012); Simmons and O'Connell (2003).

cohabiting couples is increasing, in part because people are delaying marriage. Both the number of same-sex households and the percentage of total households that same-sex couples represent increased from 1990 to 2000 and again from 2000 to 2010. This increase is likely due to more homosexuals being willing to identify themselves as members of unmarried couples rather than hide the nature of their living arrangement (Gates 2007).

Beginning in 1989, National Opinion Research Center (NORC), which administers the GSS and the NHSLS, added questions on sexual behaviors to its survey instruments. The GSS already included questions about labor market outcomes such as income and occupation. The survey now asks two questions related to sexual orientation: (1) "Now thinking about the time since your 18th birthday (including the past 12 months) how many male partners have you had sex with?" and (2) "Now thinking about the time since your 18th birthday (including the past 12 months) how many female partners have you had sex with?" (Badgett 1995, 730).

Economists classify respondents as "gay" or "lesbian" based on the responses to these questions. For example, in her groundbreaking study, Badgett (1995) uses four methods for identifying someone as a homosexual: (1) if the person had at least one same-sex sexual partner, (2) if the person had more than one same-sex sexual partner, (3) if the person had at least as many same-sex as opposite-sex sexual partners, and (4) if a person met the conditions in either (2) or (3) (731). An advantage of the GSS data is that, unlike Census data, they allow researchers to identify homosexual individuals based on individuals' responses. There are, however, three substantial disadvantages: The sample sizes are small (34 lesbian/bisexual women and 47 gay/bisexual men in Badgett's study), information about income is categorical, and some of the people who fit the definition of gay men or lesbian women identify themselves as married, which clouds the issue of whether their employers would view them as homosexuals. Because same-sex marriage was not available at the time of the survey, most researchers assumed that "married" people were married to a member of the opposite sex.

The NHSLS also contains data on sexual behavior, sexual partners, and demographic and labor market characteristics. The overall number of observations is relatively large, but, similar to the GSS, the number of gay/bisexual men and lesbian/bisexual women is relatively small. The main advantage is that the sample is randomly collected and nationally representative. Badgett (2001) provides an excellent summary of the NORC data sources.

A few more recent data sets provide information on sexual orientation and economic characteristics. The California Health Interview Survey (Carpenter 2005) is a confidential survey that was administered to approximately 50,000 households in 2001. It asked each adult, "Are you gay/lesbian or bisexual?" The survey also contained demographic, earnings, and occupational information. The Centers for Disease Control and Prevention (CDC) administers a telephone survey called the Behavioral Risk Factor Surveillance System (Carpenter 2004). Researchers identify same-sex couples the same way as they do in the Census. The CDC survey includes detailed questions about sexual behaviors and family planning that allow researchers to more accurately distinguish same-sex couples from individuals of the same sex in other living arrangements. The Third National Health and Nutrition Examination Survey (Carpenter 2005) was administered to almost 40,000 households between 1988 and 1994. Because the survey contained questions about the number of male and female sexual partners, researchers can identify homosexuals the same way as they do for the GSS.

Data exist for several countries outside of the United States—Australia (Carpenter 2008a), Canada (Carpenter 2008b), Greece (Drydakis 2011, 2012), the Netherlands (Plug and Berkhout 2004), and the United Kingdom (Arabsheibani, Marin, and Wadsworth 2004, 2005; Booth and Frank 2008; Frank 2006)—that allow researchers to compare economic outcomes for homosexuals and heterosexuals.

COUPLE FORMATION

Individuals form couples when the utility of being in a family exceeds the utility of being single (see Grossbard and Jepsen [2008] for a theoretical model). A well-developed literature models marriage markets for heterosexuals. Heterosexuals have access to legal marriage, so if they form a couple they can choose between cohabitation or marriage. Recently, homosexuals have had more options to formalize their status as a couple. Badgett and Herman (2011) provide a thorough review of the status of the legal options. At present, 22 states and the District of Columbia offer some form of legal recognition to same-sex couples. The options include marriage, civil unions, and registered domestic partnerships. Table 6.3 illustrates the available options by state.

Badgett and Herman (2011) estimate that approximately 22 percent of same-sex couples have entered into some form of legal recognition, with women more likely to take legal action than men. Almost half of all same-sex couples live in states that offer some legal recognition, meaning that they have access to legal benefits based on their partnership (Badgett and Herman 2011).

Several economic studies focus on homosexual partnerships. Carpenter and Gates (2008) analyze the prevalence of gay and lesbian partnership and cohabitation in California. Using data from two large telephone surveys (California's 2003 Lesbian, Gay, Bisexual, and Transgender Tobacco Survey and the California Health Interview Survey), they find that a lower percentage of gay men are in partnerships than heterosexual men, while the partnership rates are similar for lesbians and heterosexual women.

As illustrated in Table 6.3, registered domestic partnerships are a common alternative to marriage for same-sex couples. Like Carpenter and Gates (2008), Badgett et al. (2008) use data from the Lesbian, Gay, Bisexual, and Transgender Tobacco Survey. They find that couples who have been together longer are more likely to register for a formal domestic partnership than couples who have been together for a shorter length of time. Income is positively related to such registration, but only for men. Women are more likely to register than men, a result that is consistent with a study of civil unions in Vermont and marriages in Massachusetts (Rothblum, Balsam, and Solomon 2008). Using Granger causality tests, Graham and Barr (2008) consider whether the increasing number of same-sex couples has caused either a decrease in the number of married couples or an increase in the number of cohabiting but unmarried opposite-sex couples. Their results do not suggest causation.

Denmark, Norway, and Sweden first offered registered partnerships in 1989, 1993, and 1995, respectively (Andersson, Noack, Seierstad, and Weedon-Fekjaer 2006). The Netherlands, Belgium, Spain, and Canada followed with laws that allowed for an equivalent status to marriage. Andersson et al. (2006) profile the characteristics of couples with registered partnerships in Norway and Sweden. They find that the majority of the registered domestic partnerships in Norway and Sweden are partnered males and that the chances of divorce are higher for same-sex partnerships than opposite-sex married couples.

Jepsen and Jepsen (2002) find evidence of positive assortative mating with respect to the traits Becker categorizes as complements—age,

Table 6.3 Legal Recognition Options for Same-Sex Couples in the United States

Partnership Recognition Type		State/District	Effective
		Massachusetts	2004
		California	2008*, 2013[†]
		Connecticut	2008
		Iowa	2009
	Available to both	Vermont	2009
Marriage	same-sex and	New Hampshire	2009
	different-sex couples.	District of Columbia	2010
		New York	2011
		Washington	2012[†]
		Maine	2012[†]
		Maryland	2013[†]
		Rhode Island	2013[†]
		Delaware	2013[†]
		Minnesota	2013
		New Mexico	2013
		Hawaii	2013
		New Jersey	2013
		Utah*	2013
		Illinois	2014
		Pennsylvania	2014
		Oregon	2014
		Virginia*	2014
		California	2000, 2005
	All state-level rights	District of Columbia	2002, 2006
	and responsibilities	New Jersey	2007
Civil union/	associated with marriage.	Oregon	2007
broad	Available to same-sex	Washington	2007, 2009
domestic	couples and some	Nevada	2009
partnership	unmarried different-sex	Illinois	2011
	couples.	Rhode Island	2011
		Delaware	2012
		Hawaii	2012
		Colorado	2013*
	A limited set of rights	Hawaii	1997
	and responsibilities		
Limited	that vary by state.	Maine	2004
domestic	Sometimes available		
partnership/	only to same-sex	New Jersey	2004
reciprocal	couples, sometimes		
beneficiary/	also to unmarried	Maryland	2008
designated	different-sex couples,		
beneficiary	and sometimes to two	Colorado	2009

(*continued*)

Table 6.3   (Continued)

Partnership Recognition Type	State/District	Effective
individuals who may not be a couple.	Wisconsin	2009

*June 16 to November 5, 2008.
†Recent changes.; * Stay pending
Source: M. V. Lee Badgett and Jody L. Herman, *Patterns of Relationship Recognition by Same-Sex Couples in the United States*, (Los Angeles, CA: Williams Institute, University of California-Los Angeles School of Law, 2011), Table 1. Used by permission; recent updates from the National Gay and Lesbian Task Force www.theTaskForce.org May 20, 2014.

race, and education—for both homosexual and heterosexual couples. Members of married couples are the most alike in these traits. For labor market variables such as earnings and hours worked, these researchers find evidence of positive assortative mating, which does not support Becker's theories. The positive association is weakest for married couples, which suggests that they may specialize more than other couples.

INTRA-HOUSEHOLD BARGAINING

Economists model the bargaining process within households to analyze negotiating power and its influence on the division of household labor. Traditionally, men have had higher educational levels, more labor market experience, and higher earnings than women; hence, they have enjoyed more bargaining power. In households where men have greater bargaining power, women perform more household labor. Same-sex households may be more egalitarian in their divisions of household labor, although it is possible for one member to possess more bargaining power and negotiate an unequal division of household labor. Thus, bargaining models may suggest differences in labor market outcomes due to sexual orientation.

Grossbard-Shechtman (2003) develops a model of intra-household bargaining where one spouse specializes more in market production and the other specializes more in home production. The spouse who specializes in market production induces the other spouse to participate in some form of home production (such as doing laundry or cooking dinner) either by offering an exchange of alternative home production (e.g., "I will mow the yard if you will make dinner") or by offering what Grossbard-Shechtman calls a quasi-wage payment or transfer (e.g., "I will purchase a country club membership from my earnings for the entire family if you will make dinner each night").

Grossbard and Jepsen (2008) apply Grossbard's household bargaining theory to same-sex households. They postulate that gay men may be less likely to form couples than heterosexual men, heterosexual women, or lesbians because they may gain less from a potential mate in terms of household production. If women are more willing to supply household production than men, a lesbian couple may be more likely to have a more egalitarian division of household labor and thus market labor. If lesbians are more willing to offer household labor, they do not need a transfer from a partner who specializes in market production. This theory is consistent with the empirical results of Badgett et al. (2008), who find that higher incomes are not significantly correlated with higher probabilities of partnership for lesbians.

Klawitter (2008) considers whether bargaining differs by couple type by comparing how same-sex and opposite-sex couples hold their bank account assets. She uses intra-couple differences in education, work experience, and health as proxies for differences in bargaining power. Using banking data from the U.S. Survey of Consumer Finances, this author shows that both same-sex and opposite-sex unmarried couples are less likely to have joint banking accounts than married couples. The measures for bargaining power are not statistically significant in some models, but her results suggest that if bargaining power matters, it might matter more for same-sex and unmarried opposite-sex couples than for married couples.

Oreffice (2011) estimates the effects of bargaining within couples by analyzing the labor supply decisions of spouses with more or less power. She hypothesizes that the member of the couple who is younger and has more non-labor income has more power. Using 2000 Census data, she finds that within unmarried couples, including both same-sex and opposite-sex couples, younger and richer members work fewer hours in the labor market than their partners. Within married couples, however, older and richer members work fewer hours than their partners. Her results suggest that the characteristics that predict bargaining power, such as age, may differ by couple type.

Roommates can serve as a comparison group. Jepsen and Jepsen (2006) and Oreffice (2011) contend that roommates share the cohabiting aspects of "family" households but are unlikely to make joint decisions about allocating time to the labor market. Oreffice suggests that roommates would not bargain, so they are an appropriate reference group to the couples. As expected, she does not find any evidence of bargaining between roommates.

Jepsen and Jepsen (2006) use roommates as a comparison group for couples to look for evidence of specialization within couples. These authors find that all couple types (same sex, unmarried opposite sex, and married) are less alike in their characteristics than are roommates of the same gender composition. Their results are consistent with the idea that couples are more likely to specialize than roommates.

Social norms reinforce a division of household labor among opposite-sex couples. For example, men may do outdoor chores and women do indoor chores. Since same-sex couples have been unable to marry until recently, the risks for a partner who forgoes the accumulation of market-based capital to specialize in traditional home production can be quite high. Giddings (2003) contends that protection from discrimination in employment and access to legalized marriage could alter the market- and household-work decisions such that the division of household labor in same-sex couples might become more like the division in traditional married couples. She does not discuss whether such a move would improve the utility of members of same-sex couples. Giddings et al. (2013) explicitly model household specialization by considering the probability that each partner works in the labor force and by measuring the absolute value of the difference in hours worked within couples, which they call a "specialization gap." These researchers find that gay and lesbian couples are less likely to specialize within the household than heterosexual couples, but note that the presence of children reduces differences between homosexual and heterosexual couples. They then compare the specialization gap across three generations—Baby Boomers, Generation X, and Generation Y—and find that the gap narrows with younger generations.

Several early studies of the division of household tasks indicate that lesbian couples divide such tasks evenly (Blumstein and Schwartz 1983; Kurdek 1993). Blumstein and Schwartz (1983) suggest that gay men typically do not want a stay-at-home partner. Among lesbians with children, the biological mother tends to work fewer hours and provide more hours of child care than her partner (Chan, Brooks, Raboy, and Patterson 1998).

HUMAN CAPITAL ACQUISITION

Although Becker's theories do not directly discuss how sexual orientation could influence human capital acquisition, women's incentives to invest in market-based human capital may differ depending on the gender of their current or prospective mate. Jacobsen (2003) describes how human capital type could differ in ways associated with lower earnings for women: (1) women may be more likely to invest in human capital that has a high non-market return; (2) women may be more likely to invest in human capital that increases satisfaction with time spent in market work, non-market work, or leisure, whereas men may invest in human capital with a high return in wages but little increase in satisfaction; (3) women may invest in human capital that depreciates less rapidly than the human capital that men invest in; and (4) women may be less likely to invest in specific (rather than general) human capital (163).

Several studies compare the educational attainment of homosexuals to that of heterosexuals. All find that gay men and lesbian women have more years of schooling on average than their heterosexual counterparts. Using 1990 Census data, Allegretto and Arthur (2001) and Jepsen and Jepsen (2002) confirm that gay male heads of household, gay male partners, lesbian heads of household, and lesbian partners all have more years of schooling than cohabiting but unmarried heads of households and their partners and married heads of household and their partners. Black et al. (2007) compare educational levels using data from the 2000 Census and find that partnered gay men and lesbians are better educated than partnered heterosexual men or women. Many of the labor market studies also find similar results for heterosexual men: married men have more average education than unmarried men (Badgett 2001; Berg and Lien 2002; Carpenter 2005, 2007; Clain and Leppel 2001).

LABOR MARKETS

Badgett's 1995 seminal article compared the earnings of homosexuals to heterosexuals. Empirical studies like hers begin with a classic Mincer (1970) earnings equation that considers differences in educational levels, race, age or work experience, occupation, and industry. Some studies consider the presence of children in the household, English proficiency, or rural versus urban location. People who have higher educational levels, more work experience, stronger English proficiency, and work in urban locations have higher earnings, all else equal. Certain occupations and industries are associated with higher earnings. For example, engineers earn more, on average, than elementary school teachers. Nonwhites and Hispanics earn less than whites, on average. Women with children earn less than women without children, all else equal. After controlling for the effects of differences due to these variables, researchers can measure differences based on sexual orientation.

Theories predict that married men would earn more than either gay men or cohabiting but unmarried heterosexual men. A large literature finds statistical evidence that marriage is correlated with higher earnings for men—a phenomenon called the "male marriage premium." Married men could earn more for a variety of reasons: employers view their marital status as a sign of stability, which is a trait employers want to reward; employers believe married men must provide for their families; the same characteristics that make a man more productive in the workplace make him a more attractive husband, which economists call selection bias; or married men are more productive at work because their wives take care of household duties that could distract them, which is related to a specialization argument.

If employers discriminate against homosexuals, either in the application process or in pay once employed, gay men would earn less than heterosexual men even if in every other way a gay man was comparable to his heterosexual counterpart. In contrast, if young gay men believe that they will form a household with another man, they may have less incentive than heterosexual men to invest in market-based human capital. Alternatively, they may plan to share more household tasks with a future male partner and so may acquire more household-based human capital. If having a wife or female partner allows a man to be more productive at work, then we would predict that gay men would earn less than heterosexual men because they do not have a woman at home to specialize in household production. If gay men are more likely to work in lower-paying occupations, then they would earn less than heterosexual men. Finally, if gay men work fewer hours in the labor force than heterosexual men, then we would predict that gay men would earn less than heterosexual men.

For women, the theoretical predictions are mixed. Discrimination against homosexuals either in the hiring process or with respect to earnings would result in lesbians earning less than heterosexual women, but the reverse is also possible. Women with children earn less than women without children, all else equal (Korenman and Neumark 1992; Waldfogel 1997, 1998). If lesbians are less likely to have children than heterosexual women, therefore, we might observe that lesbians earn more than heterosexual women. Young lesbians who do not plan to marry a man may invest more in human capital than their heterosexual peers, thereby raising their earnings relative to heterosexual women. If lesbians are more likely to work in male-dominated occupations, they could earn more than heterosexual women. Lesbians could also earn more than heterosexual women because they supply more hours to the labor force. Finally, if lesbians have a partner who is willing to specialize in home production, or at least more willing to share household tasks than the male partners of heterosexual women, then lesbians could earn more than heterosexual women.

Many empirical studies find that gay men do, indeed, earn less than heterosexual men. Studies using Census or CPS data find that gay men earn between 15 percent and 30 percent less than married men (Allegretto and Arthur 2001; Antecol, Jong, and Steinberger 2008; Clain and Leppel 2001; Elmslie and Tebaldi 2007). Gay men also earn less than unmarried men who live with women, but the magnitude of the difference is smaller (Allegretto and Arthur 2001; Antecol et al. 2008; Clain and Leppel 2001; Elmslie and Tebaldi 2007).

Studies that use the GSS are able to compare homosexuals and heterosexuals without being limited to cohabiting couples. The GSS-based studies find that gay men earn roughly 10 to 30 percent less than heterosexual men (Badgett 1995, 2001; Berg and Lien 2002; Black, Makar, Sanders, and Taylor 2003; Blandford 2003; Cushing-Daniels and Yeung 2009; Zavodny 2008). Zavodny's (2008) research investigates whether a male marriage premium exists for gay men who live with their partners relative to non-cohabiting gay men. She finds no statistical differences in the earnings of cohabiting gay men relative to non-cohabiting gay men; thus she does not find evidence of a male marriage premium for gay men.

All studies using the California Health Interview Survey find that gay men suffer an earnings penalty after controlling for all the other factors that influence earnings. Carpenter (2005) uses data from the CDC's Behavioral Risk Factor Surveillance System (2004) and Third National Health and Nutrition Examination Survey (2005) and also finds that gay men earn less than heterosexual men. Studies based on data from countries other than the United States also find that homosexual men earn less than heterosexual men. The countries studied include the United Kingdom (Arabsheibani et al. 2005; Booth and Frank 2008; Frank 2006), Canada (Carpenter 2008b), Greece (Drydakis 2012), and the Netherlands (Plug and Berkhout 2004).

Antecol et al. (2008) find that neither occupational choices nor human capital investments explain the earnings gap between gay men and married men; they suggest that the remaining unexplained gap is consistent with employer-based discrimination. Berg and Lien (2002) suggest that gay male couples choose to work less and enjoy more leisure because their *combined* household income is larger than that for any other couple type. Klawitter's meta-analysis (2013) finds robust evidence of an earnings penalty for gay men and an earnings premium for lesbian women and attributes that to work intensity. Hours worked or full-time versus part-time employment status explain much of these earnings differences.

Black et al. (2003) consider the market-based human capital choices of gay men by comparing the educational attainment of both gay and heterosexual men. Fathers have similar educational attainments, but the gay sons have higher levels of education than heterosexual sons, which suggests that gay men make different choices to acquire more market-based human capital than their heterosexual peers. Blandford (2003) finds evidence of occupational clustering that explains part of the earnings gap. Gay and bisexual men are clustered in managerial and professional occupations, although the small sample sizes mean that we must refrain from drawing strong conclusions.

The majority of the studies on women find that lesbians earn more than heterosexual women. According to 2000 Census data, cohabiting lesbians earn 3 to 10 percent more than married women and 1 to 4 percent more than cohabiting but unmarried heterosexual women (Jepsen 2007). Antecol et al. (2008) also use 2000 Census data and find higher earnings for lesbians, as do Clain and Leppel (2001) using 1990 Census data.

Daneshvary et al. (2009) consider whether a lesbian previously married to a man might have made human capital investments similar to currently cohabiting or married heterosexual women. In contrast, never-married lesbians may have invested more in market-based human capital because they never intended to marry a man. According to Daneshvary et al., lesbians who were previously married earn less than lesbians who never married, and lesbians who never married earn more than all other women.

In contrast, Elmslie and Tebaldi (2007) use 2004 CPS data and find no statistical difference in the earnings of female members of same-sex couples in comparison to women who live with men. Using the GSS and the NHSLS, Badgett (1995, 2001) also finds no statistical difference in the earnings of homosexual and heterosexual women.

Using data from later years of the GSS, Berg and Lien (2002), Black et al. (2003), and Blandford (2003) find that lesbians earn 20 to 35 percent more than their heterosexual counterparts. Carpenter's (2004) study using the CDC survey finds higher earnings for lesbian households, whereas his (2005) research using the California Health Interview Survey finds no difference in earnings based on sexual orientation.

Using data from the United Kingdom, Arabsheibani et al. (2005) find no statistical differences in earnings between homosexual and heterosexual women; neither Booth and Frank (2008) nor Frank (2006) observes such differences as well. Plug and Berkhout (2004) use survey data from the Netherlands; they find that lesbians have approximately 3 percent higher incomes than heterosexual women. Using data from Canada, Carpenter (2008b) finds that lesbians have incomes that are approximately 15 percent higher than their heterosexual peers. The only study to find lower earnings for lesbians is that carried out by Carpenter (2008a) who uses data from the Australian Longitudinal Study on Women's Health.

Antecol et al. (2008) attribute the greater earnings of lesbians relative to heterosexual women to greater investments in market-based human capital, especially education, rather than occupational differences. Berg and Lien (2002) suggest that the lesbian wage premium is consistent with female homosexuals choosing to work more to compensate for the lower average household incomes because their partner is or will be a woman rather than a man. Jepsen (2007) focuses on differences in the presence of children, estimated labor market experience, and household specialization as explanations for the differences in earnings of lesbians compared to heterosexual women. She finds some support for differences in estimated labor market experience, which is consistent with other studies.

EMPLOYMENT

A few studies have attempted to measure direct discrimination in the hiring process. Weichselbaumer (2003) created fake résumés for applicants for clerical positions in Austria. The "applicants" had comparable labor-market qualifications except that some of the résumés included participation in a lesbian organization as an indicator that the applicant was a homosexual. Weichselbaumer's results reveal that lesbians are about 12 percent less likely to receive an interview than their fictional heterosexual counterparts. When Drydakis (2011) conducted a similar field experiment in Greece, he found that lesbians were almost 28 percent less likely to receive an interview than similarly qualified, fictional, heterosexual women.

If homosexuals work more or fewer hours than heterosexuals, on average, then earnings between the groups could differ. Tebaldi and Elmslie (2006) find that cohabiting gay men are more likely than either married men or men who live with women to work part-time. Gay men also work fewer hours per week than men who cohabit with women. In contrast, lesbian women are more likely to work full-time and work more hours per week than women who live with men (both cohabiting and married). Carpenter (2008b) finds similar differences in labor force participation using Canadian data.

Leppel (2009) examines the probability of being employed for members of same-sex and opposite-sex couples. She finds that members of same-sex couples (regardless of gender) are more likely to be employed than heterosexual women and less likely to be employed than married men.

Having young children in the household increases the probability of being out of the labor force for both gay men and heterosexual women. Antecol and Steinberger (2013) focus on household specialization within lesbian couples, finding that the primary earners work about 475 more hours per year than their partners. They find strong similarities between the labor supply outcomes of primary-earner lesbians and married men and also between secondary-earner lesbians and married women.

One study, carried out by Klawitter and Flatt (1998), considered whether state and local antidiscrimination policies increase earnings for members of same-sex couples by reducing discrimination in "hiring, firing, promotion, or pay" (658). Using data from the 1990 Census, these researchers do not find statistically significant evidence of higher pay for members of same-sex couples who live in areas protected by antidiscrimination policies once they control for the fact that antidiscrimination policies are more likely to have been adopted in locations with higher average earnings, and same-sex couples are more likely to live in these areas.

CHILDREN

As technological innovations reduced the demand for laborers, families had lower demands for children as inputs. More recently, economists have modeled the decision to have children as analogous to purchasing a "consumer durable" product such as a car or a washing machine (Macunovich 2003). Becker explains that children, in addition to the out-of-pocket expenses for food, clothing, and piano lessons, "cost" their parents a great deal of time. As parents' incomes rise, there may be a "quantity-quality trade-off" in numbers of children. Macunovich (2003) speculates that a declining demand for children must be associated with an increase in parental income: if a family's wages are increasing but do not rise to the level to which they aspire, children seem less affordable.

The presence of children increases the likelihood of specialization by adults. A large component of the opportunity cost of spending time with a child can be captured by a parent's hourly wage. If men have substantially higher hourly wages, then women have a lower opportunity cost of staying home to provide child care.

Married couples are more likely to have children and have a greater number of children than any other family structure (Black et al. 2007). Nevertheless, same-sex couples and cohabiting opposite-sex couples also have children. Many same-sex couples are raising children from previous relationships, often heterosexual, whom they had at a young age (Gates 2011). Until recently, Florida had a ban on foster-child adoptions by homosexuals; this ban, which had been in place for 33 years, was declared unconstitutional in September 2010 (msnbc.com).

Currently, adoption is increasing among same-sex couples (Gates 2011). Based on 2008 GSS data, 19 percent of gay/bisexual men and 49 percent of lesbian/bisexual women report having a child (Gates 2011). Badgett et al. (2008) find that children are positively correlated with the likelihood that lesbians will enter into registered domestic partnerships.

Using data from the 2000 Census, Lugaila and Overturf (2004) estimate that two-thirds of all U.S. children live in a married-couple family. Six percent live in a household with an unmarried-but-cohabiting couple. The states with the highest percentage of children living in an unmarried-partner household are Maine and Vermont. Table 6.3 shows that these states were among the first to enact some form of domestic partner recognition, albeit after the 2000 Census surveys were completed.

Gates (2011) finds some differences in the educational levels of lesbians with children. Within same-sex couples, 15 percent of women with graduate degrees have children, whereas 43 percent of women with less than a high school degree have children (p. F3, using data from the 2009 American Community Survey).

Rosenfeld (2010) finds that children living with same-sex parents are as likely to progress through school as children living with opposite-sex parents (married or unmarried) or single parents. Allen et al. (2013) dispute this finding, claiming that children raised by same-sex couples are 35 percent less likely to progress through school when compared to children raised by traditional married couples. Rosenfeld (2013) defends his conclusions by suggesting that Allen's (2013) inclusion of adopted children, foster children, and children whose family status is unknown biases his findings.

HOUSING

Housing decisions are important because they usually represent the largest consumption item in a family's budget and good housing may have direct benefits on emotional well-being and child development (Leppel 2007b). Several studies have analyzed whether housing decisions such as home ownership rates, probability of having a mortgage, home values, mortgage-to-home-value ratios, and location differ based on sexual orientation (Ahmed, Andersson, and Hammarstedt 2008; Ahmed and Hammarstedt 2009; Black, Gates, Sanders, and Taylor 2002; Jepsen and Jepsen 2009; Leppel 2007a, 2007b; Negrusa and Oreffice 2011).

Any analysis of home ownership must control for many variables to distinguish the effects of sexual orientation from other characteristics that influence the choice and ability to purchase a home. Discrimination in housing and/or mortgage lending markets may be present and may limit the choices of homosexuals in comparison to heterosexuals. Homeownership may be positively correlated with education and the number of children in the household. Because housing is a normal good, economic theory predicts that people with higher incomes will be more likely to own homes than people with lower incomes. If gay male couples have higher incomes than married couples, then, they might be more likely to own a home.

Home ownership may also be correlated with couples' preferences for permanency or stability in their living arrangements. Thus, married couples may have the greatest preferences for homeownership. Married couples may also have greater access to lending markets compared to unmarried couples or singles.

Black et al. (2002) find that adult-friendly amenities are a better predictor of where gay men will live than the area's gay-friendliness. Using GSS data, Lewis and Seaman (2004) obtain similar results. Gay men, lesbians, and bisexuals are more likely to attend art museums, classical music concerts, and dance performances than heterosexuals. These differences persist even after controlling for characteristics that predict a higher demand for art such as higher educational levels, living in urban locations, and a greater probability of being childless. In turn, such preferences are likely to affect neighborhood and housing choices.

Leppel (2007a) finds that same-sex couples are more likely to own a home than to rent when compared to unmarried opposite-sex couples, but are less likely to own than married couples. Upon studying the ratio of mortgages to home values, Negrusa and Oreffice (2011) find that lesbian couples have higher ratios than either gay or heterosexual couples. Jepsen and Jepsen (2009) find that gay male couples, lesbian couples, and cohabiting but unmarried opposite-sex couples are all less likely to own a home than married couples. Christafore and Leguizamon (2012) report that having a higher number of same-sex couples in a neighborhood is associated with higher housing prices in liberal neighborhoods and lower housing prices in conservative neighborhoods.

Two studies have focused on rental housing markets. Ahmed et al. (2008) conducted an experiment in which they responded to Internet advertisements in Sweden for rental apartments by providing two fake rental profiles: one where the couple consisted of one man and one woman and a second where the couple consisted of two homosexual women. They did not find statistical differences in the responses of landlords to the lesbian couples. Ahmed and Hammarstedt (2009) conducted a comparable experiment in Sweden but created fake profiles for two homosexual men instead of two homosexual women. Homosexual male couples were less likely to receive a response and less likely to be invited to view the apartments.

HEALTH AND WELL-BEING

A handful of studies have considered other household and personal outcomes such as health and well-being to see if there are differences correlated with sexual orientation. Ash and Badgett (2006) find that members of same-sex couples and cohabiting, opposite-sex, unmarried couples in the CPS are two to three times less likely to have health care insurance than members of married couples. Buchmueller and Carpenter (2010) analyzed health insurance coverage and access to medical care using data from the Behavioral Risk Factor Surveillance System. They report that women in same-sex relationships are less likely to have health insurance coverage than women in opposite-sex relationships. These women are also less likely to have had a medical checkup within the past year. Men in same-sex relationships are less likely to have health insurance coverage than men in opposite-sex relationships.

In 2005, California enacted legislation that required private employers to treat employees who were in committed, same-sex partnerships in the same manner they treated married employees. Buchmueller and Carpenter (2012) provide the first analysis of this law. When they consider insurance coverage for gay and heterosexual men before and after the reform, they do not find evidence that the new law increased coverage for either group or closed the modest gap in coverage correlated with sexual orientation. The results for women, however, show that the rates of employer-sponsored health insurance increased for lesbians relative to heterosexual women.

Two studies have focused on psychological well-being. Carpenter (2009) compared homosexual and heterosexual college students across a variety of measures using data from the Harvard College Alcohol Study. He reports that gay male college students have higher grade-point averages (GPAs) than their heterosexual counterparts and that they place more importance on participating in activities such as student organizations, politics, and the arts. Lesbian college students also place more importance on participating in the previously mentioned activities than their heterosexual peers. Using proprietary data from more than 9,000 Australian women aged 22–27, Carpenter (2008a) compared several measures of happiness between lesbians and heterosexual women. Lesbians report lower personal incomes than heterosexual women; they are also more likely to report harassment at work and are less satisfied and more stressed about their careers and work lives.

CONCLUSION

Becker's theories provide a framework from which to study differences between certain couple types based on the gender composition of the couple or the legal options for recognizing the couple's union.

Empirical comparisons reveal significant differences in economic outcomes by type of household. Notably, many of the results are negative for gay men and lesbians

Conversely, some comparisons show that gay men and lesbians do better than their heterosexual peers. Lesbians may earn more than heterosexual women. Homosexual college students place a greater emphasis on campus involvement and volunteerism than their heterosexual peers. Gay male college students have higher GPAs than heterosexual male students.

The increase in the opportunities for same-sex marriages may make unnecessary laws such as the one in California that mandate similar equal access to employer-based health insurance. Legalized gay and lesbian marriage may increase the opportunities for homosexual families to adopt children. In the coming decades we expect the number of nontraditional families to increase; at the same time, we expect their opportunities and legal rights to approach those of traditional families.

ACKNOWLEDGEMENTS

I thank Tyler Lange and Emily Scholtes for their excellent research assistance, Christopher Jepsen, Bryce Kanago, Ken McCormick for their helpful comments, and Lisa Giddings for her summary of legal marriage options. Special thanks go to the editor for her creative suggestions and patience.

REFERENCES

Ahmed, Ali M., Lina Andersson, and Mats Hammarstedt. "Are Lesbians Discriminated against in the Rental Housing Market? Evidence from a Correspondence Testing Experiment." *Journal of Housing Economics* 17 (2008): 234–238.

Ahmed, Ali M., and Mats Hammarstedt. "Detecting Discrimination against Homosexuals: Evidence from a Field Experiment on the Internet." *Economica* 76 (2009): 835–849.

Allegretto, Sylvia A., and Michelle M. Arthur. "An Empirical Analysis of Homosexual/Heterosexual Male Earnings Differentials: Unmarried and Unequal?" *Industrial and Labor Relations Review* 54 (2001): 631–646.

Allen, Douglas W., Catherine Pakaluk, and Joseph Price. "Nontraditional Families and Childhood Progress through School: A Comment on Rosenfeld." *Demography* 50 (2013): 955–961.

Andersson, Gunnar, Turid Noack, Ane Seierstad, and Harald Weedon-Fekjaer. "The Demographics of Same-Sex Marriages in Norway and Sweden." *Demography* 43 (2006): 79–98.

Antecol, Heather, Anneke Jong, and Michael Steinberger. "The Sexual Orientation Wage Gap: The Role of Occupational Sorting and Human Capital." *Industrial and Labor Relations Review* 61 (2008): 518–543.

Antecol, Heather, and Michael Steinberger. "Labor Supply Differences between Married Heterosexual Women and Partnered Lesbians: A Semi Parametric Decomposition Approach." *Economic Inquiry* 51 (2013): 783–805.

Arabsheibani, G. Reza, Alan Marin, and Jonathan Wadsworth. "In the Pink: Homosexual-Heterosexual Wage Differentials in the UK." *International Journal of Manpower* 25 (2004): 343–354.

Arabsheibani, G. Reza, Alan Marin, and Jonathan Wadsworth. "Gay Pay in the UK." *Economica* 72 (2005): 333–347.

Ash, Michael A., and M. V. Lee Badgett. "Separate and Unequal: The Effect of Unequal Access to Employment-Based Health Insurance on Same-Sex and Unmarried Different-Sex Couples." *Contemporary Economic Policy* 24 (2006): 582–599.

Badgett, M. V. Lee. "The Wage Effects of Sexual Orientation Discrimination." *Industrial and Labor Relations Review* 48 (1995): 726–739.

Badgett, M. V. Lee. *Money, Myths, and Change.* Chicago, IL: University of Chicago Press, 2001.

Badgett, M. V. Lee, Gary J. Gates, and Natalya C. Maisel. "Registered Domestic Partnerships among Gay Men and Lesbians: The Role of Economic Factors." *Review of Economics of the Household* 6 (2008): 327–346.

Badgett, M. V. Lee, and Jody L. Herman. *Patterns of Relationship Recognition by Same-Sex Couples in the United States.* Los Angeles, CA: Williams Institute, University of California-Los Angeles School of Law, 2011.

Becker, Gary S. *A Treatise on the Family* (enlarged ed.). Cambridge, MA: Harvard University Press, 1991.

Berg, Nathan, and Donald Lien. "Measuring the Effect of Sexual Orientation on Income: Evidence of Discrimination?" *Contemporary Economic Policy* 20 (2002): 394–414.

Black, Dan, Gary Gates, Seth Sanders, and Lowell Taylor. "Demographics of the Gay and Lesbian Population in the United States: Evidence from Available Systematic Data Sources." *Demography* 37 (2000): 139–154.

Black, Dan, Gary Gates, Seth Sanders, and Lowell Taylor. "Why Do Gays Live in San Francisco?" *Journal of Urban Economics* 51 (2002): 54–76.

Black, Dan A., Hoda R. Makar, Seth G. Sanders, and Lowell J. Taylor. "The Earnings Effects of Sexual Orientation." *Industrial and Labor Relations Review* 56 (2003): 449–469.

Black, Dan, Seth Sanders, and Lowell Taylor. "The Economics of Lesbian and Gay Families." *Journal of Economic Perspectives* 21 (2007): 53–70.

Blandford, John M. "The Nexus of Sexual Orientation and Gender in the Determination of Earnings." *Industrial and Labor Relations Review* 56 (2003): 622–642.

Blumstein, Philip, and Pepper Schwartz. *American Couples.* New York, NY: William Morrow, 1983.

Booth, Alison L., and Jeff Frank. "Marriage, Partnership and Sexual Orientation: A Study of British University Academics and Administrators." *Review of Economics of the Household* 6 (2008): 409–422.

Buchmueller, Thomas, and Christopher Carpenter. "Disparities in Health Insurance Coverage, Access, and Outcomes for Individuals in Same-Sex versus Different-Sex Relationships, 2000–2007." *American Journal of Public Health* 100 (2010): 489–495.

Buchmueller, Thomas, and Christopher Carpenter. "The Effect of Requiring Private Employers to Extend Health Benefit Eligibility to Same-Sex Partners of Employees: Evidence from California." *Journal of Policy Analysis and Management* 31 (2012): 388–403.

Carpenter, Christopher. "New Evidence on Gay and Lesbian Household Incomes." *Contemporary Economic Policy* 22 (2004): 78–94.

Carpenter, Christopher. "Self-Reported Sexual Orientation and Earnings: Evidence from California." *Industrial and Labor Relations Review* 58 (2005): 258–273.

Carpenter, Christopher. "Revisiting the Income Penalty for Behaviorally Gay Men: Evidence from NHANES III." *Labour Economics* 14 (2007): 25–34.

Carpenter, Christopher. "Sexual Orientation, Income, and Nonpecuniary Economic Outcomes: New Evidence from Young Lesbians in Australia." *Review of Economics of the Household* 6 (2008a): 391–408.

Carpenter, Christopher. "Sexual Orientation, Work, and Income in Canada." *Canadian Journal of Economics* 41 (2008b): 1239–1261.

Carpenter, Christopher. "Sexual Orientation and Outcomes in College." *Economics of Education Review* 28 (2009): 693–703.

Carpenter, Christopher, and Gary Gates. "Gay and Lesbian Partnership: Evidence from California." *Demography* 45 (2008): 573–590.

Chan, Raymond W., Risa C. Brooks, Barbara Raboy, and Charlotte J. Patterson. "Division of Labor among Lesbian and Heterosexual Parents: Associations with Children's Adjustment." *Journal of Family Psychology* 12 (1998): 402–419.

Christafore, David, and Susane Leguizamon. "The Influence of Gay and Lesbian Coupled Households on House Prices in Conservative and Liberal Neighborhoods." *Journal of Urban Economics* 71 (2012): 258–267.

Clain, Suzanne Heller, and Karen Leppel. "An Investigation into Sexual Orientation Discrimination as an Explanation for Wage Differences." *Applied Economics* 33 (2001): 37–47.

Cushing-Daniels, Brendan, and Tsz-Ying Yeung. "Wage Penalties and Sexual Orientation: An Update Using the General Social Survey." *Contemporary Economic Policy* 27 (2009): 164–175.

Daneshvary, Nasser, Jeffrey Waddoups, and Bradley Wimmer. "Previous Marriage and the Lesbian Wage Premium." *Industrial Relations* 48 (2009): 432–453.

Drydakis, Nick. "Women's Sexual Orientation and Labor Market Outcomes in Greece." *Feminist Economics* 11 (2011): 89–117.

Drydakis, Nick. "Sexual Orientation and Labor Relations: New Evidence from Athens Greece." *Applied Economics* 44 (2012): 2653–2665.

Elmslie, Bruce, and Edinaldo Tebaldi. "Sexual Orientation and Labor Market Discrimination." *Journal of Labor Research* 28 (2007): 436–453.

Ferber, Marianne A. "A Feminist Critique of the Neoclassical Theory of the Family." In *Women, Family, and Work: Writings on the Economics of Gender*, edited by Karine S. Moe, 9–23. Malden, MA: Blackwell, 2003.

Frank, Jeff. "Gay Glass Ceilings." *Economica* 72 (2006): 485–508.

Gates, Gary J. *Geographic Trends among Same-Sex Couples in the US Census and the American Community Survey: Census Snapshots*. Los Angeles, CA: Williams Institute, University of California–Los Angeles School of Law, 2007.

Gates, Gary J. *Family Formation and Raising Children among Same-Sex Couples*. Los Angeles, CA: National Council on Family Relations, Williams Institute, University of California–Los Angeles School of Law, 2011.

Giddings, Lisa. "The Division of Labor in Same-Sex Households." In *Women, Family, and Work: Writings on the Economics of Gender*, edited by Karine S. Moe, 85–102. Malden, MA: Blackwell, 2003.

Giddings, Lisa, John Nunley, Alyssa Schneebaum, and Joachim Zietz. *Children and the Specialization Gap between Same-Sex and Different-Sex Couples*. Working paper. La Crosse, WI: University of Wisconsin, 2013. http://www.uwlax.edu/faculty/giddings/Current_Research/Specialization_Giddings_7_11_2011DRAFT.pdf .

Graham, John W., and Jason Barr. "Assessing the Geographic Distribution of Same Sex and Opposite Sex Couples across the United States: Implications for Claims of Causality between Traditional Marriage and Same Sex Unions." *Review of Economics of the Household* 6 (2008): 347–367.

Grossbard, Shoshana, and Lisa K. Jepsen. "The Economics of Gay and Lesbian Couples: Introduction to a Special Issue on Gay and Lesbian Households." *Review of Economics of the Household* 6 (2008): 311–325.

Grossbard-Shechtman, Shoshana. "A Consumer Theory with Competitive Markets for Work in Marriage." *Journal of Socio-Economics* 31 (2003): 609–645.

Hobbs, Frank. "Examining American Household Composition: 1990 and 2000." *Census 2000 Special Reports* (August 2005).

Hobbs, Frank, and Nicole Stoops. "Demographic Trends in the 20th Century." *Census 2000 Special Reports* (November 2002).

Jacobsen, Joyce P. "The Human Capital Explanation for the Gender Gap in Earnings." In *Women, Family, and Work: Writings on the Economics of Gender*, edited by Karine S. Moe, 161–176. Malden, MA: Blackwell, 2003.

Jepsen, Christopher, and Lisa K. Jepsen. "The Sexual Division of Labor within Households Revisited: Comparisons of Couples and Roommates." *Eastern Economic Journal* 32 (2006): 299–312.

Jepsen, Christopher, and Lisa K. Jepsen. "Does Homeownership Vary by Sexual Orientation?" *Regional Science and Urban Economics* 39 (2009): 307–315.

Jepsen, Lisa K. "Comparing the Earnings of Cohabiting Lesbians, Cohabiting Heterosexual Women, and Married Women: Evidence from the 2000 Census." *Industrial Relations* 46 (2007): 699–727.

Jepsen, Lisa K., and Christopher A. Jepsen. "An Empirical Analysis of the Matching Patterns of Same-Sex and Opposite-Sex Couples." *Demography* 39 (2002): 435–453.

Klawitter, Marieka. "The Effects of Sexual Orientation and Marital Status on How Couples Hold Their Money." *Review of Economics of the Household* 6 (2008): 423–446.

Klawitter, Marieka. *Meta-analysis of the Effects of Sexual Orientation on Earnings.* Working paper. Seattle, WA: Evans School of Public Affairs, University of Washington, 2013.

Klawitter, Marieka, and Victor Flatt. "The Effects of State and Local Antidiscrimination Policies on Earnings for Gays and Lesbians." *Journal of Policy Analysis and Management* 17 (1998): 658–686.

Korenman, Sanders, and David Neumark. "Marriage, Motherhood, and Wages." *Journal of Human Resources* 27 (1992): 233–255.

Kurdek, Lawrence A. "The Allocation of Household Labor in Gay, Lesbian, and Heterosexual Married Couples." *Journal of Social Issues* 49 (1993): 127–139.

Leppel, Karen. "Home Ownership among Opposite-Sex and Same-Sex Couples in the U.S." *Feminist Economics* 13 (2007a): 1–30.

Leppel, Karen. "Married and Unmarried, Opposite- and Same-Sex Couples: A Decomposition of Homeownership Differences." *Journal of Housing Research* 16 (2007b): 61–81.

Leppel, Karen. "Labour Force Status and Sexual Orientation." *Economica* 76 (2009): 197–207.

Lewis, Gregory, and Bruce Seaman. "Sexual Orientation and Demand for the Arts." *Social Science Quarterly* 85 (2004): 523–538.

Lofquist, Daphne, Terry Lugaila, Martin O'Connell, and Sarah Feliz. "Households and Families: 2010." *United States Census 2010 Census Briefs* (2012).

Lugaila, Terry, and Julia Overturf. "Children and the Households They Live in: 2000." *United States Census 2000 Special Reports* (2004).

Macunovich, Diane. "Economic Theories of Fertility." In *Women, Family, and Work: Writings on the Economics of Gender,* edited by Karine S. Moe, 105–124. Malden, MA: Blackwell, 2003.

Mincer, Jacob. "The Distribution of Labor Incomes: A Survey with Special Reference to the Human Capital Approach." *Journal of Economic Literature* 8 (1970): 1–26.

Negrusa, Brighita, and Sonia Oreffice. "Sexual Orientation and Household Financial Decisions: Evidence from Couples in the United States." *Review of Economics of the Household* 9 (2011): 445–463.

Oreffice, Sonia. "Sexual Orientation and Household Decision Making: Same-Sex Couples' Balance of Power and Labor Supply Choices." *Labour Economics* 18 (2011): 145–158.

Plug, Erik, and Peter Berkhout. "Effects of Sexual Preferences on Earnings in the Netherlands." *Journal of Population Economics* 17 (2004): 117–131.

Rosenfeld, Michael J. "Nontraditional Families and Childhood Progress through School." *Demography* 47 (2010): 755–775.

Rosenfeld, Michael J. "Reply to Allen et al." *Demography* 50 (2013): 963–969.

Rothblum, Esther, Kimberly Balsam, and Sondra Solomon. "Comparisons of Same-Sex Couples Who Were Married in Massachusetts, Had Domestic Partnerships in California, or Had Civil Unions in Vermont." *Journal of Family Issues* 29 (2008): 48–78.

Simmons, Tavia, and Marin O'Connell. "Married-Couple and Unmarried-Partner Households: 2000." *Census 2000 Special Reports* (February 2003).

Tebaldi, Edinaldo, and Bruce Elmslie. "Sexual Orientation and Labour Supply." *Applied Economics* 38 (2006): 549–562.

Waldfogel, Jane. "The Effect of Children on Women's Wages." *American Sociological Review* 62 (1997): 209–217.

Waldfogel, Jane. "Understanding the 'Family Gap' in Pay for Women with Children." *Journal of Economic Perspectives* 12 (1998): 137–156.

Weichselbaumer, Doris. "Sexual Orientation Discrimination in Hiring." *Labour Economics* 10 (2003): 629–642.

Zavodny, Madeline. "Is There a 'Marriage Premium' for Gay Men?" *Review of Economics of the Household* 6 (2008): 369–389.

Chapter 7

Intergenerational Transfers and Caregiving within Families

Susan L. Averett, Asia Sikora, and Laura M. Argys

Declining fertility combined with increased longevity has caused a substantial aging of the populations in developed countries. In the United States, the number of older Americans is expected to more than double by 2050. The population older than the age of 85 will increase even faster, quadrupling in the same time period, and the rate of growth in these age groups will far outstrip the growth of those in their prime working ages (Johnson, Toohey, and Wiener 2007). Caring for these individuals represents a challenge to policymakers. There will be a burden on the next generation of adult children to provide informal care and a strain on the public coffers as the demand for publicly provided care grows.

A substantial minority of older Americans receives assistance from family members, in the form of transfers of either time or money. More than 29 percent of individuals in the Baby Boom generation in the United States report providing financial assistance to a parent (Taylor, Funk, and Kennedy 2005). Pierret (2006) reports that 27 percent of women in the United States provided financial support to their parents or parents-in-law. Only 6.2 percent reported providing support of more than $1,000 per year, yet for this group the average transfer exceeded $2,700. Time contributions to parents often take the form of informal (unpaid) caregiving. Estimates from Johnson, Toohey, and Wiener (2007) suggest that in the year 2000, more than 25 percent of the frail elderly received unpaid caregiving from a child. In 2009, more than 42 million Americans provided care for an adult relative who had limitations in daily activities. The estimated economic value of their unpaid contributions totaled approximately $450 billion (Feinberg, Reinhard, Houser, and Choula 2011). Data from Europe suggest that over one-fourth of adult parents received transfers. with contributions of time far outweighing financial contributions (Albertini, Kohli, and Vogel 2007; Attias-Donfut, Ogg, and Wolff 2005).

This chapter focuses on intergenerational transfers and caregiving in developed countries where well-developed social security systems are in place to help the elderly. We seek to understand why children might provide time and money to their elderly parents. Furthermore, we discuss how changing family patterns such as lower marriage rates, increased childlessness, smaller family size, increased women's labor force participation, and declines in intergenerational coresidence (Lundberg and Pollak 2007) have changed how the elderly live and are cared for. Finally, we discuss the role of policies and their potential to alter the provision of assistance.

ECONOMIC MODELS OF INTERGENERATIONAL TRANSFERS

Economists view families as collective units that jointly produce and consume and are characterized by unique relationships between members. In addition to being motivated to maximize one's own utility, family members may be concerned with the well-being of other family members. These altruistic preferences mean that the utility of other family members enters an individual's utility function. Within this framework, fertility and the demand for children can be motivated by a number of considerations. In some societies, children serve as productive resources that enhance the consumption possibilities of all family members (Becker 1991). Because family members share concern for one another's well-being and transfers among family members occur throughout the life cycle, children can provide insurance for parents in their old age (Cain 1982, 1983; Willis 1980). Parenthood may enhance utility simply because parents care about their children and derive utility from the quality and quantity of their offspring (Becker, Duesenberry, and Okun 1960; Becker and Lewis 1973; Cox 2008; Fuchs 1983).

The nature of the relationship among family members provides the framework for theoretical models that explain collective decision making and the allocation of resources among family members. Gary Becker developed models in which family decisions regarding fertility and the allocation of resources among family members are made by a benevolent family head who maximizes a single utility function on behalf of all family members (Becker 1991; Becker et al.1960). As an alternative to this model of unilateral decision making, economists have applied game-theoretic bargaining models to family decision making. These models suggest that an individual's utility is incorporated into family decision making based on the relative bargaining power of family members and provide a framework to think about how decisions, including those regarding financial support and coresidence, can be influenced by external opportunities (Chiappori 1988; Lundberg and Pollak 1993; Manser and Brown 1980; McElroy and Horney 1981). The decision to allocate resources takes place within a single household when an intact nuclear family coresides. In contrast, inter-household decision making may occur when family members are divided by parental separation or divorce and the creation of new households as children transition to adulthood. Changes in the health and financial well-being of family members may also result in family members making decisions to combine households throughout the life course.

The primary theoretical models of altruism and exchange that motivate *inter-vivos* intergenerational transfers are briefly summarized next, along with supporting empirical evidence from studies conducted by economists and other social scientists that examine transfers of time and money between living family members. In this chapter, we focus on the provision of support to living elderly family members. Although bequests from parents to their children account for a large proportion of intergenerational transfers, and there is a large literature examining the motives and patterns of bequests, discussion of this topic is beyond the scope of this chapter.

The Altruistic Model

The theory of altruism begins with the premise that family members care about one another. In this framework, parents' utility functions include the well-being of their children and, likewise, a child's utility function includes the well-being of her parents. Recognizing that parents and adult children face time and budget constraints, the altruistic model of intergenerational transfers suggests that parents will provide financial transfers to children when child income is low and parental income is high, and vice versa. This suggests a life-cycle model in which parents invest in their children through young adulthood, assisting their children with the acquisition of human capital and family formation. In turn, in their prime working years, adult children may provide financial assistance to parents, a period in which elderly parents may experience declining income in retirement or be in ill health (Becker 1988; Cigno 1993; Ribar and Wilhelm 2006). A model of pure altruism predicts behavior that is consistent with income pooling across family members. Utility maximization in the income-pooling model suggests that an increase in parental income of $100 accompanied by a decrease in child income of the same amount will result in a transfer of $100 from the parents to their child.

The Model of Exchange

An alternative economic model suggests that the transfer of resources between family members is part of an exchange in which one member provides resources to another because that member expects the resources to be returned in a reciprocal relationship (Bernheim, Schleifer, and Summers 1985). Such exchanges could take place simultaneously, if, for instance, children provide assistance in the form of time, services, or direct caring for elderly parents, while parents might provide financial assistance to these same children. In other families, retired parents might provide time resources in the form of child care while adult children make financial contributions to their parents. Reciprocal relationships may not always occur simultaneously, however. Parents may provide assistance to children in the form of investments in schooling or help buying a house when their children are young adults; these children, in turn, may provide help to their parents as they age or experience declining health. In a model motivated solely by exchange (i.e., in the absence of altruism), enforcement of future transfers may be difficult. To secure assistance in old age, parents may engage in exchanges with children whom they feel that they can trust. Alternatively, parents may ensure continued interactions from children in their old age by playing the final trump card in this exchange relationship through their allocation of bequests.

A model closely related to the exchange theory of transfers recognizes that exchanges may take place across multiple generations. Through what is referred to as the "demonstration effect," parents may provide assistance to their own elderly parents in the hope of modeling such behavior for their children (Cox and Stark 1994). In this fashion, parents may provide care for their elderly parents in exchange for care from their own children in later years. Using an intergenerational sample of Mexican Americans, Ribar and Wilhelm (2006) find evidence consistent with a demonstration effect, particularly for young men.

EMPIRICAL EVIDENCE

Empirical analyses provide no consensus regarding which of the motives for intergenerational transfers dominates. Some studies, for example, provide more support for the exchange model. Using data on extended family members in the United States from the National Survey of Families and Households, Cox and Rank (1992) find evidence that intergenerational transfers are not compensatory. The altruism model predicts that transfers are more likely to be made to family members with low income, but these authors' results suggest precisely the opposite: larger transfers are more likely made to those with higher socioeconomic status. In addition, Cox and Rank find that the probability of a transfer is related to the receipt of child services. They conclude that financial transfers are more in keeping with the exchange hypothesis than a motive of pure altruism.

Analyses of data from Great Britain (Grundy 2005) also documents behavior most closely associated with the exchange model of intergenerational transfers. While nearly 75 percent of older British parents are engaged in exchange relationships with their adult children, there is some evidence of altruistic transfers as well.

Other studies demonstrate exchange of money for time. Using longitudinal Dutch data, Geurts, Poortman, and van Tilburg (2012) report that parents who provide child care for their grandchildren receive financial support in return. U.S. data reveal a similar pattern. Norton and Van Houtven (2006) find that *inter-vivos* transfers seem to be motivated by exchange as compensation for informal care. According to these authors, the inequality of transfers from parents to adult children and the inequality between children who provide care for their parents, primarily daughters and unmarried children, result in parents trying to offset costs for those children who provide care.

The evidence regarding altruistically motivated transfers is mixed. Although Altonji, Hayashi, and Kotlikoff (1997) find evidence of larger transfers in response to decreases in the recipient's income, the effect is not large enough to provide convincing evidence that transfer behavior reflects complete income pooling among family members as predicted by the pure altruism model. Other studies also indicate that transfers occur in response to the needs of the recipient (McGarry and Schoeni 1995, 1997). Laferrère and Wolff (2006) show that in an altruistic framework, parental distribution of financial resources across siblings is unequal and undertaken to compensate for endowment differences among siblings. Research also suggests that the socioeconomic status of the donor affects the amount and type of transfer. Rising children's wages have been found to increase financial transfers to parents and reduce assistance in the form of time (Couch, Daly, and Wolf 1999; Zissimopoulos 2001).

The lack of consensus regarding empirical support for the altruism versus exchange models of transfer behavior has led economists to recognize that both theories provide motives for intergenerational transfers. Cox and Rank (1992) and Arrondel and Masson (2004) have developed theoretical models that allow for both altruism and exchange to play a role in determining transfers between the elderly and their adult children.

Demographic Change and Intergenerational Support for the Elderly

Need for support for the elderly, both in terms of financial transfers and physical care, will continue to rise steeply in Organization for Economic and Cooperative Development (OECD) countries[1] as the Baby Boom generation reaches old age. Figure 7.1 depicts the proportion of the population older than ages 65 and 85 for selected OECD countries in the years 2000 and 2009. In virtually all cases, the proportion represented by each age group increased during this period.

The strain on the working-age population created by an aging population is reflected in the old age dependency ratio, as shown in Figure 7.2. Japan's old age dependency ratio has risen nearly 50 percent since 1980. The old age dependency ratio in the United States

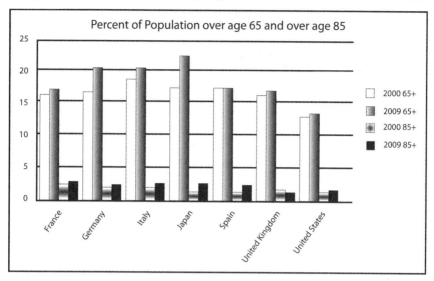

Figure 7.1 (World Bank Data Indicators (http://data.worldbank.org/indicator/))

and European countries is starting to rise and is expected to increase even faster as the Baby Boom generation retires (Johnson et al. 2007; Rechel, Doyle, Grundy, and McKee 2009).

Fertility

The rise in the old age dependency ratio has its roots in decreasing fertility and increasing longevity. Figure 7.3 shows the total fertility rate (TFR) for selected OECD countries between 1980 and 2010. The TFR is the average number of children a woman would expect to

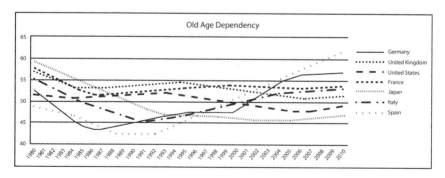

Figure 7.2 (World Bank Data Indicators (http://data.worldbank.org/indicator/))

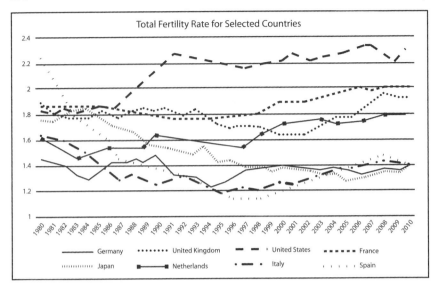

Figure 7.3   (World Bank Data Indicators (http://data.worldbank.org/indicator/))

have if she were to experience all of the age-specific birth rates occurring in that year over her lifetime; it is often interpreted as the average number of children per woman. Figure 7.3 indicates that the TFR has declined substantially and in many countries is now at historically low rates. In a developed country, replacement rate fertility is considered to be a TFR of 2.1— the average number of births per woman that will maintain a country's current population level. Over the time frame shown in Figure 7.3, Germany's lowest fertility rate was 1.24, Japan's was 1.26, Italy's was 1.18, and Spain's was 1.15. These very low fertility rates eventually lead to reductions in the number of young skilled workers—a trend that could affect economic growth if not offset by an increase in productivity (Bloom, Canning, and Fink 2010).

Labor Force Participation

Women's labor force participation rates and the TFR are closely related (Feyrer, Sacerdote, and Stern 2008). Because women's earnings potential represents the opportunity cost of fertility, economic theory predicts a negative correlation between the female labor force participation rate and the TFR. Typically, when fertility rates have fallen, women's labor force participation has increased (Figure 7.4).

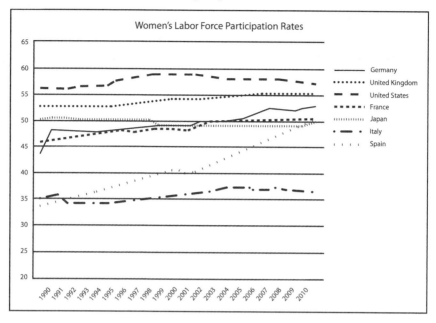

Figure 7.4　(World Bank Data Indicators (http://data.worldbank.org/indicator/))

In general, a negative correlation between fertility and labor force participation seems evident when we compare the data in Figures 7.3 and 7.4, yet substantial variations occur across countries and over time. Of particular concern is the fact that in Japan and some European countries there has been a reversal in the correlation between fertility rates and labor force participation (Adsera 2005; Apps and Rees 2004; Del Boca and Locatelli 2006). Adsera (2005) notes that in 1975, the correlation between fertility rates and labor force participation of women in 23 OECD countries was –0.18. However, by the late 1980s, those countries with the lowest levels of labor force participation, such as Spain and Italy, also had the lowest levels of fertility, such that the correlation was a positive 0.43.

Entrenched gender inequality within families in some countries has been implicated as a driver of lower fertility rates and lower labor market opportunities for women (Feyrer et al. 2008; Repo 2012). Currently, Japan, Spain, and Italy offer relatively sparse labor market opportunities for women; at the same time, men in these countries participate much less in the production of household goods than they do in other countries (Feyrer et al. 2008). These countries also have low fertility rates. Such a pattern may have implications for gender differences in elder care. Although the existence of fewer market opportunities for women lowers the opportunity cost of elder care, the low rates of fertility in these countries suggest that the provision of care by adult children will not meet the increased demand for elder care in the future.

Marital Disruption

Changes in marital stability also impact intergenerational transfers. Divorce rates in the United States and Europe have increased since the 1970s (OECD 2011a). These increases have altered the pattern of transfers between adult children and their parents. Research in the United States suggests that the ties between children and their nonresident parent (typically the father) weaken if a divorce happens during childhood (McLanahan and Sandefur 1994). Researchers have examined the impact of marital dissolution on intergenerational transfers and have identified a negative impact on both financial and time transfers to parents (Furstenberg, Hoffman, and Shrestha 1995; Pezzin, Pollak, and Schone 2008; Pezzin and Schone 1999).

For single and divorced men, who would otherwise be dependent on care from their spouse or children in their old age, the disrupted family environment may reduce the support available. For divorced fathers, relationships with their children are more strained if they remarry shortly after divorce from the children's biological mother or if they were not actively involved with their children after divorce (Ahrons and Tanner 2003). After divorce, the opportunity for a father to invest in his relationship with his children is generally diminished through reduced contact (Kalmijn 2007). In addition, as Kalmijn notes, mothers help facilitate intergenerational support between their children and their husbands while still married, but after divorce they may no longer be willing to facilitate such interactions.

INTERGENERATIONAL CAREGIVING: THE DEMAND FOR LONG-TERM CARE

Family decisions concerning the time-intensive care of frail elderly members are complex; consequently, a single economic model cannot hope to capture all the dimensions of this choice. This section high-lights a few of the modeling strategies and empirical results from this literature (For more detail, readers are referred to Goree, Hiedemann, and Stern [2011]). In some models, family decision makers (usually the adult children of the elderly family member) are assumed to maxi-mize a single family utility function (Hoerger, Picone, and Sloan 1996; Stabile, Laporte, and Coyte 2006). Other authors use a game-theoretic framework that allows for the possibility that adult children may have different preferences regarding care for their parents (e.g., Hiedemann and Stern 1999, Pezzin, Pollak, and Schone 2007; Sloan, Picone, and Hoerger 1997). Finally, the researcher must allow for multiple types of arrangements. Typically decision makers must choose between informal care provided by an adult child, institutional care, or contin-ued independence of their elderly parents if possible.

As an example of this type of modeling, Pezzin, Pollak, and Schone (2007) propose a theoretical two-stage bargaining model to analyze the living arrangements of an elderly parent and the assistance that children provide to that parent. In their model, the parent can live with one of two children, alone, or in a nursing home. Using backward induction, these authors examine the second stage of the level of assistance that each child would provide to the parent under each living arrangement. Based on the second-stage outcome, they determine the living arrange-ment that would emerge in the first stage. They find that the two-stage game may not be Pareto efficient if coresidence reduces the bargaining power of the coresident child relative to her siblings.

Of particular interest in this literature is whether formal care and informal care are substitutes or complements. Van Houtven and Norton (2004; also Van Houtven and Norton, 2008) and Hanaoka and Norton (2008) develop models of children's provision of informal care and parents' use of formal care. They find that informal care comple-ments formal care if the parent requires follow-up after outpatient sur-gery. They also find that formal care is a substitute for informal care when the requirement is for long-term care rather than acute interven-tion. Others have found more mixed evidence on this topic (Charles and Sevak 2005). Similar analysis of informal care by children in Europe suggests that informal care and formal care are substitutes (Bonsang 2009). Such substitution raises concerns that public provi-sion of elder care may crowd out informal care (Zissimopolous 2001).

Patterns of Caregiving and Elderly Needs

Most Americans older than the age of 65 do not live with their children. According to the 2010 U.S. decennial Census, the majority (55 percent) of non-institutionalized adults older than age 65 live with their spouses, while another 30 percent live alone (U.S. Census Bureau 2012). Living arrangements of the elderly vary substantially by their level of independence. Typically a person is defined as needing care if he or she has trouble with one or more activities of daily living (ADLs) or with one or more instrumental activities of daily living (IADLs). An individual with an ADL has need of help with bathing, getting in and out of bed, eating, dressing, walking across a room, and/or using the toilet. IADLs encompass tasks such as shopping for groceries, preparing hot meals, using the phone, taking medications, and managing money.

In 2002, approximately 8.7 million people aged 65 or older living at home in the United States had some sort of disability that required assistance. Most of these individuals were of modest means and lived alone but had children nearby who could provide care (Johnson and Wiener 2006).

The U.S.-based National Long Term Care Survey of persons 65 and older examines the caregiving arrangements for elderly respondents who had trouble with either an ADL or an IADL. In 1999, more than one-third of these individuals received care from their children. Among children caring for elderly parents, one-third were coresident. Another 24 percent of the frail elderly were cared for by their spouses (Wolf 2004). Research, however, suggests that approximately 20 percent of older individuals who need care do not have a caregiver (Roth, Haley, Wadley, Clay, and Howard 2007).

Figure 7.5 presents data from several countries showing the percentage of the population older than the age of 65 in 2009 that received long-term care either at home or in an institution. Long-term care is defined as care provided by someone who is paid (OECD 2011b). Care at home may be care either in the elderly person's own home or in the home of the caregiver (who is often a spouse or child). Institutional care is that care received either in a nursing facility or in a long-term care facility that provides both accommodations and caregiving. In Spain, elderly persons receive relatively little institutional care; by comparison, the elderly in Nordic countries are more likely to be cared for in an institutional setting.

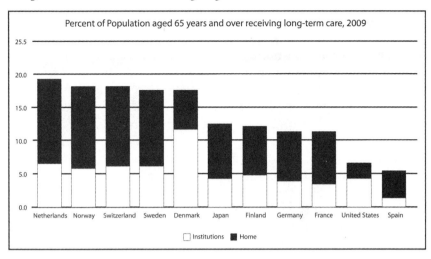

Figure 7.5 (OECD (2011), Health at a Glance 2011: OECD Indicators, OECD Publishing, http://dx.doi.org/10.1787/health_glance-2011-en. Used by permission.)

There is substantial variation across countries in the percentage of the elderly needing care. Only 6.5 percent of the elderly in the United States are long-term care recipients and only 5.1 percent receive such care in Spain. These low levels of long-term care could arise either because there is more informal (unpaid) care for the elderly or because the elderly are less likely to have disabilities. Some evidence suggests this specific pattern is the result of the scarce availability of institutional care in Spain and the generally better health status of the elderly in the United States (Adsera 2004; OECD 2011b).

In the United States, approximately two-thirds of the elderly requiring care are women. Married men and women often remain in their homes late into life with their spouses. Married individuals are, therefore, more likely to receive partner care than unmarried cohabiting individuals (Nöel-Miller 2011), and are less likely to enter into institutional care or reside with children than their unmarried counterparts (Freedman 1996). Because of the age gap in marriage[2] and well-known gender differences in longevity, women are more likely to care for an older husband until his death and then often live a number of years as widows. As her health fails or her financial resources run short, children are often faced with a decision regarding how to take care of their aging mother.

Who Provides Care?

Nearly two-thirds of unpaid caregivers are women. Daughters are more often than not the caregivers for their elderly parents in the United States (Johnson and Wiener 2006). These patterns are similar in much of Europe (OECD 2011b); however, gender roles in caregiving often differ by ethnic origin. In particular, in some Asian and African societies, male children (particularly the oldest male child) are expected to provide care for elderly parents (Bongaarts and Zimmer 2002). In contrast, in the United States, African American women are more likely to expect care from their daughters (Roth et al. 2007). In Japan, low fertility rates and the increasing labor force attachment of women have led men to increasingly take on caregiving duties (Hanaoka and Norton 2008).

Caregiving arrangements in the United States differ systematically by the gender, family composition, and socioeconomic status of the recipient and his or her family. The provision of care is likely to fall to the sibling with the lowest opportunity cost of time, reflecting differences in wages, schooling, marital status, and own family responsibilities. McGarry and Schoeni (1995) show that children are less likely to provide time transfers when their own income is higher and they have higher education.

A higher value for their own time leads children to shift from providing personal assistance to providing either financial transfers or an outsourcing of help with caregiving tasks. In the United States, it is not uncommon for individuals who are unable to live alone to purchase in-home caregiving assistance or institutional care (Johnson and Wiener 2006). This preference may reflect the fact that wages in the United States are high and well-educated children, facing a high opportunity cost of time, choose instead to contribute financial resources that allow the purchase of institutional or in-home care. It is also possible that the prevalence of non-family caregiving in the United States may be due to the availability of publicly provided long-term care options. These institutional differences are discussed in a later section of this chapter.

Informal care is more common among the less educated and among blacks and Hispanics in the United States (Johnson and Wiener 2006). These patterns are consistent with the prediction that informal care is more common when wage rates are low. In addition, children who receive financial transfers from their parents during young adulthood are more likely to provide assistance to their aging parents (Henretta, Hill, Li, Soldo, and Wolf 1997)—a finding that supports the economic theory of exchange.

Caring for Parents in Poor Health

Informal caregivers provide services to their elderly family members that save millions of dollars. The total estimated savings from such informal care in the United States was valued at $375 billion in 2007 (Houser and Gibson 2008). Patients undergoing cancer treatment in 2000 received, on average, 3 more hours of informal care per week, which translates to a cost of $1 billion per year nationally (Hayman et al. 2001). The annual cost of caregiving for persons with diabetes mellitus is estimated at between $3 billion and $6 billion (Langa et al. 2002), caregiving after a stroke amounts to $6.1 billion (Hickenbottom, Fendrick, Kutcher, Kabeto, Katz, and Langa 2002), and caregiving for those with depressive symptoms totals approximately $9 billion (Langa, Valenstein, Fendrick, Kabeto, and Vijan 2004). In comparison to persons with normal cognitive functioning, who average 4.6 hours of care, individuals with mild dementia receive 8.5 additional hours of care and those with moderate and severe dementia receive 17 and 41 more hours of care, respectively. The annual national cost of care for dementia is estimated at more than $18 billion (Langa et al. 2001).

Consequences to Caregivers

Time commitment of caregivers can be substantial. Respondents to a national survey of caregiving who reported caring for an elderly person older than the age of 50 for at least 5 hours per week in the past month with a need related to either an ADL or an IADL stated that they spent an average of 35.4 hours per week in caregiving, with the median response being 20 hours (Evercare and National Alliance for Caregiving 2007).

In addition to the time spent in care, noneconomic costs can be physical, social (e.g., relationship problems and a decrease in personal activities), or emotional (e.g., stress, morale, and lack of independence) (Fast, Williamson, and Keating 1999). A large body of literature deals with the psychological and mental strain that adult caregivers experience (e.g., Amirkhanyan and Wolf 2006; Evercare and National

Alliance for Caregiving 2007; Merz, Schulze, and Schuengel 2010). In a 2006 survey of caregivers, 55 percent of respondents reported that caregiving resulted in worsening health and more than half stated that these declines in health affected their ability to provide care (Evercare and National Alliance for Caregiving 2007).

The most common symptoms reported by caregivers are a decrease in energy and sleep; increases in stress and panic attacks; increases in pain, aching, and headaches; increased levels of depression; and weight gain/loss. Mui (1995) reports that daughters experience higher levels of psychological strain than sons do, which may reflect to some extent the tendency of daughters to wait longer to seek external help with caregiving compared to sons. This contention is supported by recent evidence from the Longitudinal Survey of Aging, which examined transitions in the provision of primary care (Allen, Lima, Goldscheider, and Roy 2012). Husband and son caregivers are more likely to transfer out of care responsibilities than wife and daughter caregivers, although gender-matched caregivers are less likely to transfer out of caregiving. According to Allen et al., coresidence with the primary caregiver places an individual at greater risk to transition to another formal caregiver within two years, although coresidence also lowers the probability of transitioning into formal care (e.g., a nursing home).

In the United States, several types of resources are available to help caregivers in their provision of care for an elderly family member. The 2000 amendments to the Older American Act of 1965 established the National Family Caregiver Support Program (Administration on Aging 2012). Under this program, all states, working in partnership with Area Agencies on Aging and local community service providers, must provide information for caregivers about available services; assistance to gain access to services; individual counseling, organized support groups, and caregiver training; respite care; and supplemental services, on a limited basis, to complement the care provided by family caregivers.

Out-of-pocket expenses for caring for an elderly parent are not trivial—an estimated $5,531 per year per caregiver (Evercare and National Alliance for Caregiving 2007). Expenses are higher for long-distance caregivers compared to coresident caregivers and those caring for someone nearby. The most common out-of-pocket expenses are purchases of household goods, food, and meals (42 percent), travel and transportation costs (40 percent) and medical care copayments and pharmaceuticals (31 percent) (Evercare and National Alliance for Caregiving 2007).

There is a growing interest in determining how caring for the elderly impacts the labor supply of the caregiver. Because women represent the majority of caregivers, this literature has, therefore, focused on female labor supply. This concern is particularly salient in Europe, where the Lisbon Agenda proposed that member states strive to increase female workforce participation rates to 60 percent by 2010 in an effort to emphasize the importance of women's role in the economy and to enhance economic growth (Viitanen 2007). Theoretically, the impact of providing informal care on the individual's labor market participation depends on the context in which care is negotiated (Heitmueller 2007). For example, is time spent caring negotiated between a mother and a daughter, or is it negotiated in a family setting where many siblings and perhaps extended family members are involved?

The option to provide informal caregiving means that individuals must choose between three uses of time: work, leisure, and informal caregiving. The opportunity cost of caregiving comprises some combination of forgone earnings and leisure, depending on how that time is reallocated. Whether formal care is available and affordable to the individual needing care also factors into the caregiver's decision-making process.

Researchers have noted that women with lower labor market attachment are more likely to be caregivers (Lilly, Laporte, and Coyte 2007). This negative relationship may not reflect the impact of caregiving on labor supply *per se* but rather be due to unobservable factors that systematically influence the employment and caregiving decisions. For instance, women who place a high value on caregiving may opt out of the labor market to care for children and then transition into caregiving for an elderly parent.

A small but growing body of literature aims to determine the causal effect of informal care on female labor supply by carefully taking into account the joint nature of these decisions. This literature uses both European and U.S. data. Early studies using U.S. data by Wolf and Soldo (1994) and Stern (1995) concluded that there was no effect of caregiving on women's labor force activity at either the extensive margin (participation) or the intensive margin (hours of work). Using data from France, Wolff and Dimova (2009) reached the same conclusion. Pagani and Marenzi (2008) note that older relatives requiring care may contribute to the household by providing household services, thereby making it more likely that their informal caregivers can work. Using data from Italy, these authors model a trivariate choice: to work, to use informal help from older relatives, and to care for older relatives. They find no evidence that caring for an older relative reduces women's labor supply. In a study examining caregiving in 13 European countries, Viitanen (2007) also finds little evidence that informal caregiving negatively affects employment. (The exception is in Germany, where a reduction in employment among caregivers is apparent.)

In contrast, Johnson and Lo Sasso (2006) find that for U.S. women in midlife, caring for an elderly parent substantially reduces hours of work. A study using data from the United Kingdom likewise determined that caregiving negatively affects employment and that employment negatively affects caregiving (Michaud, Heitmueller, and Nazarov 2010). Heitmueller (2007); Bolin, Lindgren, and Lundborg (2008); and Lilly, Laporte, and Coyte (2007) report that this strong negative relationship between caregiving and work is most significant for those involved in *intensive* elder care.

The decision to remain in the labor force becomes more complicated when caregivers have children of their own who also need care. Such women (and some men) make up the "sandwich generation"— individuals who juggle their place in the workforce with the need to provide or find care for both their children and aging parents (Spillman and Pezzin 2002). Dimova and Wolff (2008) extend the theoretical framework related to monetary transfers to encompass downward transfers of child care. In particular, they examine how grandchild care is distributed across the children of the elderly and how this type of care impacts the labor supply of the mothers of the grandchildren. These authors report that grandchild care is not distributed equally across siblings and that, in fact, grandchild care is directed toward those siblings who have better market opportunities. Extending their work to use data from 10 different European countries, Dimova and Wolff (2011) confirm that when grandparents provide care to their grandchildren, it facilitates the labor force participation of the mothers of the grandchildren and that this care is typically provided to daughters who have better human capital endowments and, therefore, a higher opportunity cost of not participating in the formal labor market.

POLICY IMPLICATIONS

Financial and material security in old age and the mix of public and private sources of support for the elderly have long been a concern of policymakers. As dependency ratios rise, policymakers and adult children will be faced with the growing needs of aging parents.

All OECD countries rely on various pay-as-you-go (PAYG) social security programs to provide financial support for the oldest generations (Ehrlich and Kim 2007). A PAYG plan is designed so that payments to retirees are supported by payroll taxes applied to the next generation of workers. Although total benefits to retirees must ultimately be balanced by the total contributions coming from their children's generation, retirees themselves do not need to have children to collect benefits. An increase in the dependency ratio suggests that total contributions will be declining relative to the demand for benefits and that governments' continued reliance on these policies places support for the elderly at risk.

Governments are well aware of the demographic issues that plague PAYG systems. The European Commission in 2012 issued a white paper in which it noted the demographic threats faced by PAYG systems and suggested three ways to address these challenges: privatization of retirement accounts, reductions in benefits, and increased labor market participation by the elderly. Between 1981 and 2007, more than 30 countries, predominantly in Latin America, Asia, and Africa, established fully or partially privatized pension systems.

While in general pension privatization has been slower to come about in OECD countries, in the 2000s Germany made some inroads to privatization by introducing a system of voluntary, state-subsidized pension savings accounts (Orenstein 2011). In the United States, George W. Bush unsuccessfully urged "privatization" of the country's social security system in 2005 in part to stave off the large payments due to retirees. The expansion of private pension systems has slowed in the aftermath of the 2008 financial crisis. The European Commission recommended keeping the elderly in the labor market longer by raising the retirement age. Proposals in the United States have focused on removing the disincentives for labor force participation for those who are elderly, including but not limited to the removal of the social security earnings tax (Nizalova 2012).

The public provision of elder care in the United States differs dramatically by the degree of need for care and by socioeconomic status.

Funding for elder care is provided through a variety of programs. The federal Medicare program is the primary source of health insurance for those aged 65 and older in the country. It covers short-term rehabilitation from injury or illness either in home or at a skilled nursing facility. However, Medicare does not cover long-term care either at home or in a skilled nursing facility for the frail or incapacitated elderly.

If an elderly individual needs long-term nursing care, coverage must be paid for either out-of-pocket or with privately held long-term care insurance or, for those who have inadequate assets, through the Medicaid program. Long-term care insurance policies have grown in number over time, yet currently only 12 percent of the U.S. population has long-term care insurance (NHEA 2010). Norton (2000) concludes that expenditures on long-term care are the greatest risk to financial security facing the elderly in the United States.

Medicaid pays for long-term care in skilled nursing facilities once an elderly individual falls below the asset eligibility level. Shortly after it was first enacted in 1965, Medicaid became the major source of payments for long-term care services for the elderly. For the first two decades after its inception, almost all elderly long-term care paid for by Medicaid was received in nursing homes.

In the 1980s, states began experimenting with home- and community-based services (HCBS) programs that allow the elderly to receive assistance but remain in their homes. Medicaid HCBS spending has since risen faster than spending on nursing homes, although Medicaid spending on the latter is still higher (Kaye, LaPlante, and Harrington 2009). Studies have shown that it is less expensive to provide comparable care in a non-institutionalized setting compared to a nursing home, yet the concern is that the availability of subsidies for in-home care may induce many more elderly to demand such care, thereby increasing overall costs. Recent evidence suggests that states allowing more generous HBCS assistance have experienced slower growth in Medicaid payments for long-term care overall than states that rely more heavily on institutional care (Kaye et al. 2009).

Although little compelling evidence indicates that in-home care yields better outcomes than institutional care (Mottram, Pitkala, and Lees 2002), most elderly would prefer to live in a home setting (Costa 1999; McGarry and Schoeni 2000). Given that most elderly individuals still rely on informal care, policymakers have to grapple with whether and how to support informal caregivers. For example, should governments provide pension credits for time spent on caregiving and payments to caregivers to compensate them for their loss of earnings? If so, what are the consequences of providing such incentives to caregivers to take time out of the labor market? Most caregivers are women who often leave the labor market to care for an elderly parent. Their reentry into the labor market can be difficult due to both depreciation of human capital and exogenous changes in the labor market (Lovejoy and Stone 2011; Van Houtven, Coe, and Skira 2010).

Policymakers in many countries are developing initiatives to support informal care. In the United States, tax policies exist to help children of elderly parents. The Elderly Dependent Care Tax Credit (also known as the Child and Dependent Care Credit) helps alleviate some of the financial burden incurred through caregiving for coresident elderly dependents by lowering the total tax burden faced by their caregivers (Wisensale 2009). Employers may offer Dependent Care Assistance Programs (DCAPs), which are flexible spending accounts that allow employees to set aside up to $5,000 of annual income to cover out-of-pocket elder-care costs. Finally, the Family and Medical Leave Act allows for eligible working individuals to help balance their work and caregiving responsibilities by taking up to 12 weeks of unpaid leave in a 12-month period to care for a sick spouse or parent (U.S. Department of Labor, n.d.).

In England and Wales, the Carers and Disabled Children Act was passed in 2000 to provide direct payments and respite care for informal caregivers. In 2002, Scotland introduced the Free Personal Care program, which provides generous personal and nursing care for those age 65 and older (Mentzakis, McNamee, and Ryan 2009). In 2000, in response to its rapidly aging population, Japan introduced public long-term care insurance (Hanaoka and Norton 2008).

In 1997 in the United States, the Program of All-inclusive Care for the Elderly (PACE) was founded. This program serves elderly adults who need nursing-home-level care but who can reside in a community setting. Often, PACE takes the form of an adult daycare program. This program, funded through both Medicare and Medicaid, is designed to allow people who otherwise need nursing-home-level care to remain at home (Petigara and Andersen 2009).

The recently passed Affordable Care Act (ACA) in the United States does not include specific provisions for long-term care. The Community Living Assistance Services and Supports Act (CLASS) was introduced as part of the ACA to provide a voluntary long-term care insurance program. At the time of this chapter's writing, the program was not functional because of concerns over premium costs due to adverse selection—the voluntary nature of the program makes it likely that only the most frail will purchase the insurance, driving up premiums and making it unaffordable (Miller 2011). Ultimately, as part of the American Taxpayer Relief Act of 2012, Congress formally repealed CLASS.

Policymakers are also addressing the issues that arise when families turn to the market to deal with their elder-care needs. A recent report commissioned by the World Health Organization argued that all European countries should ensure that an appropriate amount of formal and informal care for the elderly is provided (Rechel et al. 2009). To meet the growing demand for care, many OECD countries have made use of immigrants to care for the elderly. In the United Kingdom in 2008 it, was estimated that 18 percent of care workers were foreign born (a higher proportion than in the U.K. workforce as a whole) and that 23 percent of nurses were foreign born (Cangiano, Shutes, Spencer, and Leeson 2009). The United States also relies on a cadre of migrants to fill the gap in elder care (Browne and Braun 2008). Generally, the supply of migrant long-term care workers comes from developing countries where there are fewer labor market opportunities. These workers seek employment in developed nations with rapidly aging populations (Bettio, Simonazzi, and Villa 2006).

CONCLUSION

In the near future, policymakers and adult children alike will face the challenge of meeting the growing needs of the aging population. Public and private sources of support are already strained by increased longevity, lower fertility, and increased childlessness—demographic trends that are increasing the elderly population while shrinking the pool of individuals available to support and care for them. Projections for the United States suggest a quadrupling of the oldest segment of the population, including those persons older than the age of 85, in the next 40 years (Johnson et al. 2007). The same trends are evident in Europe, where below-replacement-level fertility threatens to exacerbate an already tenuous demographic situation (Rechel et al. 2009). Higher disability rates and the prevalence of more severe disabilities among the elderly, who now live longer, will also increase the difficulty and expense of serving this population. The growing number of frail elderly coupled with a far slower increase in the working-age population highlights the potential crisis that the American, Japanese, and European long-term care systems will face.

Projections by the Urban Institute suggest that unpaid informal care will increase, but the proportion of the elderly relying on formal care or having unmet care needs will also rise (Johnson et al. 2007). Current PAYG social security systems will have difficulty keeping pace with the growing elderly population as the working-age population shrinks. Increased childlessness and higher rates of divorce and non-marital childbearing add to this threat. Fewer children and weakened ties between parents and children mean that fewer elderly individuals will be able to rely on informal support from relatives in their old age. It is clear that expecting families in general, and adult daughters in particular, to meet the increased demand for long-term elder care is not a feasible option. Policymakers will need to grapple with the difficult task of developing a financially sustainable public care system and creating a market environment that promotes affordable long-term care options.

Many countries have dealt with this issue by providing incentives for formal and informal in-home care. Any shift to a lower-cost care alternative affords the opportunity to care for a larger number of elderly without breaking the budget (Kaye et al. 2009). The success of these kinds of policies will depend on the market for long-term care workers. Predicted job growth in the long-term care sector exceeds that of many other sectors in the economy (U.S. Department of Labor 2012). Yet, this industry remains plagued by low wages, high turnover, and lack of upward mobility (Stone and Harahan 2010). Additional increases in migration or adjustments in compensation and working conditions may be necessary to meet the growing need.

NOTES

1. A complete list of the OECD member countries can be found at http://www.oecd.org/document/58/0,3746,en_2649_201185_1889402 _1_1_1_1,00.html.

2. In the United States, women typically marry men nearly two years their senior. The marriage age gap is larger in many other

countries (Esteve, Cortina, and Cabré 2009; Hancock, Stuchbury, and Tomassini 2003).

REFERENCES

Administration on Aging. "National Family Caregiver Support Program (OAA Title IIIE)." 2012. http://www.aoa.gov/aoa_programs/hcltc/caregiver/index.aspx. Accessed January 22, 2013.

Adsera, A. "Changing Fertility Rates in Developed Countries." *Journal of Population Economics* 17 (2004): 17–43.

Adsera, A. "Vanishing Children: From High Unemployment to Low Fertility in Developed Countries." *American Economic Review* 95, no. 2 (2005): 189–93.

Ahrons, C. R., and J. L. Tanner. "Adult Children and Their Fathers: Relationship Changes 20 Years after Parental Divorce." *Family Relations* 52, no. 4 (2003): 340–351.

Albertini, M., M. Kohli, and C. Vogel. "Intergenerational Transfers of Time and Money in European Families: Common Patterns, Different Regimes?" *Journal of European Social Policy* 17, no. 4 (2007): 319–334.

Allen, S. M., J. C. Lima, F. K. Goldscheider, and J. Roy. "Primary Caregiver Characteristics and Transitions in Community-Based Care." *Journals of Gerontology Series B: Psychological Sciences and Social Sciences* 67B, no. 3 (May 1, 2012): 362–371.

Altonji, J. G., F. Hayashi, and L. J. Kotlikoff. "Parental Altruism and *Inter-vivos* Transfers: Theory and Evidence." *Journal of Political Economy* 105 (1997): 1125–1166.

Amirkhanyan, A. A., and D. A. Wolf. "Parent Care and the Stress Process: Findings from Panel Data." *Journals of Gerontology: Series B, Psychological Sciences and Social Sciences* 61 (2006): S248–S255.

Apps, P., and R. Rees. "Fertility, Taxation and Family Policy." *Scandinavian Journal of Economics* 106, no. 4 (December 2004): 745–763.

Arrondel, L., and A. Masson. "Altruism, Exchange or Indirect Reciprocity: What Do the Data on Family Transfers Show?" In *Handbook of the Economics of Giving, Altruism and Reciprocity*, Vol. 2, edited by S. Kolm and J. Ythier, 971–1053. Amsterdam: Elsevier, 2004.

Attias-Donfut, C., J. Ogg, and F-C Wolff. "European Patterns of Intergenerational Financial and Time Transfers." *European Journal of Ageing* 2 (2005): 161–173.

Becker, G. S. "Family Economics and Macro Behavior." *American Economic Review* 78, no. 1 (March 1988): 1–13.

Becker, G. S. *A Treatise on the Family* (enlarged ed.). Cambridge, MA: Harvard University Press, 1991.

Becker, G. S., J. S. Duesenberry, and B. Okun. "An Economic Analysis of Fertility." In *Demographic and Economic Change in Developed Countries*, edited by Universities-National Bureau, 225–256. UMI, 1960. http://www.nber.org/chapters/c2387.pdf.

Becker, G. S., and H. G. Lewis. "On the Interaction between the Quantity and Quality of Children." *Journal of Political Economy* 81 (1973): S279–S288.

Bernheim, B. D., A. Shleifer, and L. H. Summers. "The Strategic Bequest Motive." *Journal of Political Economy* 93, no. 6 (December 1985): 1045–1076.

Bettio, F., A. Simonazzi, and P. Villa. "Change in Care Regimes and Female Migration: The 'Care Drain' in the Mediterranean." *Journal of European Social Policy* 16, no. 3 (August 1, 2006): 271–285.

Bloom, D. E., D. Canning, and G. Fink. "Implications of Population Ageing for Economic Growth." *Oxford Review of Economic Policy* 26, no. 4 (2010): 583–612.

Bolin, K., B. Lindgren, and P. Lundborg. "Your Next of Kin or Your Own Career?: Caring and Working among the 50+ of Europe." *Journal of Health Economics* 27, no. 3 (2008): 718–738.

Bongaarts, J., and Z. Zimmer. "Living Arrangements of Older Adults in the Developing World: An Analysis of Demographic and Health Survey Household Surveys." *Journal of Gerontology, Series B: Psychological Sciences and Social Sciences* 57, no. 3 (2002): S145–S157.

Bonsang, E. "Does Informal Care from Children to Their Elderly Parents Substitute for Formal Care in Europe?" *Journal of Health Economics* 28, no. 1 (2009): 143–154.

Browne, C. V., and K. L. Braun. "Globalization, Women's Migration, and the Long-Term-Care Workforce." *Gerontologist* 48, no. 1 (February 1, 2008): 16–24.

Cain, M. "Perspectives on Family and Fertility in Developing Countries." *Population Studies* 36, no. 2 (1982): 159–175.

Cain, M. "Fertility as an Adjustment to Risk." *Population and Development Review* (1983), 688–702.

Cangiano, A., I. Shutes, S. Spencer, and G. Leeson. *Migrant Careworkers in Ageing Societies.* Oxford, UK: ESRC Centre on Migration, Policy and Society, 2009.

Charles, K. K., and P. Sevak. "Can Family Caregiving Substitute for Nursing Home Care?" *Journal of Health Economics* 24, no. 6 (2005): 1174–1190.

Chiappori, P-A. "Rational Household Labor Supply." *Econometrica* 56, no. 1 (January 1988): 63–90.

Cigno, A. "Intergenerational Transfers without Altruism: Family, Market and State." *European Journal of Political Economy* 9, no. 4 (1993): 505–518.

Costa, D. "A House of Her Own: Old Age Assistance and Living Arrangements of Older Nonmarried Women." *Journal of Public Economics* 72 (1999): 39–60.

Couch, K., M. Daly, and D. Wolf. "Time? Money? Both? The Allocation of Resources to Older Parents." *Demography* 36, no. 2 (1999): 219.

Cox, D. "Intergenerational Caregiving and Exchange: Economic and Evolutionary Approaches." In *Intergenerational Caregiving*, edited by A. Booth, A. Crouther, S. Bianchi, and J. Seltzer, 81–126. Washington, DC: Urban Institute, 2008.

Cox, D., and M. R. Rank. "*Inter vivos* transfers and intergenerational exchange." *Review of Economics and Statistics* 74 (1992): 305–314.

Cox, D., and O. Stark. "Intergenerational Transfers and the 'Demonstration Effect.' " Working paper. Boston, MA: Boston College, 1994. http://fmwww.bc.edu/EC-P/WP329.pdf.

Del Boca, D., and M. Locatelli. "The Determinants of Motherhood and Work Status: A Survey." IZA Discussion Paper No. 2414. October 2006. http://ssrn.com/abstract=947056.

Dimova, R., and F-C. Wolff. "Grandchild Care Transfers by Ageing Immigrants in France: Intra-household Allocation and Labour Market Implications." *European Journal of Population/Revue Européenne de Démographie* 24, no. 3 (2008): 315–340.

Dimova, R., and F-C. Wolff. "Do Downward Private Transfers Enhance Maternal Labor Supply? Evidence from around Europe." *Journal of Population Economics* 24, no. 3 (2011): 911–933.

Ehrlich, I., and J. Kim. "Social Security and Demographic Trends: Theory and Evidence from the International Experience." *Review of Economic Dynamics* 10, no. 1 (2007): 55–77.

Esteve, A., C. Cortina, and A. Cabré. "Long Term Trends in Marital Age Homogamy Patterns: Spain, 1922–2006." *Population* (English edition, 2002–) 64, no. 1 (January-March 2009): 173–201.

Evercare and National Alliance for Caregiving. *Family Caregivers: What They Spend, What They Sacrifice.* Bethesda, MD: National Alliance for Caregiving, 2007.

Fast, J. E., D. L. Williamson, and N. C. Keating. "The Hidden Costs of Informal Elder Care." *Journal of Family and Economic Issues* 20, no. 3 (1999): 301–326.

Feinberg, L., S. Reinhard, A. Houser, and R. Choula. *Valuing the Invaluable: 2011 Update. The Growing Contributions and Costs of Family Caregiving.* Washington, DC: AARP Public Policy Institute, 2011.

Feyrer, J., B. Sacerdote, and A. D. Stern. "Will the Stork Return to Europe and Japan? Understanding Fertility within Developed Nations." *Journal of Economic Perspectives* 22, no. 3 (2008): 3–22.

Freedman, V. A. "Family Structure and the Risk of Nursing Home Admission." *Journals of Gerontology Series B: Psychological Sciences and Social Sciences* 51B, no. 2 (1996): S61–S69.

Fuchs, V. *How We Live: An Economic Perspective on Americans from Birth to Death.* Cambridge, MA: Harvard University Press, 1983.

Furstenberg, F. F. Jr., S. D. Hoffman, and L. Shrestha. "The Effect of Divorce on Intergenerational Transfers: New Evidence." *Demography* 32, no. 3 (August 1995): 319–333.

Geurts, T., A-R Poortman, and T. G. van Tilburg. "Older Parents Providing Child Care for Adult Children: Does It Pay off?" *Journal of Marriage and Family* 74, no. 2 (2012): 239–250.

Goree, M., B. Hiedemann, and S. Stern. *Will You Still Want Me Tomorrow? The Dynamics of Families' Long-Term Care Arrangements.* Working Paper # 2011–035. Chicago, IL: University of Chicago, Economic Research Center, Human Capital and Economic Opportunity Working Group, 2011.

Grundy, E. "Reciprocity in Relationships: Socio-economic and Health Influences on Intergenerational Exchanges between Third Age Parents and Their Adult Children in Great Britain." *British Journal of Sociology* 56, no. 2 (2005): 233–255.

Hanaoka, C., and E. Norton. "Informal and Formal Care for Elderly Persons: How Adult Children's Characteristics Affect the Use of Formal Care in Japan." *Social Science & Medicine* 67, no. 6 (2008): 1002–1008.

Hancock, R., R. Stuchbury, and C. Tomassini. "Marital Age." *Population Trends* 114 (2003): 19–23.

Hayman, J. A., K. M. Langa, M. U. Kabeto, S. J. Katz, S. M. DeMonner, M. E. Chernew, M. B. Slavin, and A. M. Fendrick. "Estimating the Cost of Informal Caregiving for Elderly Patients with Cancer." *Journal of Clinical Oncology* 19, no. 13 (July 1, 2001): 3219–3225.

Heitmueller, A. "The Chicken or the Egg? Endogeneity in Labour Market Participation of Informal Carers in England." *Journal of Health Economics* 26, no. 3 (2007): 536–559.

Henretta, J. C., M. S. Hill, W. Li, B. J. Soldo, and D. A. Wolf. "Selection of Children to Provide Care: The Effect of Earlier Parental Transfers." *Journals of Gerontology Series B: Psychological Sciences and Social Sciences* 52B (Special Issue, May 1, 1997): 110–119.

Hickenbottom, S. L., A. M. Fendrick, J. S. Kutcher, M. U. Kabeto, S. J. Katz, and K. M. Langa. "A National Study of the Quantity and Cost of Informal Caregiving for the Elderly with Stroke." *Neurology* 58, no. 12 (2002): 1754–1759.

Hiedemann, B., and S. Stern. "Strategic Play among Family Members When Making Long-Term Care Decisions." *Journal of Economic Behavior & Organization* 40, no. 1 (1999): 29–57.

Hoerger, T. J., G. A. Picone, and F. A. Sloan. "Public Subsidies, Private Provision of Care and Living Arrangements of the Elderly." *Review of Economics and Statistics* 78, no. 3 (1996): 428–440.

Houser A., and M. J. Gibson. "Valuing the Invaluable: The Economic Value of Family Caregiving, 2008 Update." *AARP Insight on the Issues* 13 (2008): 1–8.

Johnson, R. W., and A. T. Lo Sasso. "The Impact of Elder Care on Women's Labor Supply at Midlife." *Inquiry* 43, no. 3 (2006): 195–210.

Johnson, R. W., D. Toohey, and J. M. Wiener. *Meeting the Long-Term Care Needs of the Baby Boomers: How Changing Families Will Affect Paid Helpers and Institutions.* Washington, DC: Urban Institute, 2007.

Johnson, R., and J. M. Wiener. *A Profile of Frail Older Americans and Their Caregivers.* Occasional Paper #8. Washington, DC: Urban Institute, The Retirement Project, 2006.

Kalmijn, M. "Gender Differences in the Effects of Divorce, Widowhood and Remarriage on Intergenerational Support: Does Marriage Protect Fathers?" *Social Forces* 85, no. 3 (March 2007): 1079–1104.

Kaye, H. S., M. P. LaPlante, and C. Harrington. "Do Noninstitutional Long-Term Care Services Reduce Medicaid Spending?" *Health Affairs* 28, no. 1 (2009): 262–272.

Laferrère, A., and F.-C. Wolff. "Microeconomic Models of Family Transfers." In *Handbook of the Economics of Giving, Altruism and Reciprocity*, Vol. 2., edited by S. Kolm and J. Ythier, 971–1053. Amsterdam: Elsevier, 2006.

Langa, K. M., M. E. Chernew, M. U. Kabeto, A. R. Herzog, M. B. Ofstedal, R. J. Willis, et al. "National Estimates of the Quantity and Cost of Informal Caregiving for the Elderly with Dementia." *Journal of General Internal Medicine* 16, no. 11 (2001): 770–778.

Langa, K., M. Valenstein, A. Fendrick, M. Kabeto, and S. Vijan. "Extent and Cost of Informal Caregiving for Older Americans with Symptoms of Depression." *American Journal of Psychiatry* 161, no. 5 (2004): 857–863.

Langa, K. M., S. Vijan, R. Hayward, M. Chernew, C. Blaum, M. Kabeto, et al. "Informal Caregiving for Diabetes and Diabetic Complications among Elderly Americans." *Journals of Gerontology Series B: Psychological Sciences and Social Sciences* 57, no. 3 (2002): S177–S186.

Lilly, M. B., A. Laporte, and P. C. Coyte. "Labor Market Work and Home Care's Unpaid Caregivers: A Systematic Review of Labor Force Participation Rates, Predictors of Labor Market Withdrawal, and Hours of Work." *Milbank Quarterly* 85, no. 4 (December 2007): 641–690.

Lovejoy, M., and P. Stone. "Opting Back in: The Influence of Time at Home on Professional Women's Career Redirection after Opting out." *Gender, Work & Organization* 19, no. 6 (2011): 631–653.

Lundberg, S., and R. A. Pollak. "Separate Spheres Bargaining and the Marriage Market." *Journal of Political Economy* 100, no. 6 (1993): 988–1010.

Lundberg, S., and R. A. Pollak. "The American Family and Family Economics." *Journal of Economic Perspectives* 21, no. 2 (2007): 3–26.

Manser, M., and M. Brown. "Marriage and Household Decision-Making: A Bargaining Analysis." *International Economic Review* 21, no. 1 (1980): 31–44.

McElroy, M. B., and M. J. Horney. "Nash-Bargained Household Decisions: Toward a Generalization of the Theory of Demand." *International Economic Review* 22, no. 2 (1981): 333–349.

McGarry, K., and R. Schoeni. "Transfer Behavior in the Health and Retirement Study: Measurement and the Redistribution of Resources within the Family." *Journal of Human Resources* (1995), S184–S226.

McGarry, K., and R. Schoeni. "Transfer Behavior within the Family: Results from the Assets and Health Dynamics Survey." *Journal of Gerontology* 52b (1997): 82–92.

McGarry, K., and R. Schoeni. "Social Security, Economic Growth, and the Rise in Elderly Widows' Independence in the Twentieth Century." *Demography* 37 (2000): 221–236.

McLanahan, S., and G. Sandefur. *Growing up with a Single Parent: What Hurts, What Helps.* Cambridge, MA: Harvard University Press, 1994.

Merz, E-M., H-J. Schulze, and C. Schuengel. "Consequences of Filial Support for Two Generations: A Narrative and Quantitative Review." *Journal of Family Issues* 31 (2010): 1530–1554.

Mentzakis, E., P. McNamee, and M. Ryan. "Who Cares and How Much: Exploring the Determinants of Coresidential Informal Care." *Review of Economics of the Household* 7, no. 3 (2009): 283–303.

Michaud, P., A. Heitmueller, and Z. Nazarov. "A Dynamic Analysis of Informal Care and Employment in England." *Labour Economics* 17, no. 3 (2010): 455.

Miller, E. A. "Flying beneath the Radar of Health Reform: The Community Living Assistance Services and Supports (CLASS) Act." *Gerontologist* 51, no. 2 (2011): 145–155.

Mottram, P., K. Pitkala, and C. Lees. "Institutional versus At Home Long Term Care for Functionally Dependent Older People." Cochrane Library (2002). www.cochrane.org/cochrane/revabstr/AB003542.htm.

Mui, A. C. "Caring for Frail Elderly Parents: A Comparison of Adult Sons and Daughters." *Gerontologist* 35, no. 1 (February 1, 1995): 86–93.

National Health Expenditure Accouts (NHEA) by Type of Service and Source of Funds. Baltimore, MD: Center for Medicare and Medicaid Services, 2010.

Nizalova, O. "The Wage Elasticity of Informal Care Supply: Evidence from the Health and Retirement Study." *Southern Economic Journal* 79, no. 2 (2012): 350–366.

Noël-Miller, C. M. "Partner Caregiving in Older Cohabiting Couples." *Journals of Gerontology Series B: Psychological Sciences and Social Sciences* 66B, no. 3 (May 1, 2011): 341–353.

Norton, E. C. "Long-Term Care." In *Handbook of Health Economics*, Vol. 1, 955–994. New York, NY: Elsevier Science, 2000.

Norton, E. C., and C. H. Van Houtven. "*Inter-vivos* Transfers and Exchange." *Southern Economic Journal* 73, no. 1 (July 2006): 157–172.

Orenstein, M. A. "Pension Privatization in Crisis: Death or Rebirth of a Global Policy Trend?" *International Social Security Review* 64, no. 3 (2011): 65–80.

Organization for Economic and Cooperative Development (OECD). "Family Database." 2011a. http://www.oecd.org/dataoecd/4/19/40321815.pdf. Accessed June 16, 2012.

Organization for Economic and Cooperative Development (OECD). "Health at a Glance 2011: OECD Indicators." 2011b. http://dx.doi.org/10.1787/health_glance-2011-en.

Pagani, L., and A. Marenzi. "The Labor Market Participation of Sandwich Generation Italian Women." *Journal of Family and Economic Issues* 29, no. 3 (2008): 427–444.

Petigara, T., and G. Andersen. "Program of All-Inclusive Care for the Elderly." *Health Policy Monitor* (April 2009). http://www.hpm.org/us/b13/2.pdf

Pezzin, L. E., R. A. Pollak, and B. S. Schone. "Efficiency in Family Bargaining: Living Arrangements and Caregiving Decisions of Adult Children and Disabled Elderly Parents." *CESifo Economic Studies* 53, no. 1 (March 1, 2007): 69–96.

Pezzin, L. E., R. A. Pollak, and B. S. Schone. "Parental Marital Disruption, Family Type, and Transfers to Disabled Elderly Parents." *Journals of Gerontology Series B: Psychological Sciences and Social Sciences* 63, no. 6 (2008): S349.

Pezzin, L. E., and B. S. Schone. "Parental Marital Disruption and Intergenerational Transfers: An Analysis of Lone Elderly Parents and Their Children." *Demography* 36, no. 3 (1999): 287–297.

Pierret, C. "The Sandwich Generation: Women Caring for Parents and Children." *Monthly Labor Review* (September 2006): 3–9.

Rechel, B., Y. Doyle, E. Grundy, and M. McKee. *How Can Health Systems Respond to Population Aging?* Policy Brief 10. Geneva, Switzerland: World Health Organization, 2009.

Repo, J. "The Governance of Fertility through Gender Equality in the EU and Japan." *Asia Europe Journal* 10, no. 2–3 (2012): 199–214.

Ribar, D., and M. Wilhelm. "Exchange, Role Modeling and the Intergenerational Transmission of Elder Support Attitudes: Evidence from Three Generations of Mexican-Americans." *Journal of Socio-Economics* 35, no. 3 (2006): 514–531.

Roth, D., W. Haley, V. Wadley, O. Clay, and F. Howard. "Race and Gender Differences in Perceived Caregiver Availability for Community-Dwelling Middle-Aged and Older Adults." *Gerontologist* 47, no. 6 (2007): 721–729.

Sloan, F., G. Picone, and T. Hoerger. "The Supply of Children's Time to Disabled Elderly Parents." *Economic Inquiry* 35, no. 2 (1997): 295–308.

Spillman, B. C., and L. E. Pezzin. "Potential and Active Family Caregivers: Changing Networks and the 'Sandwich Generation.'" *Milbank Quarterly* 78, no. 3 (2002): 347–374.

Stabile, M., A. Laporte, and P. C. Coyte. "Household Responses to Public Home Care Programs." *Journal of Health Economics* 25, no. 4 (2006): 674–701.

Stern, S. "Estimating Family Long-Term Care Decisions in the Presence of Endogenous Child Characteristics." *Journal of Human Resources* 30, no. 3 (1995): 551–580.

Stone, R., and M. Harahan. "Improving the Long-Term Care Workforce Serving Older Adults." *Health Affairs* (January 29, 2010): 1109–1115.

Taylor, P., C. Funk, and C. Kennedy. "Baby Boomers Approach Age 60: From the Age of Aquarius to the Age of Responsibility." PEW Research Center Social Trends Reports. 2005. http://pewsocial trends.org/files/2010/10/socialtrends-boomers120805.pdf. Accessed June 25, 2012.

U.S. Census Bureau. "Table 58: Living Arrangements of Persons 15 Years Old and Over by Race and Age: 2010." In *Statistical Abstract of the United States*. 2012. http://www.census.gov/prod/2011 pubs/12statab/pop.pdf. Accessed May 25, 2012.

U.S. Department of Labor, Bureau of Labor Statistics. "Occupational Outlook Handbook." 2012. http://www.bls.gov/ooh/home.htm. Accessed June 1, 2012.

U.S. Department of Labor. "Family and Medical Leave Act (FMLA)." n.d. http://www.dol.gov/compliance/laws/comp-fmla.htm. Accessed January 22, 2013.

Van Houtven, C., N. Coe, and M. Skira. *Effect of Informal Care on Work, Wages, and Wealth.* Working paper. Boston, MA: Boston College Center for Retirement Research, 2010.

Van Houtven, C. H., and E. C. Norton. "Informal Care and Health Care Use of Older Adults." *Journal of Health Economics* 23, no. 6 (2004): 1159–1180.

Van Houtven, C. H., and E. C. Norton. "Informal Care and Medicare Expenditures: Testing for Heterogeneous Treatment Effects." *Journal of Health Economics* 27, no. 1 (2008): 134–156.

Viitanen, T. K. "Informal and Formal Care in Europe." IZA Discussion Paper No. 2648. 2007. http://ssrn.com/abstract=970484.

Willis, R. "The Old Age Security Hypothesis and Population Growth." In *Population, Environment and Development*, edited by T. Burch, 43–69. Boulder, CO: Westview Press, 1980.

Wisensale, Steven K. "Aging Policy as Family Policy: Expanding Family Leave and Improving Flexible Work Policies." In *Boomer Bust?: Economic and Political Issues of the Graying Society*, edited by Robert B. Hudson, 253–270. Westport, CT: ABC-CLIO, 2009.

Wolf, D. A. "Valuing Informal Elder Care." In *Family Time*, edited by N. Folbre and M. Bittman, 110–130. London, UK: Routledge Press, 2004.

Wolf, D. A., and B. J. Soldo. "Married Women's Allocation of Time to Employment and Care Of Elderly Parents." *Journal of Human Resources* 29, no. 4 (Special Issue: The Family and Intergenerational Relations, Autumn 1994): 1259–1276.

Wolff, F-C., and R. Dimova. "Upstream Transfers and the Donor's Labour Supply: Evidence from Migrants Living in France." *Manchester School* 77, no. 2 (2009): 204–224.

Zissimopoulos, J. *Resource Transfers to the Elderly: Do Adult Children Substitute Financial Transfers for Time Transfers?* RAND Labor and Population Working Paper DRU-2542. Santa Monica, CA: Rand Corporaton, 2001. http://www.rand.org/content/dam/rand/pubs/drafts/2008/DRU2542.pdf

Chapter 8

Household Labor Supply and Dynamic Macroeconomic Analysis

Mark C. Kelly and Ronald S. Warren, Jr.

The theory of individual labor supply has been an integral part of *microeconomics*, as an application of the neoclassical theory of consumer behavior, since the pioneering work of Robbins (1930). The analysis of labor supply decisions made by individuals in the context of membership in a household can be traced to the early, influential studies of Becker (1981) on fertility and Mincer (1962) on female labor force participation. Subsequently, Becker (1965) introduced the concept of *home work*, or *home production,* which he defined to be the productive use of time not spent working for pay in the private or public sector. Lawn care, cooking, shopping, and time spent on the care of other adults are all typical examples of home work. Thus, home work can be thought of as the portion of productive time undertaken that occurs outside of the formal labor market.

The implications for *macroeconomic* analysis of modeling labor supply in a household setting were initially explored by Benhabib et al. (1991) and Greenwood and Hercowitz (1991). Changes in market wages affect not only the decisions of existing workers concerning how many hours to work, but also the decisions of potential workers about whether to allocate time away from leisure and household production toward work in the formal labor market. Traditionally, econometric studies using individual-level data have reported estimates of the wage elasticity of labor supply derived from what is termed the "intensive margin." The intensive margin refers to changes in the hours worked by *employed* individuals in response to a change in their wage rates. These intensive-margin estimates of labor-supply elasticities are typically very small in magnitude (Pencavel 1998, 2002). This conclusion stands in sharp contrast to the much larger values of the wage elasticity of labor supply commonly used in the macroeconomics literature.

Estimates of the wage elasticity of labor supply at the labor-force-participation or "extensive" margin are typically much higher than the corresponding intensive-margin estimates (Kimmel and Kniesner 1998). Labor supply decisions at the extensive margin are often made by individuals in the context of their membership in a household, where the time allocations of one member may be complements to or substitutes for the allocations of other members of the same household (Grossbard-Shechtman 1984). Labor force participation within a household framework has most often been studied as the outcome of decisions made by husbands and wives about the specialization and division of labor between market and non-market production. The existence of an additional extensive margin between market work and home work provides, in principle, a means of reconciling the consistently small estimates of the wage elasticity of labor supply found in microeconometric research with the much larger estimates required by simulations of widely used macroeconomic models to reproduce the observed cyclical correlations among, and volatility of, various aggregate variables.

A burgeoning literature has attempted, with varying degrees of success, to bridge the gap between empirically estimated labor-supply elasticities and the calibrated values for aggregate labor supply typically found in Real Business Cycle (RBC) models of the macroeconomy. We begin by reviewing some of the stylized facts that motivated much of this recent research.

Figure 8.1 depicts the unemployment rate and labor force participation rate (LFPR) for the 10-year period from January 2003 through May 2013. The unemployment rate reached a peak of 6.3 percent in June 2003 and declined to 4.4 percent several times before climbing back to 5 percent in December 2007, when the Great Recession officially began. The unemployment rate increased sharply thereafter, reaching a high of 10 percent in October 2009. The unemployment rate remained near 10 percent for the next 6 months, after which it began to fall slowly but steadily to 7.6 percent in May 2013.

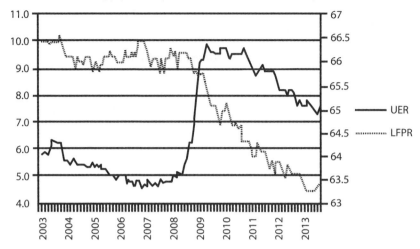

Figure 8.1 Unemployment Rate and Labor Force Participation Rate, 2003–2013 (U.S. Department of Labor, Bureau of Labor Statistics. Unemployment Rate (UER): http://data.bls.gov/timeseries/LNS14000000 Labor-force Participation Rate (LFPR): http://data.bls.gov/timeseries/LNS11300000)

From January 2003 to July 2009, the LFPR remained relatively stable, fluctuating between 65.5 percent and 66.5 percent. From August 2009 to May 2013, however, the LFPR steadily declined, from 65.4 percent to a low of 63.3 percent in March and April of 2013, and was at 63.4 percent in May 2013. In all, the LFPR declined by 2.6 percentage points from the beginning of the recession in December 2007 to May 2013.

When viewed in the context of household decision making, the cyclical patterns of unemployment and labor force participation raise several interesting and important questions: Do households pool resources in a risk-sharing manner to cope with rising unemployment? Does home production increase during a recession and, if so, by whom? Is access to credit markets effective in dampening the effects of cyclical shocks on household well-being? The answers to these questions depend, in part, on how and to what extent households change their allocation of time over the business cycle. This, in turn, will affect estimates of the elasticity of aggregate labor supply and bring greater clarity to the evaluation of alternative models of the macroeconomy.

The next section of this chapter reviews the static and dynamic theories of labor supply, giving particular emphasis to the conceptual distinction among various measures of the responsiveness of hours of work to changes in wages and to alternative assumptions about the structure of household decision making. We then set out the neoclassical model of economic growth, which serves as the foundation for the modern theory of business cycles, and discuss the extent to which the observed cyclical fluctuations of key macroeconomic variables match the simulated values of these variables based on a stylized model of the macroeconomy. Next, we describe how the introduction of household production has played a critical role in attempts to develop a more accurate model of the cyclical fluctuations in employment and hours of work. We then review the recent scholarly literature that has addressed the disparity between individual-level and economy-wide estimates of the wage elasticities of labor supply. In the final section, we provide a summary of our review and evaluation, and suggest several possible avenues for future research.

THE THEORY OF LABOR SUPPLY

In the textbook model of labor supply, the unit of analysis is interpreted to be either an individual or, equivalently, a multi-person, "unitary" household. In the latter interpretation, choices are assumed to be made by either a benevolent dictator, as in Becker (1976), or through an unspecified consensual process, as in Samuelson (1956) and Chiappori (1988), and the collective preferences are represented by a social welfare function. It is straightforward to show in this model that labor-supply choices made at the extensive (participation) margin imply a larger wage elasticity than decisions made at the intensive (hours) margin.

In the standard model, an individual (or other decision-making unit) simultaneously chooses the amount of goods and services to consume and the number of hours to work to maximize utility, subject to a resource or budget constraint. Utility is given by the function $U(c, h)$, where c is the quantity of a composite consumption commodity and h is the number of hours worked. The budget constraint can be written $Pc = Wh + Y$, where P is the price of the composite commodity c (P is interpreted as a price index), W is the wage rate, and Y is non-wage income. P, W, and Y are assumed to be exogenous; that is, they are not affected by the individual's behavior. The solution functions for the individual's problem are the uncompensated (Marshallian) demand function for goods and services $c^*(P, W, Y)$ and the supply function for labor $h^*(P, W, Y)$.

The uncompensated own-wage effect on labor supply can be written using the Slutsky decomposition:

$$\partial h^*/\partial W = \partial h^*/\partial W \,|\,_{dU=0} + h^*(\partial h^*/\partial Y)$$

The first term is the substitution effect, which is unambiguously positive. The second term is the income effect, and it is negative assuming leisure is a normal good. Thus, $\partial h^*/\partial W$ is generally ambiguous in sign because of the opposing substitution and income effects. However, at the extensive margin, where the individual's market wage equals the reservation wage (or the minimum supply price of labor), $h^* = 0$ so that there is only a substitution effect and, therefore,

$$\partial h^*/\partial W \,|\,_{h^*=0} = \partial h^*/\partial W \,|\,_{dU=0} > 0$$

The individual model of labor supply has been extended to encompass the behavior of multi-person households. The household utility function can be written as $U(c_m, c_f, h_m, h_f, z)$, where the subscripts m and f denote male and female household members, respectively, c_m and c_f are the quantities of a (private) composite commodity consumed by each member, with $c = c_{m+c_f}$, and z is a household public good produced with the technology $z = f(x, h_m, h_f)$, where x is a market-purchased, composite private good with price normalized to 1. Quantities of the composite commodity and amounts of labor market time for each individual are chosen to maximize household utility subject to the budget constraint $Pc + x = W_m h_m + W_f h_f + Y$. Although there is only one (household) utility function in this model, Grossbard (2011) has argued that the model can be interpreted as one in which each individual in the household independently maximizes his or her own utility with respect to consumption and labor-supply choices, but nevertheless takes into account the choices of the other individual(s) in the household. Individual-specific *conditional* labor-supply functions and demand functions for the private consumption good can be then derived in the usual manner, and they inherit some (but not all) of the properties of unconditional demand and supply functions in the individual case (Pollak 1969).

As a framework for understanding the labor supply decisions made by individuals who are members of households, however, the unitary approach is unsatisfactory on both theoretical and empirical grounds. From a theoretical perspective, this approach ignores all of the problems, emphasized by Samuelson (1954) and Arrow (1963), associated with the aggregation of individual preferences and the social choice process that characterize decision making in a collective setting. Moreover, among the most notable (and counterfactual) implications of this model are that each household member treats the labor-market income of the other members as non-labor income, and household non-labor income is pooled among the members. These implications are typically rejected in empirical studies—for example, by Lundberg (1988), Phipps and Burton (1992), and Browning et al. (1994).

In the non-unitary approach, explicit recognition is given to the existence of separate (but possibly interrelated) preferences of individual household members. An alternative for modeling household labor-supply decisions in a non-unitary framework is the cooperative bargaining approach, pioneered by Manser and Brown (1980) and McElroy and Horney (1981). One possibility for representing household preferences in this context is with a weighted-average utility function of the general form

$$sU_m(c_m, c_f, h_m, h_f, z) + (1 - s)U_f(c_m, c_f, h_m, h_f, z)$$

where $0 < s < 1$ is the weight attached to the male's utility and can be interpreted as reflecting the distribution of power in the household. Decisions are made in a two-stage process, with bargaining over the value of s taking place in the first stage and individual choices of h and c, as well as the joint choice of z, being made in the second stage, conditional on the first-stage value of s. These models, and their implications for household consumption and labor supply decisions, are admirably surveyed and critiqued by Lundberg and Pollak (1996) and, more recently, by Donni and Chiappori (2011).

However, it is not clear how the introduction of interdependent labor supply decisions affects the size of the Marshallian and Hicksian wage elasticities at the household level. Income effects arising from increases in others' incomes will reduce the Marshallian labor-supply elasticities, assuming leisure is a normal good, but will not affect the Hicksian elasticities. In contrast, cross-substitution elasticities may raise or lower the Hicksian elasticities, depending on whether members' time spent in household production and leisure consumption is a complement or a substitute. Finally, specifying that the husband's hours adjustments are made on the extensive margin while the wife's adjustments occur on the intensive margin, as is done by Donni and

Moreau (2007), would seem to *increase* the Marshallian wage elasticity of household labor supply because there would then be only a substitution effect on the husband's labor supply of an increase in his wage rate. However, if the husband's labor supply is actually fixed exogenously (by either custom or demand-side conditions), *household* labor supply will be *less* wage-elastic.

In any case, for business-cycle analysis, the relevant wage elasticity of labor supply is not the static (Marshallian or Hicksian) wage elasticity but rather a dynamic or intertemporal one. This intertemporal (or Frisch) wage elasticity of labor supply gives the response of labor supply in the current time period to a temporary change in the current-period wage rate. In other words, the intertemporal wage elasticity reveals by how much households are willing to reallocate their multiperiod labor supply toward times in which the reward from working is (temporarily) relatively high and away from periods when the reward is relatively low. To investigate this issue, we need to recast the choice problem in an explicitly dynamic setting in which the entire time paths of labor supply and consumption are chosen to maximize the discounted present value of (lifetime) utility subject to a multiperiod budget constraint.

In the basic dynamic labor-supply model, it is assumed that there is no uncertainty about the future values of the wage rate, the decision maker can borrow and lend at the same, certain market interest rate r, human capital is accumulated on the job through work experience, the length of the relevant time horizon is known with certainty, and utility is intertemporally separable (so that, for example, the marginal utility of consumption or leisure in one period is unaffected by the amount consumed and worked in any other period, MaCurdy, 1981). Non-wage income Y in any given time period is not exogenous, as in the static labor-supply model, but rather depends in part on how much was saved (and how much interest was earned on this saving) in previous periods.

The household chooses c_t and h_t in each time period to maximize the present value of discounted utility (Altonji, 1986),

$$\sum_{t=0}^{N} (1/(1 + r))^t \, U(c_t, h_t)$$

where $N + 1$ is the number of periods in the time horizon, subject to the intertemporal budget constraint

$$K_0 + \sum_{t=0}^{N} \left[(1/(1 + r))^t \, W_t h_t \right] = \sum_{t=0}^{N} \left[(1/(1 + r))^t \, P_t c_t \right]$$

where K_0 is the initial level of assets. The intratemporal budget constraint, $Pc = Wh + Y$, does not bind in every time period in this model because of the ability to borrow or lend.

The Frisch labor-supply and commodity-demand functions are $h_t (\lambda, W_t \lambda, P_t \lambda)$ and $c_t (\lambda, W_t \lambda, P_t \lambda)$, respectively, where λ is the marginal utility of intertemporal wealth. In contrast to the Marshallian and Hicksian labor-supply functions, which hold constant lifetime money income and utility, respectively, the Frisch labor-supply function holds constant the marginal utility of wealth. If the wage rate W increases in time period t, holding λ constant, the household will unambiguously work more in period t. That is, $\partial h_t / \partial W_t |_{d\lambda=0} = (\partial h_t / \partial W_t \lambda)(\partial W_t \lambda / \partial W_t) > 0$.

$$\partial h_t / \partial W_t |_{d\lambda=0} = (\partial h_t / \partial W_t \lambda)(\partial W_t \lambda / \partial W_t) > 0.$$

This intertemporal substitution effect differs both conceptually and in magnitude from the (intratemporal) Hicksian substitution effect in the Slutsky equation. With regard to the relative size of the two substitution effects, we can infer unambiguously that the Frisch substitution effect is larger than the Hicksian substitution effect:

$$\partial h^* / \partial W |_{dU=0} < \partial h_t / \partial W_t |_{d\lambda=0}$$
$$\partial h^* / \partial W |_{dU=0} < \partial h_t / \partial W_t |_{d\lambda=0}.$$

This result follows from the fact that the marginal utility of wealth λ is affected by the parameters W, P, and K_0 as follows: $\partial \lambda / \partial W_t < 0$; $\partial \lambda / \partial P > 0$, and $\partial \lambda / \partial K_0 < 0$.

The implications of modeling household labor supply in a non-unitary choice framework for the size of Frisch elasticities are not entirely clear. The extent of efficient risk sharing within the household in the face of cyclical shocks to the incomes of one or more family members would be critical to such an investigation. The relationship between the structure of household decision making and the elasticity of household and aggregate labor supply is a promising area for future theoretical and empirical research.

BUSINESS-CYCLE DYNAMICS

The primary challenge for any model of business-cycle dynamics is to generate predictions about the cyclical behavior of key

Table 8.1 Actual Empirical Moments of the Aggregate U.S. Economy

Variable	(A)	(B)	(C)	(D)
Output	0.017	1.00	0.85	1.00
Consumption	0.009	0.53	0.79	0.76
Investment	0.047	2.76	0.87	0.79
Total Hours	0.019	1.12	0.90	0.88
Average Hours	0.005	0.29	0.69	0.71
Employment	0.012	0.71	0.91	0.80
Labor Productivity	0.011	0.65	0.72	0.42

Sources: Sims (2012) [used by permission]; all series are expressed in per capita terms after dividing by the civilian, non-institutionalized population age 16 and older. All series are in real (inflation-adjusted) terms and in natural logarithms. The output measure is gross domestic product from the Census Bureau's Bureau of Economic Analysis (BEA) accounts. Consumption is the sum of expenditures on non-durables and services, also from the BEA accounts. Investment is measured as total private fixed investment plus consumption expenditures on durable goods from the BEA. Total hours are measured in the non-farm business sector, and were taken from the Department of Labor, Bureau of Labor Statistics (BLS). Productivity is defined as output per hour in the non-farm business sector, also from the BLS.

macroeconomic variables that match their observed movements, and co-movements, over the business cycle. There is widespread agreement among macroeconomists about these "stylized facts": (1) consumption, investment, total hours worked, employment, and labor productivity are pro-cyclical in the sense that their de-trended, cyclical component appears to be positively correlated with the cyclical component of output; (2) consumption is much less volatile than output, while investment is much more volatile than consumption or output; (3) total hours worked and total employment are both approximately as volatile as output, while average hours worked per worker is much less volatile than output; (4) labor productivity is pro-cyclical, but is less volatile than output; and (5) all of these series are strongly persistent in the sense that a positive or negative realization tends to be followed by subsequent realizations of the same sign. Table 8.1 gives empirical justification for these stylized facts by providing for each of the listed, de-trended variables its (A) volatility (standard deviation), (B) volatility relative to output (the ratio of standard deviations), (C) autocorrelation, and (D) contemporaneous correlation with output.

The finding that total hours worked and employment are almost as volatile as output, whereas average hours worked is not nearly as volatile as employment, suggests that it is the *extensive* margin of adjustment (increases or decreases in the number of workers) that is more important in explaining changes in labor utilization over the business cycle than the *intensive* margin (increases or decreases in the hours of work of employed workers). This turns out to be an important short-coming of the standard real business-cycle model, as that model incorporates only an intensive (hours) adjustment margin.

The benchmark model for the modern, dynamic analysis of business cycles is based on the neoclassical growth model originally developed by Ramsey (1928) and extended by Cass (1965) and Koopmans (1965). A focal objective of any growth model is to determine the allocation of current output (or non-wage [i.e., "capital"] income) between current consumption, on the one hand, and saving and investment, on the other hand. The Ramsey-Cass-Koopmans (RCK) model posits an omniscient, benevolent central planner who chooses consumption at each point in time to maximize the present value of discounted social utility over an infinite horizon, subject to a technologically determined "law of motion" for investment per capita and the initial capital stock. The behavior of the central planner in the RCK model can be "decentralized" by replacing her with a fixed number of identical, immortal individuals or unitary households, each endowed with perfect foresight over an infinite future, and adding identical firms that have access to a perfectly competitive rental market for capital goods. The "households" maximize the present value of discounted utility, subject to an intertemporal wealth constraint, and firms with constant-returns-to-scale technologies maximize instantaneous profits on a period-by-period basis. The steady states can be characterized by the following two results: (1) the rate of growth of the capital stock and output equals the (exogenous) rate of growth of the labor force (or size of the household) and (2) the ratio of saving (and investment) to output is a constant.

The canonical RCK growth model has been generalized to allow for human capital accumulation (Mankiw, Romer, and Weil 1992), exhaustible natural resources (Solow 1974), imperfect competition, and increasing returns to scale. The uncomfortable assumption of an immortal household with an infinite planning horizon can be circumvented by populating the model economy with finite-lived, overlapping generations, each of which maximizes its own utility and leaves no bequest to succeeding generations. Although this overlapping-generations (OG) model has its origin in an analysis of interest rate determination by Samuelson (1958), its implications for neoclassical growth theory were first examined by Diamond (1965). The central result of the OG and RCK models is the same: the rate of growth of output equals the (exogenous) growth rate in the labor force. Moreover, if the generational utility function in the OG model takes the logarithmic form, each generation saves a constant fraction of its earnings, as in the RCK model.

In the neoclassical growth model, whether of the Solow-Swan or RCK variety, the economy always converges to a steady-state growth path from any point off that path, and then grows smoothly thereafter (Solow, 1956; Solow and Swan, 1956). Such a model is especially well suited to the analysis of the long-run issues that arise in the study of economic development. To adapt the model for use in the analysis of short-run, cyclical fluctuations around the steady state, some type of random disturbance or shock must be introduced. Brock and Mirman (1972) introduced a stochastic component into the neoclassical growth model by assuming that the production function is subject to random shocks to total factor productivity, resulting in an early, prototype Real Business Cycle (RBC) model. In their seminal contribution to business-cycle analysis, Kydland and Prescott (1982) followed Brock and Mirman (1972) by adding random shocks to technology in the neoclassical growth model that serve as the driving force or "propagation mechanism" behind the short-run fluctuations. Most importantly, Kydland and Prescott (1982) allowed labor supply (and, therefore, employment), as well as consumption, to respond to the resulting changes in equilibrium output and input prices.

To see how well the RBC model performs in terms of matching the empirical features of the macroeconomic variables displayed in Table 8.1, one must specify in sufficient detail the dynamic structure of the model economy and then choose values for certain key parameters (for example, the capital depreciation rate, the steady-state rate of technological progress, and labor's share of the value of income received or output produced) such that, when the model is perturbed with a random, exogenous shock, the resulting predictions match the empirical moments as closely as possible. The selection of these parameter values, which is called "calibration," is the most innovative and controversial aspect of the methodological approach initiated by Kydland and Prescott (1982) and elaborated upon by Prescott (1986). Sims (2012) calibrated a conventionally specified RBC model of the U.S. economy, introduced a technological shock, and compared the resulting predictions. The results are shown in Table 8.2.

Table 8.2   Calibrated Moments of the U.S. Economy

Variable	(A)	(B)	(C)	(D)
Output	0.016	1.00	0.73	1.00
Consumption	0.007	0.44	0.78	0.95
Investment	0.050	3.13	0.71	0.99
Total hours	0.007	0.44	0.71	0.98
Average hours	—	—	—	—
Employment	—	—	—	—
Labor productivity	0.010	0.63	0.23	0.99

Source: Sims (2012), 6 [used by permission].

   In Table 8.2, there are no calibrated values for the separate moments of average work hours and employment because the model does not contain an extensive margin with which movements in total hours can be decomposed into changes in hours per worker and in the number of workers. Nevertheless, the calibrated model does well at matching the observed volatilities of output, consumption, investment, and labor productivity, as indicated by a comparison of the first three rows and the last row of column A in Tables 8.1 and 8.2. The model also does a good job of matching the autocorrelations of each of the series; all of the series exhibit substantial levels of persistence, with autocorrelations typically approximating 0.75. Finally, the calibrations capture the property that consumption, investment, total hours, and labor productivity are highly pro-cyclical, as evidenced by the large contemporaneous correlations with output, although these correlations are much too large relative to the empirical moments. However, the calibrated values for the volatility of total hours of work and the volatility of total hours relative to output substantially understate the (absolute and relative) volatility of work hours in the data. Specifically, the calibrated volatility for total hours of work is only approximately one-third of both its absolute and relative observed volatility. The inability of the standard RBC model to replicate these central features of real-world business cycles is an important and widely acknowledged shortcoming of that framework for understanding the cyclical dynamics of the labor market.

LABOR SUPPLY IN THE REAL BUSINESS CYCLE MODEL

The formulation of the labor-leisure choice in the RBC model presented by Prescott (1986) reveals both the theoretical strength and the empirical fragility of the Kydland-Prescott framework. Prescott (1986) observed that time devoted to non-market ("leisure") activities in the United States exhibited essentially no secular trend over the 40-year period from 1946 to 1985, whereas the average real wage increased steadily over that same time. From this stylized fact, Prescott inferred that the *intra*temporal elasticity of substitution between consumption and leisure is approximately 1. Prescott then cited several empirical papers reporting estimates of the *inter*temporal elasticity of substitution of the composite consumption-leisure "commodity" as being near 1. Together, the assumptions of unit intratemporal and intertemporal substitution elasticities imply that the limiting form of the instantaneous aggregate utility function in Prescott's model can be written as

$$U(c, \ell) = (1 - \varphi) \log c + \varphi \log \ell$$

where ℓ is time spent in leisure and φ is the share of leisure in "full" income or expenditure, $Pc + W\ell$.

The assumption of a unit elasticity of intratemporal substitution between consumption and leisure implies that the Frisch (constant marginal utility of income) wage elasticity of the demand for leisure is -1. Prescott interprets Ghez and Becker (1975) as finding that the typical household allocates approximately one-third of its productive time to market work and two-thirds to non-market activities, so that φ is assumed to be $2/3$. Since $h = T - l$, the Frisch intertemporal wage elasticity of *labor supply* implied by Prescott's calibrations is simply $\varphi/(\varphi - 1)(-1) = 2$. However, the Frisch elasticity in the Kydland-Prescott RBC model is highly sensitive to assumptions about both the intratemporal elasticity of substitution and the leisure-share parameter, φ. For example, Summers (1986), in his critical comments on Prescott (1986), cites Eichenbaum et al. (1986) as providing evidence that $\varphi = 5/6$, in which case the Frisch elasticity is 5, which is 6 times larger than the typical micro-based estimate. Summers's (1986) criticism of the large macro labor-supply elasticities embedded in most RBC models has remained one of the most persistent criticisms of the equilibrium approach to business-cycle analysis.

RECONCILING MICRO AND MACRO ESTIMATES OF THE ELASTICITY OF LABOR SUPPLY

Raj Chetty, along with various co-authors, has published several recent papers comparing labor-supply elasticity estimates obtained from macro and micro data (Chetty, Friedman, Olsen and Pistaferri, 2011; Chetty 2012). In particular, Chetty's work tends to focus on how micro and macro estimates differ by both the nature of the elasticity estimated (i.e., Hicksian versus Frisch elasticities) and the margin of adjustment considered (i.e., intensive versus extensive). Hicksian and Frisch labor-supply elasticities can be estimated on either the intensive margin or the extensive margin. Recall that labor-supply elasticity estimates of the intensive margin measure the response of hours worked to a change in the wage rate for *employed* individuals. Estimates of the extensive-margin elasticity, by contrast, measure the effect of a change in the wage rate on labor force participation. While microeconomists are concerned with understanding how individuals respond to shocks to their real wage rate, macroeconomists are interested in the aggregate response to real-wage shocks. More specifically, macroeconomists use assumptions about the size of aggregate labor-supply elasticities to calibrate representative-agent models of business-cycle dynamics. The aggregate labor-supply elasticities are the sum of the intensive-margin and extensive-margin elasticities, weighted by hours of work when there are individuals with heterogeneous preferences.

There is considerable disparity between the findings of the macro and micro literatures on the cyclical elasticity of labor supply. According to Chetty, Guren, Manoli, and Weber (2011; Chetty, Guren, Manoli and Weber, 2012), both the macro and the micro estimates of the Hicksian aggregate labor-supply elasticity are in rough agreement. The same can be said of the macro and micro Frisch intensive-margin estimates. However, the aggregate Frisch elasticity estimate is nearly three and a half times larger than the micro estimate, with the macro estimate appearing to be the outlier when compared to the Hicksian estimates. This evidence supports Summers's (1986) criticism of the labor-supply elasticity assumptions in RBC models. The challenge for proponents of the RBC framework has been to find support for the relatively large aggregate Frisch elasticities required in RBC models to match the cyclical volatility of employment.

Much of the research on RBC models since Prescott (1986) has involved various attempts to determine the degree to which the addition of an extensive margin of adjustment to the labor supply enables calibrations of a suitably modified RBC model to match more closely the observed volatility of total work hours, and this volatility relative to the volatility of output, that is documented in Table 8.1 (Krusell et al. 2012). Hansen (1985) considered the polar case in which there is *only* an extensive margin on which work hours can adjust; the labor supply decision in that case is a binary one in which an individual determines whether to work but not how many hours to work once employed. This assumption has been justified by an appeal to the existence of fixed costs of employment, arising from either the demand side, as in Oi (1962), or the supply side, as in Cogan (1981). For example, initial hiring and training costs incurred by firms and the costs borne by workers of commuting to and from work or arranging child care place a lower bound on the optimal (profit- or utility-maximizing) hours of work demanded or supplied. At the intensive (hours) margin, the labor supply response of (employed) married women to a wage increase is similar in magnitude to that for (married or unmarried) employed men. However, Hansen (1985) emphasizes that it is the presence of an operative extensive (labor force participation) margin that drives the relatively large wage elasticity of labor supply for married women.

Cho and Rogerson (1988)

Cho and Rogerson (1988) extend the RBC model by introducing heterogeneity within the family with respect to the labor supply responses of spouses to a change in their respective wage rates arising from a common technology shock. Husbands and wives are initially assumed to have identical (linear) preferences regarding consumption and market labor supply. However, Cho and Rogerson assume further that the family incurs a fixed utility cost when both the husband and the wife supply labor simultaneously. If the wife has a lower market productivity (relative to the value of time spent in household production) than the husband, this fixed cost is borne by the wife. As a result, there is always some fraction of all families in the economy where the husband is working and the wife is not. In such families, a positive technology shock that increases market productivities (and market wage rates) equally for the husband and wife results in a household labor supply response only along the extensive margin; the intensive (hours) response of the husband is zero.

With this feature of an otherwise standard RBC model in place, simulations reveal that the response of aggregate hours of work in the model economy to a technology shock is very similar to that observed for the U.S economy. Moreover, fluctuations in the total work hours of married females in response to the shock are approximately 20 times larger than the resulting fluctuations in the hours of married men, closely matching estimates of the relative intertemporal wage elasticities of labor supply for married men and women reported in the microeconometric literature. Thus, the model is capable of replicating the large difference in the wage elasticities of labor supply between married men and women, while generating aggregate labor-supply elasticities that are large enough to explain fluctuations in total hours over the business cycle as an equilibrium response to exogenous shocks.

These results seem at first glance to be at odds with the model specified and estimated by Donni and Moreau (2007), who note that men either are employed, in which case their average hours per week are closely clustered around a 40-hour full-time work week, or are unemployed, in which case their work hours are zero. In contrast, women who are employed in the formal labor market have greater flexibility in their work hours. However, a reconciliation of the findings of Cho and Rogerson (1988) and Donni and Moreau (2007) is possible once it is understood that there is no unemployment in the Cho-Rogerson model; all cyclical labor-supply adjustments by men and women in their model are equilibrium in nature. Consequently, a reduction in male employment during a recession would be classified by Cho and Rogerson (1988) as a voluntary reduction in labor force participation but an increase in unemployment in the Donni-Moreau framework.

Benhabib, Rogerson, and Wright (1991)

Despite the widespread interest generated by the concept of home work, introduced by Becker (1965), its implications for business-cycle analysis were not immediately appreciated. The RBC model of Kydland and Prescott (1982) and Prescott (1986) assumed that households allocate their time solely between market work and leisure. Thus, the large changes in aggregate hours worked implied by productivity shocks in their model were explained entirely by the decisions of employed workers along the intensive margin.

Benhabib, Rogerson, and Wright (1991; henceforth BRW) were the first to include home work as a third use of time in the standard RBC model. The addition of home work not only provided a more complete depiction of labor supply changes over the business cycle but also,

BRW claimed, substantially improved the quantitative performance of the standard RBC model. In particular, BRW sought to demonstrate how the inclusion of home work could address five notable criticisms of the standard RBC model: when compared with business-cycle data, the standard RBC model predicts that (1) output fluctuates too little; (2) relative to output, labor hours fluctuate too little; (3) relative to output, consumption fluctuates too little; (4) relative to output, investment fluctuates too much; and (5) the correlation of productivity with output or hours is far too high.

BRW began their analysis by citing Eisner's (1988) survey of the home production literature, which concluded that the value of home production in the United States is equivalent to 20 to 50 percent of the measured gross national product. Similarly, Benhabib, Rogerson, and Wright (1990) used the Michigan Time Use Survey to show that the average married couple in the sample devoted almost as much discretionary time to non-market production (28 percent) as they did to market production (33 percent). BRW noted that there is a positive relationship between the labor-supply elasticity and the elasticity of substitution in production between market and non-market consumption. In particular, if market and non-market goods are highly substitutable, then, when faced with a temporary decline in wages, the household will reduce work hours in favor of home work. This finding implies that the wage elasticity of labor supply will be higher the greater is the substitutability in *production* between market-purchased and home-produced goods.

In calibrating their model, BRW attempted to match the proportion of time devoted to market work (33 percent) and non-market work (28 percent) cited in Benhabib, Rogerson, and Wright (1990). BRW defined total household production C as a composite good produced by combining market-purchased goods C_m and non-market goods C_n according to the household production function:

$$C = (a_m C_m^e + a_n C_n^e)^{\frac{1}{e}}$$

They identified the intratemporal input substitution parameter $e = 1 - 1/\sigma$ the missing symbol is lower case sigma for both boxes below. I enlarged just to make it easier to see.

$e = 1 - 1/\sigma$ as crucial for matching the model's predictions with the observed volatility in the data, where σ is the elasticity of substitution between C_m and C_n in production and a_m and a_n are input-share parameters for market and non-market goods, respectively.

Using data from the Panel Study of Income Dynamics (PSID) previously analyzed by Rios-Rull (1993), BRW estimated a value of 0.6 for e. This estimate suggests that market and non-market inputs in household production are highly (albeit not perfectly) substitutable. However, BRW noted that their micro-based approach to estimating e is quite different from that of Eichenbaum and Hansen (1990), who used aggregate data and assumed there are no household time-allocation decisions. Based on their findings, as well as those of Eichenbaum and Hansen (1990), who made a case for $e = 1$, BRW decided to set $e = 0.8$.

BRW compared the simulated results from their RBC model with home production to the simulated results of the standard RBC model and to U.S. data. The addition of home production in their RBC model substantially improved its performance relative to the data. For example, the standard deviation of output obtained from simulations of the home-production model is almost identical to that found in the data. Moreover, the simulated volatility of consumption and investment relative to output volatility in the BRW model is significantly improved when compared to the standard RBC model. The most important contribution of the inclusion of home-production model in the RBC model is with respect to labor hours. The volatility of labor hours relative to output implied by the BRW model comes much closer to matching the relative volatility observed in the data. However, the correlation of labor hours and output is still too high relative to the U.S. data.

Domeij and Floden (2006)

Prior to the work of Domeij and Floden (2006), models that reported estimates of the Frisch elasticity failed to consider the impact that borrowing constraints may have on household labor supply decisions. From a theoretical standpoint, when credit markets are introduced, the household has an additional means for smoothing consumption. The household can now borrow in the credit market during periods where there has been a negative shock to its wage income, and pay off the loan later when its income has returned to the pre-shock level. In other words, the ability to borrow leaves the household's lifetime income relatively unaffected by the shock (i.e., the income effect is small). As a result, the intertemporal substitution effect dominates, and the household will devote more time to leisure. Thus, the Frisch labor-supply elasticity is expected to be higher when households have access to credit markets.

Consider, for example, a representative household that lives in a world with no credit markets. Now imagine a negative shock that temporarily decreases the wages received by the household. The substitution effect implies that the household's hours of work will decrease because the opportunity cost of leisure has declined. However, this substitution effect will be offset to some degree by an income effect. The size of the income effect is determined by the household's preference for current consumption and its ability to smooth consumption over time, among other factors. In the absence of a credit market, the most efficient way for the household to smooth consumption over time is to leave its work hours relatively unaltered (implying the income effect is relatively large). Consequently, the Frisch elasticity will be small because the response of current hours of work by the household is small relative to the temporary decline in the wage rate.

Domeij and Floden (2006) assume that there are two types of households: unconstrained (which have a low default risk and can easily borrow) and constrained (which have a high default risk and cannot readily borrow). Using evidence from the credit market literature, they assume that approximately 20 percent of U.S. households are credit-constrained. Domeij and Floden then extend the standard RBC model to include an imperfect credit market, and introduce stochastic shocks to labor productivity. Using data from the Panel Study of Income Dynamics (PSID), they show that estimates of the Frisch labor-supply elasticity rise as credit-constrained households are eliminated from the sample, consistent with the theoretical prediction.

Aguiar, Hurst, and Karabarbounis (2012)

Aguiar et al. (2012) use the American Time Use Survey (ATUS) 2003–2010 to examine the extent to which workers substitute away from market work toward other uses of time during a recession. Survey respondents in the ATUS are drawn from the out-rotation groups in the Current Population Survey (CPS). These respondents are asked to keep a 24-hour time diary. Every event recorded in the time diary is assigned to one of 400 time-use categories. Aguiar et al. aggregate these into seven broad categories: (1) market work, (2) other income-generating activities, (3) job search, (4) child care, (5) non-market work, (6) leisure, and (7) other.

When the Great Recession began, time devoted to market work fell by 2.11 hours per week in the ATUS. Aguiar et al. explored the relative importance of the substitution toward non-market work (including household production) during this recession by computing the share of the overall decrease in aggregate hours of market work that was reallocated to each of the other time-use categories. Additionally, they estimated the fraction of the decrease in aggregate market-work hours that occurred at the intensive and extensive margins.

For the entire sample, Aguiar et al. found that leisure accounted for nearly 80 percent of respondents' time when they were not engaged in market work, while non-market work and job search accounted for approximately 13 percent and 0.21 percent, respectively. However, during the Great Recession, 30 percent of the decline in market work was reallocated to non-market work, 50 percent to leisure, and 2 to 6 percent to job search. Similarly, Aguiar et al. estimated that approximately 74 percent of the decrease in aggregate market-hours worked was the result of extensive-margin adjustments, while only 26 percent represented adjustments to hours of market work by employed workers.

Aguiar et al. also compared the time reallocations of men and women, and married and single individuals. They failed to reject the hypothesis of no difference in the reallocations of men and women. However, they did find some evidence that women reallocated more of their reduced market-work hours to "core home production activities" (cooking, cleaning, and laundry) and sleep, while men devoted more of their time formerly spent in market work to leisure (especially, watching television) and "other" activities (in particular, investing in human capital).

Married individuals, in contrast, responded much differently than single individuals to the reduction in hours of market work. Married individuals allocated 34 percent of their additional non-market time to household production, whereas single individuals allocated only 15 percent to that category. Similarly, married individuals reported an 8 percent increase in time devoted to child care. Single individuals did not allocate any of the additional time to child care. Instead, they devoted more time to leisure (with almost all of the difference relative to married individuals accounted for by increased sleep time) and human capital investment.

Aguiar et al. concluded that increased time spent in home production accounts for a substantial portion of the decline in aggregate market-work hours caused by a business-cycle downturn. They find that the elasticity of non-market work with respect to market work is approximately 0.50. This is consistent with the relationship between non-market work and leisure hours reported by Benhabib, Rogerson, and Wright (1991) under the assumption that the elasticity of substitution in production between market-produced and home-produced goods in their model is 2.5.

Imai and Keane (2004)

In the benchmark RBC model, wage changes over the life cycle are assumed to be exogenous. This assumption is somewhat problematic because it presupposes that a household's accumulation of human capital (defined here as education, work experience, and training) has no effect on observed wage changes. In other words, as Keane and Rogerson (2012, 468) state, "these models assume that the approximate doubling of wages that is observed for the average person as they go from their early twenties to their mid-forties would still be realized if members of these households were to stay home and watch television for twenty years and then suddenly decide to look for a job." Instead, it is most likely the case that, over those 20 years, the average person has acquired additional human capital through education, on-the-job training, or learning-by-doing. As human capital accumulates, workers become more productive, causing their wages to rise.

Imai and Keane (2004) incorporate human capital accumulation into the standard life-cycle labor-supply model and find that doing so has important implications for the analysis of aggregate labor-supply elasticities. Throughout their analysis, Imai and Keane refer to the return from an hour of work as the "opportunity cost of time" (OCT). The OCT is the after-tax wage rate plus the expected present value of the increased (after-tax) earnings in all future periods obtained by working an extra hour at time t. Imai and Keane identify the latter term as the "human capital term" (HC).

Imai and Keane (2004) provide a stylized representation of how wages, hours, OCT, and HC evolve over a representative male's life cycle. In the early stages of the individual's career (i.e., at a young age), hours worked rise slowly. As the individual ages, hours worked eventually peak and then fall sharply as he moves toward retirement. The individual's wages follow a similar pattern. However, Imai and Keane show that wages rise far more sharply than hours when the individual is young and fall slightly less sharply as he nears retirement. When considered together, these two stylized facts imply that labor-supply elasticities will be low, as the large wage increases that occur when the worker is young will lead to relatively small adjustments to hours worked.

However, this model fails to account for the effect of human capital accumulation on hours worked. Consider what happens when HC is added to the model. The value of HC is initially high when the individual is young, but then falls at a decreasing rate owing to diminishing returns from HC over time. Moreover, as the individual nears retirement, the potential returns from additional HC will also fall. When the worker makes his labor-supply decision, he considers the full OCT inclusive of wages and HC. As Imai and Keane demonstrate, the life-cycle profile for OCT is much smoother than the wage profile, and is almost parallel to the hours-worked profile. In other words, as OCT rises, there will be a similar response of hours worked. Imai and Keane conclude that the inclusion of HC in the model implies that the wage elasticity of labor supply may be much higher than estimates from the micro literature that do not include human capital accumulation.

Rogerson and Wallenius (2009)

Rogerson and Wallenius (2009) extend the benchmark RBC model to consider two very important aspects of lifetime labor supply: the fraction of the individual's life spent in employment and the time devoted to work when employed. The individuals in this model have a fixed length of life that is normalized to 1, derive utility from consumption, and receive disutility from the hours they devote to work. Productivity varies over the life cycle and will ultimately diminish toward the end of the individual's life. Rogerson and Wallenius assume that producers require that individuals work some minimum number of hours to remain employed. Thus, labor supply $g(h)$ is equal to

$$g(h) = \max\{h - \bar{h}, 0\}$$

where h denotes the individual's instantaneous, optimal number of hours worked, and $\bar{h}$ is the minimum-hours requirement. When $h < \bar{h}$, the agent chooses to retire; that is, his labor supply equals zero. Thus, the model includes both intensive-margin adjustments (changes to h) and an extensive-margin adjustment (retirement).

Rogerson and Wallenius use the model to analyze the potential effect of a reform to a basic tax-and-transfer scheme. In particular, they are concerned with studying how the response of aggregate labor supply differs with different values of γ. Rogerson and Wallenius calibrate the model for different values of γ (0.1, 0.5, 1.0, 2.0), and then use the conventional labor-supply model to estimate γ. They first consider the impact of changes in the wage rate on the number of hours worked, and find that the estimated Frisch elasticities are consistently around one-half of their true value. Rogerson and Wallenius then investigate the response of aggregate hours to a rise in the marginal tax rate on labor income from 30% to 50%. They find that the change in aggregate hours worked is relatively large (an increase of more than 20 percent) for all four stipulated values of γ. This increase occurs despite the fact that the estimated micro labor-supply elasticities vary considerably (from 0.05 to 1.29).

In other words, the aggregate response to the increased tax rate remains approximately constant, at approximately 20 percent, even though the individual-level (micro) Frisch elasticities differ substantially. Therefore, Rogerson and Wallenius show that the small Frisch elasticities found in the micro literature can exist alongside large estimated aggregate Frisch elasticities that fall in a range between 1 and 2.

CONCLUDING REMARKS

The neoclassical model of economic growth provides an insightful framework for the analysis of the determinants of the long-run trends in savings, investment, employment, and output. A major attraction of this model is the ability to interpret it in terms of the outcomes of the optimizing behavior of individuals and firms, giving it "microeconomic foundations." It is not well suited, however, for the study of short-run, cyclical fluctuations of employment and output around these long-run trends. Extensions of the model to accommodate random shocks and, subsequently, the labor-leisure choice have given macroeconomists a toolkit with which to analyze business-cycle dynamics within an equilibrium environment.

An important shortcoming of the equilibrium or "real" approach to the study of business cycles is its inability to provide an understanding of the cyclical volatility of employment as an optimal response of work hours to temporary changes in productivity. The incorporation of labor-supply decisions, especially on the extensive margin of labor-force participation, has been a key advance in the quest for concordance between the predictions of this theory and the observed reality. Placing labor-supply decisions in a household or family setting where choices about the allocation of time are made among leisure, market work, and home work (or household production) has put researchers on a fruitful path toward reconciling the large body of empirical findings of a small elasticity of labor supply at the micro level with the much larger elasticity required of macro models to make sense of the magnitude of the cyclical fluctuations in employment.

While some progress has been made toward achieving this reconciliation, much theoretical and empirical work remains to be done and several challenges remain. For example, it may be possible to use results from the literature in public finance on the elasticity of taxable income, emphasized by Feldstein (1995) and recently surveyed by Saez et al. (2012), to examine decision margins, such as effort level and occupational choice, that have been unexplored in the business-cycle literature. These additional dimensions are, in principle, relevant for the estimation of aggregate labor-supply elasticities and may contribute to a further narrowing of the gap between the micro and macro results. It is also imperative to confront the fact—inconvenient for RBC adherents—that demographic groups such as prime-age males, for whom labor supply is the most wage-inelastic, counterfactually experience the largest cyclical fluctuations in employment. The model introduced by Donni and Moreau (2007) may point the way for proponents of the RBC framework to respond to that concern. Finally, more realistic assumptions about the structure of family decision making will undoubtedly have an effect on empirical estimates of the responsiveness of household labor supply to macroeconomic shocks.

REFERENCES

Aguiar, Mark, Erik Hurst, and Loukas Karabarbounis. "Time Use during the Great Recession." *American Economic Review* 103 (2012): 1664–1696.

Altonji, Joseph G. "Intertemporal Substitution in Labor Supply: Evidence from Micro Data." *Journal of Political Economy* 94 (1986): S176–S215.

Arrow, Kenneth J. *Social Choice and Individual Values*, 2nd ed. New Haven, CT: Yale University Press, 1963.

Becker, Gary S. "A Theory of the Allocation of Time." *Economic Journal* 75 (1965): 493–517.

Becker, Gary S. "Altruism, Egoism, and Genetic Fitness: Economics and Sociobiology." *Journal of Economic Literature* 14 (1976): 817–826.

Becker, Gary S. *A Treatise on the Family.* Cambridge, MA: Harvard University Press, 1981.

Benhabib, Jess, Richard Rogerson, and Randall Wright. *Homework in Macroeconomics I: Basic Theory.* National Bureau of Economic Research Working Paper No. 3344. Cambridge, MA: NBER, 1990. http://www.nber.org/papers/w3344.

Benhabib, Jess, Richard Rogerson, and Randall Wright. "Homework in Macroeconomics: Household Production and Aggregate Fluctuations."*Journal of Political Economy* 99 (1991): 1166–1187.

Brock, William A., and Leonard J. Mirman. "Optimal Economic Growth and Uncertainty: The Discounted Case." *Journal of Economic Theory* 4 (1972): 479–513.

Browning, Martin, Francois Bourguignon, Pierre-Andre Chiappori, and Valerie Lechene. "Income and Outcomes: A Structural Model of Intrahousehold Allocation." *Journal of Political Economy* 102 (1994): 1067–1096.

Cass, David. "Optimum Growth in an Aggregative Model of Capital Accumulation." *Review of Economic Studies* 32 (1965): 233–240.

Chetty, Raj. "Bounds on Elasticities with Optimization Frictions: A Synthesis of Micro and Macro Evidence on Labor Supply."*Econometrica* 80 (2012): 969–1018.

Chetty, Raj, John N. Friedman, Tore Olsen, and Luigi Pistaferri. "Adjustment Costs, Firm Responses, and Micro vs. Macro Labor Supply Elasticities: Evidence from Danish Tax Records." *Quarterly Journal of Economics* 126 (2011): 749–804.

Chetty, Raj, Adam Guren, Day Manoli, and Andrea Weber. "Are Micro and Macro Labor Supply Elasticities Consistent? A Review of Evidence on the Intensive and Extensive Margins." *American Economic Review Papers and Proceedings* 103 (2011): 1–6.

Chetty, Raj, Adam Guren, Day Manoli, and Andrea Weber. "Does Indivisible Labor Explain the Difference between Micro and Macro

Elasticities? A Meta-analysis of Extensive Margin Elasticities." *NBER Macroeconomics Annual* 27 (2012): 1–56.

Chiappori, Pierre-Andre. "Rational Household Labor Supply." *Econometrica* 56 (1988): 63–90.

Cho, Jang-Ok, and Richard Rogerson. "Family Labor Supply and Aggregate Fluctuations." *Journal of Monetary Economics* 21 (1988): 233–245.

Cogan, John F. "Fixed Costs and Labor Supply." *Econometrica* 49 (1981): 945–963.

Diamond, Peter. "National Debt in a Neoclassical Growth Model." *American Economic Review* 55 (1965): 1126–1150.

Domeij, David, and Martin Floden. "The Labor-Supply Elasticity and Borrowing Constraints: Why Estimates Are Biased." *Review of Economic Dynamics* 9 (2006): 242–262.

Donni, Olivier, and Pierre-Andre Chiappori. "Nonunitary Models of Household Behavior: A Survey of the Literature." In *Household Economic Behaviors: International Series on Consumer Science*, edited by Jose Alberto Molina, 1–40. New York, New York: Springer Science+Business Media, 2011.

Donni, Olivier, and Nicolas Moreau. "Collective Labor Supply: A Single-Equation Model and Some Evidence from French Data." *Journal of Human Resources* 42 (2007): 214–246.

Eichenbaum, Martin, and Lars Hansen. "Estimating Models with Intertemporal Substitution Using Aggregate Time Series Data." *Journal of Business and Economic Statistics* 8 (1990): 53–69.

Eichenbaum, Martin, Lars Hansen, and Kenneth J. Singleton. *A Time Series Analysis of Representative Agent Models of Consumption and Leisure Choice under Uncertainty.* National Bureau of Economic Research Working Paper No. 1981. Cambridge, MA: NBER, 1986.

Eisner, Robert. "Extended Accounts for National Income and Product." *Journal of Economic Literature* 26 (1988): 1611–1684.

Feldstein, Martin. "The Effect of Marginal Tax Rates on Taxable Income: A Panel Study of the 1986 Tax Reform Act." *Journal of Political Economy* 103 (1995): 551–572.

Ghez, Gilbert, and Gary S. Becker. *The Allocation of Time and Goods over the Life Cycle.* New York, NY: National Bureau of Economic Research, 1975.

Greenwood, Jeremy, and Zvi Hercowitz. "The Allocation of Capital and Time over the Business Cycle." *Journal of Political Economy* 99 (1991): 1188–1214.

Grossbard, Shoshana. "Independent Individual Decision-Makers in Household Models and the New Home Economics." In *Household Economic Behaviors: International Series on Consumer Science*, edited by Jose Alberto Molina, 41–56. New York, New York: Springer Science+Business Media, 2011.

Grossbard-Shechtman, Amyra. "A Theory of Allocation of Time in Markets for Labor and Marriage." *Economic Journal* 94 (1984): 863–882.

Hansen, Gary D. "Indivisible Labor and the Business Cycle." *Journal of Monetary Economics* 16 (1985): 309–327.

Imai, Susumu, and Michael P. Keane. "Intertemporal Labor Supply and Human Capital Accumulation." *International Economic Review* 45 (2004): 601–641.

Keane, Michael, and Richard Rogerson. "Micro and Macro Labor Supply Elasticities: A Reassessment of Conventional Wisdom." *Journal of Economic Literature* 50 (2012): 464–476.

Kimmel, Jean, and Thomas J. Kniesner. "New Evidence on Labor Supply: Employment versus Hours Elasticities by Sex and Marital Status." *Journal of Monetary Economics* 42 (1998): 289–301.

Koopmans, Tjalling C. "On the Concept of Optimal Economic Growth." In *The Economic Approach to Development Planning.* Amsterdam, Netherlands: Elsevier, 1965.

Krusell, Per, Toshihiko Mukoyama, Richard Rogerson, and Aysegul Sahin. *Is Labor Supply Important for Business Cycles?* National Bureau of Economic Research Working Paper No. 17779. Cambridge, MA: NBER, 2012.

Kydland, Finn E., and Edward C. Prescott. "Time to Build and Aggregate Fluctuations." *Econometrica* 50 (1982): 1345–1370.

Lundberg, Shelly. "Labor Supply of Husbands and Wives: A Simultaneous Equations Approach." *Review of Economics and Statistics* 70 (1988): 224–235.

Lundberg, Shelly. "Bargaining and Distribution in Marriage." *Journal of Economic Perspectives* 10 no. 4 (Autumn 1996): 139–158.

MaCurdy, Thomas E. "An Empirical Model of Labor Supply in a Life Cycle Setting." *Journal of Political Economy* 89 (1981): 1059–1085.

Mankiw, N. Gregory, David Romer, and David N. Weil. "A Contribution to the Empirics of Economic Growth." *Quarterly Journal of Economics* 107 (1992): 407–448.

Manser, Marilyn, and Murray Brown. "Marriage and Household Decision Making: A Bargaining Analysis." *International Economic Review* 21 (1980): 31–44.

McElroy, Marjorie B., and Mary Jane Horney. "Nash Bargained Household Decisions: Toward a Generalization of the Theory of Demand." *International Economic Review* 22 (1981): 333–349.

Mincer, Jacob. "Labor Force Participation of Married Women: A Study of Labor Supply." In *Aspects of Labor Economics*, 63–106. Princeton, NJ: Princeton University Press and the NBER, 1962.

Oi, Walter Y. "Labor as a Quasi-fixed Factor." *Journal of Political Economy* 70 (1962): 538–555.

Pencavel, John H. "The Market Work Behavior and Wages of Women: 1975–1994." *Journal of Human Resources* 33 (1998): 771–804.

Pencavel, John H. "A Cohort Analysis of the Association between Work Hours and Wages among Men." *Journal of Human Resources* 37 (2002): 251–274.

Phipps, Shelley, and Peter Burton. "What's Mine Is Yours? The Influence of Male and Female Incomes on Patterns of Household Expenditure." *Economica* 65 (1992): 599–613.

Pollak, Robert A. "Conditional Demand Functions and Consumption Theory." *Quarterly Journal of Economics* 83 (1969): 70–78.

Prescott, Edward C. "Theory ahead of Business Cycle Measurement." *Quarterly Review of the Federal Reserve Bank of Minneapolis* 10 (1986): 9–22.

Ramsey, Frank P. "A Mathematical Theory of Saving." *Economic Journal* 38 (1928): 543–559.

Rios-Rull, Jose-Victor. "Working in the Market, Home Production and the Acquisition of Skills: A General Equilibrium Approach." *American Economic Review* 83 (1993): 893–907.

Robbins, Lionel. "On the Elasticity of Demand for Income in Terms of Effort." *Economica* 10 (1930): 123–129.

Rogerson, Richard, and Johanna Wallenius. "Micro and Macro Elasticities in a Life Cycle Model with Taxes." *Journal of Economic Theory* 144 (2009): 2277–2292.

Saez, Emmanuel, Joel Slemrod, and Seth H. Giertz. "The Elasticity of Taxable Income with Respect to Marginal Tax Rates: A Critical Review." *Journal of Economic Literature* 50 (2012): 3–50.

Samuelson, Paul A. "The Pure Theory of Public Expenditure." *Review of Economics and Statistics* 36 (1954): 387–389.

Samuelson, Paul A. "Social Indifference Curves." *Quarterly Journal of Economics* 70 (1956): 1–22.

Samuelson, Paul A. "An Exact Consumption-Loans Model of Interest, with or without the Social Contrivance of Money." *Journal of Political Economy* 66 (1958): 467–482.

Sims, Eric. "Stylized Business Cycle Facts and the Quantitative Performance of the RBC Model." 2012. http://www3.nd.edu/~esims1/stylized_facts_rbc_sp12.pdf.

Solow, Robert M. "A Contribution to the Theory of Economic Growth." *Quarterly Journal of Economics* 70 (1956): 65–94.

Solow, Robert M. "Intergenerational Equity and Exhaustible Resources." *Review of Economic Studies* 41 (1974): 29–45.

Summers, Lawrence H. "Some Skeptical Observations on Real Business Cycle Theory." *Quarterly Review of the Federal Reserve Bank of Minneapolis* 10 (1986): 23–27.

Swan, Trevor W. "Economic Growth and Capital Accumulation." *Economic Record* 32 (1956): 334–361.

About the Editor

ESTHER REDMOUNT, PhD, is an associate professor of economics at Colorado College in Colorado Springs, Colorado. She holds a doctorate from the University of Virginia and was a Lady Davis postdoctoral fellow in agricultural economics at the Faculty of Agriculture of the Hebrew University in Rehovot, Israel. Among her published works are "Cyclical Patterns in School Attrition and Attendance: A Study in the Labor Market Behavior of Children" in *Economic Development and Cultural Change* (51:1, October 2002) and "The Effect of Wage Payment Reform on Workers' Wages, Labor Supply and Welfare," with Ronald G. Warren, Jr., and Arthur Snow in the *Journal of Economic History* (72:4, December 2012).

About the Contributors

Laura M. Argys
Professor of Economics, University of Colorado–Denver; Interim Dean of the College of Liberal Arts and Sciences, University of Colorado, Denver, Colorado

Susan L. Averett
Charles A. Dana Professor of Economics, Lafayette College, Easton, Pennsylvania; Research Fellow IZA (Institute for the Study of Labor), Bonn, Germany; Co-editor, *Eastern Economics Journal.*

Rachel Connelly
Bion R. Cram Professor of Economics, Bowdoin College, Brunswick, Maine; Research Fellow IZA (Institute for the Study of Labor), Bonn, Germany; Associate Editor, *Feminist Economics.*

Joyce P. Jacobsen
Dean of the Social Sciences and Director of Global Initiatives, and Andrews Professor of Economics, Wesleyan University, Middletown, Connecticut.

Lisa K. Jepsen
Faculty, Department of Economics, College of Business Administration, University of Northern Iowa, Cedar Falls, Iowa.

Mark C. Kelly
Department of Economics, Terry School of Business, University of Georgia, Athens, Georgia.

Jean Kimmel
Faculty, Department of Economics, Western Michigan University, Kalamazoo, Michigan; Research Fellow IZA (Institute for the Study of Labor), Bonn, Germany.

Karine Moe
F. R. Bigelow Profess or Economics, Macalester College, St. Paul, Minnesota; Editor of the Springer Publisher Series *Economics of Gender.*

Solomon W. Polachek
Distinguished Research Professor of Economics and Political Science, Department of Economics, Department of Political Science, Binghamton University (SUNY), Binghamton, New York; Research Fellow IZA (Institute for the Study of Labor), Bonn, Germany.

Asia Sikora
Faculty, Department of Health Promotion and Social and Behavioral Health, University of Nebraska Medical Center, College of Public Health, Omaha, Nebraska.

Ronald S. Warren, Jr.
Faculty, Department of Economics, Terry School of Business, University of Georgia, Athens, Georgia.

Jun Xiang
Faculty, Department of Economics; Faculty, Division of Global Affairs, Rutgers University-Newark, Newark, New Jersey.

Index